MW01029420

CHARLOTTE'S STORY

A Florida Keys Diary
1934 & 1935

by
Charlotte Arpin Niedhauk

Laurel & Herbert
Lower Sugarloaf Key
Florida

Second Edition

Edited by Mary-Alice Herbert

© 1998 by the Friends of the Islamorada Area State Parks

Cover © 1998 by Jo Cooper

This work was originally published in different form by Exposition Press.

First Edition
© 1973 by Charlotte Arpin Niedhauk
First Printing 1973
Second Printing 1977
Third Printing 1983

Second Edition
First Printing 1998
Second Printing 2002

Library of Congress Catalog Card Number: 73-89522

Library of Congress Cataloging-in-Publication Data

Niedhauk, Charlotte Arpin. 1910-1983
    Charlotte's story: A Florida Keys Diary, 1934 & 1935/Charlotte Arpin Niedhauk
    Foreword by Al Burt.
        p.   cm.
    Originally published: Islamorada, Fla.: Niedhauk, 1973 © 1973
    Includes index.   Illus. Photos. Maps.
    ISBN 0-9619155-4-4 (pbk. : alk. Paper)
    1. Niedhauk, Charlotte Arpin—Childhood and youth. 2. Florida Keys (Fla.)
    Biography. 3. Florida Keys (Fla.)—Social life and customs. 4. Elliott Key (Fla.)—
    Biography. 5. Elliott Key (Fla.)—Social life and customs. 6. Depressions—
    1929—Florida—Elliott Key. I. Title.

    F317.M7N53 1998
    975.9' 41062'092—dc21
    [b]   98-39527
                                                                                    CIP

ISBN 0-9619155-4-4

Printed in the United States of America

ACKNOWLEDGEMENTS

Publishing this new edition of *Charlotte's Story* has been a project blessed from the beginning. In memory of Charlotte Niedhauk, the publishers wish to thank Gary A. Bremen, park ranger, Biscayne National Park; Jim Clupper, director of the Helen Wadley Branch Library of Monroe County; Irving Eyster, president, Matecumbe Historic Trust; Alison Fahrer, president, Friends of the Islamorada Area State Parks; Tom Hambright, director of the Florida History Department at Monroe County Public Library; Rebecca A. Smith and Dawn Hugh, curators of Research Materials, The Historical Museum of Southern Florida; Luciann Niebler-Spare, chairman of the FIASP Lignumvitae Committee; Karen Strobel, secretary of FIASP; Pat Wells, park manager, Florida State Parks, Jerry Wilkinson, president of the Historical Preservation Society of the Upper Keys.

The publishers are grateful to the **Friends of the Islamorada Area State Parks**, without whom this book would not have come to fruition. FIASP is a non-profit organization, chartered by the State of Florida in 1987, whose mission is to promote and assist the seven Islamorada Area State Parks: Indian Key State Historic Site, Lignumvitae State Botanical Site, Windley Key State Geologic Site, Curry Hammock, Long Key State Recreation Area, Shell Key State Preserve, and San Pedro Underwater Archeological Site. FIASP membership includes more than 150 volunteers. Its projects include purchases of park equipment, housing for park workers, and college scholarships. Its annual events include the Indian Key Festival in October, Windley Quarry Day, and Lignumvitae Christmas.

The voices in "About Charlotte" are DeeDee Lynn, a friend living in Islamorada; Carol Cepress, *The Daily Tribune,* Wisconsin Rapids; Martha Canfield, *Key Largo Bureau,* Lucille E. Moran, the Foreword to the first edition.

Cover art by Jo Cooper. Typography and pre-press by Fonts & Film, Key West, Florida. Proofreader, Margaret Montana. Printed by Central Plains Book Manufacturing.

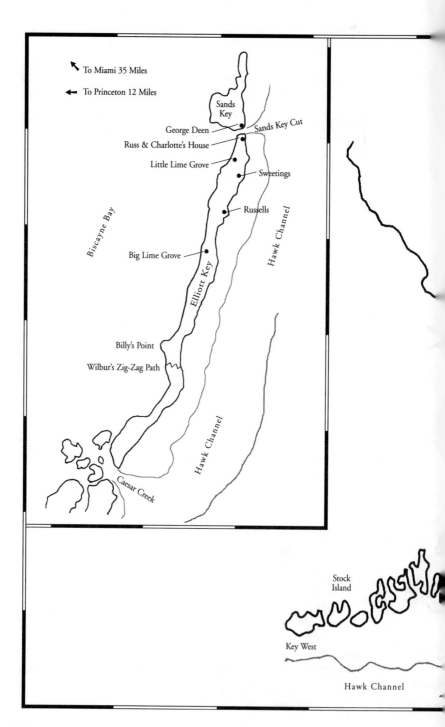

To Miami 35 Miles

To Princeton 12 Miles

Sands Key

George Deen

Sands Key Cut

Russ & Charlotte's House

Little Lime Grove

Sweetings

Biscayne Bay

Russells

Hawk Channel

Big Lime Grove

Elliott Key

Billy's Point

Wilbur's Zig-Zag Path

Hawk Channel

Caesar Creek

Stock
Island

Key West

Hawk Channel

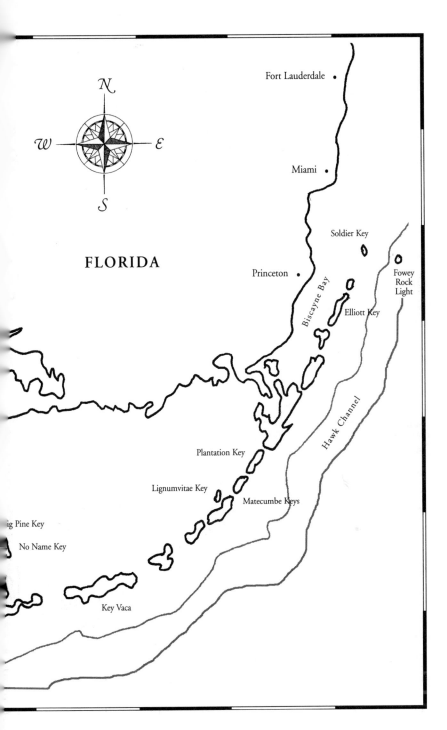

N

W E

S

Fort Lauderdale •

Miami •

Soldier Key

Princeton •

Biscayne Bay

Fowey
Rock
Light

Elliott Key

FLORIDA

Hawk Channel

Plantation Key

Lignumvitae Key

Matecumbe Keys

ig Pine Key

No Name Key

Key Vaca

FOREWORD

In 1934 the Florida Keys were backcountry islands linked to the United States by Flagler's Overseas Railroad. Prohibition outlawed whiskey and the Depression made jobs scarce. Smugglers and fugitives prowled the waters. Into that frontier wandered an unlikely pair, Charlotte and Russell Niedhauk, two intrepid Lilliputians (each stood 5 feet, 4 inches) who overflowed with inventive imagination.

Neither were native Floridians. As teenagers each had moved to Florida from the north with their parents. She had been a legal stenographer and flapper. He had operated a towboat on a Fort Lauderdale canal, had been a licensed radio operator, a machinist and mechanic, an engineer, a naturalist, a woodworker. Whatever needed to be done, he could do it.

That spring of 1934 they moved to Elliott Key, an island 12 miles offshore from Princeton in southern Dade County. The Key had no electricity, running water, telephones or law. The Niedhauks survived by improvising.

Charlotte's Story tells their two-year island adventure. Charlotte wrote it almost a quarter-century after the experience, when the two of them were living on another island, Lignum Vitae Key. She details their life as a housewife might, and therefore it includes the routine things that both focus history into human scale and slow its telling. The story moves at an island pace with home-made style and delivers a valuable account of a special place and time.

The Niedhauks tell us about preserving rainwater in a cistern, devising home remedies, scavenging for necessities, coping with the nuisances of bugs and snakes and rats, and much more. It is a tale of remarkable self-dependence. Above all, they tell us what the natural Keys were like.

Most striking, perhaps, is an inside-the-storm account of the Labor Day hurricane of 1935, the Keys' worst ever. The Niedhauks rode it out on their island, but the damage was so severe that it ended their island adventure.

I first met the Niedhauks in 1981. They were living on a 65-foot boat tied up at Islamorada. With Charlotte hovering nearby, constantly interrupting, Russell patiently explained his nearly half-century addiction to the isolation and unique beauty of islands. Finally, he would say, sweetly but firmly, "Hush, Charlotte, don't butt in for a minute." She would hush.

Charlotte's Story, explaining how it all began, already had been told. It follows...

-Al Burt

CONTENTS

CHARLOTTE'S STORY

Russell and Charlotte Niedhauk

CHAPTER ONE

Who? Why? What? Where? "Bill."

I had just signed for the telegram that was to change my entire way of life. It was delivered just a few minutes before my husband, Russell, returned home from his temporary job at the Atlantic Marine filling station. During most of the year, he worked as chief engineer on a 77-foot yacht. During stand-by time, as now, he took temporary work.

Russ opened it and read aloud, "GOING ON A SIX MONTHS' CRUISE, COME AT ONCE. LEAVE YOUR WIFE AT HOME." It was signed, "Captain Winskell."

I stuttered a bit and then started to protest. I didn't consider the salary as important as the six months' separation.

"Charlotte, two hundred dollars a month and all my expenses is a hell of a lot right now when millions are out of work!"

"If you go, I'll go back to work as a legal stenographer."

"No. My wife isn't going to work."

We were interrupted by a knock at the door. Russ went down the stairs to answer it. As he opened the door, I heard a strange voice say, "Douse that light!" He did, and the person outside darted in and closed the door.

The unfamiliar voice said, "Quiet now, Russ. I smuggled some liquor ashore, and now I'm afraid I'll be hijacked. Hide it for me, will ya?"

After a moment of silence, Russ said, "Okay." Then, "Charlotte, turn off the upstairs lights." I did, and sat down to listen.

"Russ, I gotta do this in a hurry. Give me a hand, please!"

1

For a while I heard sounds of bumping as things were brought inside and set down in the hallway. The door was closed, and Russ said, "Put the lights on. We are coming up."

As he came up the steps, in each hand he grasped a bulky burlap bag by its top. The bags looked heavy. He introduced me to the man following him, a man I'll refer to as "Bill." He was an acquaintance from the Atlantic Marine, a foot taller and a hundred pounds heavier than Russ. Merely nodding to acknowledge the introduction, he asked, "Where are we going to put these?"

"I guess the best place to hide them is under our bed," Russ said. He led the way into the bedroom and they started to stow the things. I counted twenty bags as they brought them up.

Finished now, Russ called me. "Come look."

I saw nothing different except that the bedspread was pulled down to the floor. Somehow they managed to stow the twenty bags of liquor. A dozen bottles to the bag.

It was pretty hot that March night and they were both perspiring, so I suggested some iced tea. As they followed me to the kitchen, Bill said, "I didn't know where to turn, then I thought of you. I sorta figured you would help a guy out. I surely appreciate it, Russ."

The telegram was open on the table and Bill looked at it as he sat down. "Bad news?"

I said, "Read it, it's not good."

"Six months! Wow! Russ, I've been telling you about that island proposition. Why don't you consider it? It's just right for you two people."

"What island, Bill?"

"Well, it's one of the offshore keys south of here. There is a house on the north end, quite livable. No rent, no time limit. You can stay there in exchange for clearing out two lime groves on the property. One of them is small. You can get crawfish to sell for groceries. Limes bring in a good price, too."

That sounded interesting to me.

Bill continued, "Russ, what does that yacht job pay you?"

"Two hundred a month and all expenses for me."

"Russ, you could make that much down there and be your own boss and be together! Why don't you go down to the island?"

"I'm not going to make up my mind right now."

"Think about it. I can arrange things with Fossey, the owner, and borrow Flip's boat to take you down there. Let me know."

I guess he noticed the frown on Russ' face. He stood up. Then, walking towards the steps, he said, "Thanks a lot. Good-bye for now."

After Russ walked to the door with Bill, he returned and sat down to supper. We ate in a more or less silent manner. Now and then I would hopefully say something about the possibility of going to the "romantic island." Dishes done, we listened to the radio for a time and then went to bed.

When I tried to find a soft spot in the bed, I grumbled a lot about Russ' generous gesture. There was no give to the spring now that it was so firmly supported by liquor, 240 bottles of it, but neither one of us considered removing it.

I was almost asleep when Russ said, "I'll have to wire Captain Winskell in the morning." I didn't say anything and drifted off to sleep.

As he left for work in the morning, Russ said, "I'll call you if I come to a decision."

At noon he phoned the good news, "We are going to the island. I wired the Captain to get a replacement for me. Bill dropped in about an hour ago and I told him. He was sort of funny. Jubilant about my decision, and then strangely reluctant to find another hiding place for his liquor. He finally said he would come get it tonight.

"Now, I want you to sort everything in the apartment. Make two piles in the spare bedroom, things to be stored and the necessities for living on an island. I'll bring some boxes home tonight to pack things.

"By the way, my boss, Mr. Everett said I could come back to work for him if we change our minds. Contact the landlady and pay her an extra month's rent. That will give us six weeks to decide. You might not be able to take island living. It will be a wild and woolly life for a city gal like you. I know *I* can take it. Can *you*?"

Anything was possible now! "I know I can. I'll get busy and sort things out. Thanks so much for deciding this way. Good-bye now, I'm going to start work."

We hadn't brought too many things from Fort Lauderdale when we moved to Miami, and I soon had things sorted. Then I got busy with my washing and ironing. The day passed swiftly and supper was ready when Russ returned.

Dishes done, we got to work packing. I was amazed at the number of things Russ removed from the necessary pile and packed for storage. Having packed the boxes in our car, we were on our way to his parents' home in Fort Lauderdale.

"Where does Bill work?"

"As far as I know, he doesn't. He drops in at the Atlantic Marine at all hours of the day. He drives a nice car and always seems to have money. Guess he's a rum runner."

Taking a notebook and pencil from his pocket, Russ said, "Here, I'll give you a list of things which we will get from the folks' attic to take down with us. A good handsaw, hammer, fishing equipment, I'll think of other things as we go along. Now, start another page for groceries we will need."

I was amazed at the number of dried foods he named, and the amounts of each startled me. When I asked if we needed that much, he said that he figured for five weeks' supply and a small amount for emergencies.

At that time, in 1934, five dollars would buy all the meat and groceries a couple would need for a week. I don't mean rice! We had all the pickles, jam and other goodies we wanted and our bills seldom ran over that.

At his parents' home we stored our boxes of town clothes, except one outfit for each of us. From other boxes stored previously, Russ filled the list of things we needed for the island, including some motor tools. His parents were dismayed about his decision; they couldn't understand that he would give up such a good job during the Depression. There wasn't much they could do about it, though, since Russ was thirty and I was twenty-four. The atmosphere was sort of tense and we didn't visit long.

At my parents' home, we got the same reaction. My parents insisted that we leave our daughter Jan with them. They said a deserted island was no place for a three-year-old. They did agree to allow us to borrow her if we stayed for any length of time. Even though we weren't sure how we would do it, we promised to keep in touch with them.

On our return trip, we completed the grocery list and planned to shop the next evening after supper. We were to leave for the island the following day.

It was quite late when we got back to Miami and we retired immediately.

With Russ on his way to work in the morning, I started house-cleaning. Things must be in perfect condition in case we stayed on the island. A minimum of dishes and cooking utensils must be left in case we returned for a visit. While preparing supper, I also prepared some potato salad for lunch the next day. I was putting it in a large glass jar when Russ got home.

During supper Russ told me about his friend Flip. He had dropped by the filling station that morning and told Russ that he was happy to do him the favor of loaning Bill the boat for our trip to the island. He described him to be five foot, four inches tall, around a 120 pounds, much the same size as Russ. A blue-eyed blond. With a speech impediment. "A really pleasant sort of guy. He lives with his girlfriend about a block from the Atlantic Marine."

"By the way, he told me he is retired. A retired rum runner."

Our apartment was the entire upstairs of one of the older houses in Miami. That area has long since been developed into a business district. We drove the few blocks to the equivalent of a modern-day supermarket. There were long counters in front of the shelves of groceries, and a clerk was amazed when Russ put the long list of multiple items on the counter in front of him and asked that the things be put into boxes. He called for a bag boy to bring them. People expressed amazement as the stack of boxes grew. It was a bit impressive to me, too!

In those days, most people bought their supplies daily in order to take advantage of the daily specials. All together we bought over fifty dollars' worth of groceries. Roach paste, soap, and other incidentals accounted for the extra.

With the help of the bag boys, we packed the rumble seat high and then found that we would have to use the floor space and part of the passenger's seat for the overflow. I had to ride on Russ' lap on the way home, but he seemed to enjoy it.

Back home Russ drove the car over the lawn to the back

door. "If I park this close to the house, things will be safer. Now, you go on up and pack everything that isn't already packed. I'll go down to the corner drugstore and fill the list I have. I also have to get some oilcloth to put on those boxes for tonight. I won't be long."

When he returned, he left the bundle in the hall and brought up some ice cream. "It will be quite a while before we have any more of this. Did you realize that?"

"Not exactly, but you won't hear me complaining!"

The House

CHAPTER TWO

The House. City of Roaches, Buzzards, Rats, Ants, Conch Stew.
Repair Boat. Make Coconut Shell Items.

I straightened the apartment while Russ found room in and on the car for the medical supplies, clothing and a few other things that we were taking with us. Finished, I closed the windows, skipped down the stairs and announced, "I'm all ready to leave for the island!"

"I'm all ready, but you aren't, not dressed as you are. Your dress and shoes are suitable–for Miami. I figured you'd do that so I unpacked one of my shirts for you. Our first stop will be down at the clothing store. You go in, buy a couple of pair of dungarees, high-top tennis shoes, and some socks. You can change in the store."

I did this while he stayed in the car and guarded our many boxes. With my city dress and shoes in a package, I got into the car. Now it was my turn to wait while he went to a little store nearby to buy the fresh vegetables and meat, the last we would have in a long time.

When he returned, we left for the dock where Bill had arranged to meet us with a boat for the trip to the "romantic island."

We never knew whether Bill owned a boat of his own or not. For this trip, he had borrowed Flip's boat. It was a 25-foot motor launch. As we drove into the filling station, Mr. Everett waved us towards the dock as he said, "You should have had a truck. By the looks of this load, you intend to stay a while!"

Russ parked, and I slid off his lap just as Bill climbed up onto the dock. He looked especially happy to see us. I thought it odd. I didn't know then that this was the first step in his plan.

Loading didn't take long at all. Everybody there helped, including Flip. At the last minute, Russ drove to a nearby ice house and bought a hundred-pound chunk of ice and a burlap bag in which to put it. When he returned, Mr. Everett said, "Leave your car here. I'll take care of it." That settled our last problem, and we thanked him.

Moving a few boxes around, we made a place in the middle for the ice, which was wrapped now in the oilcloth, meat on top, and insulated with the morning's *Miami Herald* and a box of clothing.

Bill impatiently started the motor with a roar that drowned out our friends' voices as they called out their good-byes and best wishes. Casting off the lines, we started off. We were on our way to a different mode of life.

Like most folks who have lived in Florida, I had been out deep-sea fishing before. Five miles out to the fishing ground never seemed to take long, but this was really different. It was a straight run, thirty-five miles to an offshore island.

Perched there on the boxes, I was thrilled, but still I felt a bit worried about whether I could qualify as a companion in some of the circumstances that might arise. I knew nothing about being isolated from civilization. Russ had given up a well-paying job at a time when millions were out of work, and he loved me enough to do it. I hoped and prayed that I wouldn't disappoint him.

I knew that I was to live under somewhat primitive conditions, but I didn't realize it until I saw the little dock on the edge of the land surrounded by jungle. It was small and wobbly, about ten feet long and six feet wide. The shore end of the dock was about twelve feet from shore, and this space was spanned by a two-by-six plank. Could I manage to walk that? Would I get to shore dry? I was glad I had tennis shoes. It would have been impossible in my usual high heels. While I hesitated, Russ said, "Don't try walking that plank. Put that box down and wait a minute."

He took his box ashore, put it down and came back for me. "Now, put your hands on my shoulders, watch where you put your feet." Success! Ashore and dry!

I picked up the box and started up the rocky path towards the house, which I had been told was about a city block away. As I couldn't see over the box, I just went stumbling up the path. I had determined to carry my own weight, literally, in this adventure.

I didn't know exactly what to expect in the way of living quarters there on the north end of Elliott Key, but I was surprised and pleased when I saw the wooden house. It was twenty by forty feet and not quite as open as a porch because it had wooden drop shutters which doubled as awnings all around the house. The open areas were screened and almost ceiling height. The shutters had wooden props to hold them up, so it was evident that one had to go outside and get thoroughly wet while letting them down and buttoning them with the wooden turn buttons.

Looking up at the second story, I wondered whether it had been an afterthought. It looked as though part of the roof peak had been sawed off and raised three feet on corner posts and frames. I saw a small four-paned window in the middle front, facing the ocean.

Bill arrived then and said, "Just a second—I'll unlock the door." It was my first sight of a padlocked front door. When he opened it, I saw the kitchen. Looking to the left, I saw a stove and a four-foot partition towards the back of the room. I put down the box and went back for more. Remembering my stumbling progress on the way up, I removed some of the rocks from the path as I went along.

It didn't take forever—I just thought it did. We finally had all our supplies in the house. By that time I was pooped, but determined not to show it. In the living-dining room area, we had piled up boxes of linen. I noticed the ice making a puddle on the kitchen floor, but it didn't seem to matter as it was running towards the door.

I went through the walk-through space by the kitchen partition and found shelves on which we could put our groceries later. The living room was divided lengthwise, making a bedroom area. Further partitions made it into three bedrooms. The dividing partition was four feet high, making a kind of window. This space had white cotton curtains, floor to ceiling, that could be drawn closed for privacy.

The back porch had been an addition to the house and ran the full width. It had screened areas between it and the living room. The only door inside the house was there, and it, too, was screened. I didn't appreciate this arrangement at the time. Later, during mosquito season, I saw how useful it was. Looking towards the left, I saw a wooden door and to the right, another in the far corner. On opening this, I saw the bathroom facilities. Some thoughtful soul had added this small room to the porch. I had expected to find an outside one of the Chic Sales variety, and although this was of that type, it was a U-Dump-It.

In the living area again, I decided to look upstairs. A ladder had been built against the wall between the second and third bedrooms, giving only three inches of toe space. I climbed it. Pushing the hinged trap door open, I found it formed part of the upstairs floor. At that time, I noticed another little four-paned window at the back of the house. The only way to raise the shutters was from the outside, so I unbuttoned the turn-buttons on the window, set them aside, and crawled around on the roof raising the shutters. There was a double-sized mattress on the floor—not enough height in the room for a bed frame. I could have used a spring! Oh well, that would come later.

Right then I decided that was going to be our room. The trap door would provide more privacy than the curtains.

As I backed down the ladder to get the linen, I remembered the ice. The men were outside talking and I heard Bill say, "Hawk Channel is just a couple of miles off shore."

I yelled, "Where's the icebox? The ice is melting!"

"Mr. Fossey told me there is one, but I didn't see it."

As they entered the house, Russ said, "Maybe they have one like the old-timers used to have, set under the floor!"

I remembered seeing a wide right-angled crack near where the box of linen was. I said, while moving the box off the crack, "Could this be it?"

It was. Russ pried up the lid (a piece of wood) and I saw this luxurious treasure was a box with sawdust in the bottom.

Russ slapped the lid back, "Boy, city of roaches! Come on, let's put all the boxes on the table and bench before we open that again. Get something to swat them with. I'll find the flit gun."

"I'll use my tennis shoes, " I said, and I sat down to take them off.

Bill picked up one of my science fiction magazines from its box and said, much to my silent dismay, "This will work fine!"

At the thought of those darn bugs crawling around I tucked my pants' legs into my socks. Russ had located the flit gun and told Bill to lift the lid, "Here we go!"

Russ started spraying and the bugs crawled out of the box onto the floor. They were over an inch long and looked like monsters. I started swatting those that came in my direction and was sure that I killed at least half of them. They ran so fast and erratically I was surprised they didn't fly. I must have said so out loud because Russ said, "They can't. Too much spray on them."

Soon the floor was strewn with dead roaches, and no more were coming out. There were still more in the sawdust, though. Bill discovered that when, with his longer arms, he reached in and stirred with my precious magazine. When these came out, I was more efficient with my shoes and none got past me. I thought of the roaches that had gotten past me, those I would have to kill later. I took the magazine from Bill and put it back in its box. It was still in one piece, more or less.

Russ wrapped the ice in the morning paper, put the meat on top of it, and put more paper on that. Had I known that it would be a month before I saw another paper, I think I would have said something.

Russ was looking for the Coleman lantern when I went into the kitchen to get the broom to sweep up the mess. In the tropics, night falls as though someone had pulled the shade, and I stepped into the ice water without seeing it. I swept up bugs, used a piece of cardboard for a dustpan, and then flung the things outside. Then, with my shoes on, I got busy prying some of the squashed ones from the floor. Ugh!

I finally located the pillows and linen necessary to make the bed; naturally, they were in the bottom boxes now. I gathered the bulky bundle together and realized that I would need two hands to climb the ladder. The men were outside again, so I solved my problem by balancing some things on my head and slowly climbing, pushing them onto the floor when I got high enough. I only dropped things three or four times before I got everything up.

11

My miniature muscles were complaining as I went back down again to get a flashlight so I could see up there.

Make the bed. It sounds easy, but it wasn't. I stood up to flip the mattress pad, hit my head on the roof and fell, almost going through the hole in the floor. Muttering obscenities, I closed the trap door and managed to complete the job by crawling around on the floor. During this time I had heard most of the conversation Bill and Russ were having downstairs where they were making up a bed for Bill. Wow, thin floors! They were talking about supper, so I called down that they would find cold cuts and jars of potato salad in one of the paper bags on the table.

"Charlotte, I'll set the table if you can remember what kind of a box you put the silverware in."

"All I remember is that it is square and big enough for plates."

Russ had things organized when I went down to eat my first meal on the island. Our six-pack of Cokes lasted only a few minutes. No more of those for a while. The men were still talking when I went up to bed. I was half asleep before they finished eating.

I shut the trap door, but they sounded as loud as before. I dropped off, and nothing disturbed me until morning when the sun came up–right in my face. No window shades, no possibility of dimming that light so I could catch another forty winks.

It took me quite a few minutes to get up. My muscles rebelled. I never knew I had so many, particularly in my legs. Then I developed a hurtful knotty condition in my legs.

"Just a charley-horse," said Russ, as he rubbed it away.

I was still dressing as he backed down the ladder. I followed him shortly and found that he had lit the stove in the kitchen. This was the most expensive item in the house, and it was a darling. It was a four-burner Detroit Red Wheel vapor stove. A dipstick, a four-inch piece of wire with asbestos on the end, was used to light it. The dipstick lived in its own little fuel reservoir on the front of the stove. Using the dipstick to light the stove was safe, but using a match was risky. I know–burnt fingers!

At that time I saw one faucet set over the sink. Later, I found out that we had a three-hundred-gallon rainwater tank outside near the back corner of the kitchen. It was almost half full.

I soon had bacon and eggs ready. And, I made toast on an unfamiliar piece of equipment Russ had bought, one of those pyramid-shaped toast scorchers that sit over the open flame. Burnt my fingers, and then used a fork to turn the bread.

Breakfast tasted marvelous! I hope someday to again have the taste treat I had with my first rainwater coffee.

Bill left for Miami right after breakfast.

We were on our own. No power boat to depend on. Twelve miles to the nearest part of the Florida mainland, Princeton, just north of Homestead.

"Charlotte, I'm going outside. They must have a scythe or something to cut the weeds. If we keep the weeds down, we keep the bugs away from the house."

"Okay, I'll straighten up in here."

I painfully worked some of the soreness out of my legs by moving some of the boxes of clothing and other supplies up the ladder to our bedroom. The packed suitcases almost finished me. I fastened two of Russell's belts together to hoist them up. It was awkward turning the suitcases sideways to get them through the trap door, but I managed. Now my neck ached more than ever. I found my only dress in a paper bag, scrunched up. I smoothed it out as best I could and put it on the boxes.

Thirsty now, I went down for a glass of water and sat down to drink it. I woke up from my unscheduled nap when Russ came in for lunch.

"Hey, I saw a lot of buzzards to the north of us, just circling. From the dock it looked like they were over the north end of Sands Key—that's the key just north of us. Gotta be something dead there. I'm not interested in seeing what."

I shuddered. I had only read about buzzards or seen them in the movies. I wasn't curious either.

Lunch was the rest of the salad and cold cuts, and we treated ourselves to ice water.

"Charlotte, this bread will get moldy unless you stack it. Take care of it after lunch. Stack it log cabin style with air spaces so it will dry. It'll be a little tough, but you'll get used to it." I stacked four loaves on our large platter and put them in the safe. That was an indispensable item. It was a two-shelf, two-door, screened

13

cabinet, suspended from the ceiling on three-eighths inch iron rods. About six inches below the ceiling, there were funnels with cotton in them. The rods went through these and fitted tightly. You needed to soak the cotton with kerosene or some other deterrent to the bugs to keep them from using the rods as highways to the food supplies. From then on, we ate dried bread, except for the day we bought it, not crisp, but crunchy.

During lunch I mentioned to Russ that we would need some large jars into which we could put leftovers.

"Let's see what we can find by beachcombing. No stores here."

I sort of woke up to the fact that our needs in that respect were to be supplied, or not, according to who had thrown what overboard from a boat and in what condition.

We put on our swimsuits so we could have a cooling swim before returning to the house. Also tennis shoes—no telling what we might step on while beachcombing. Before we left, Russ got out a small notebook and pencil and put them on the table. "That's for our 'want list.' We are going to find a lot of things we didn't bring."

I was wondering how I could take a shower after swimming when Russ said that he had investigated, and if we wanted to have enough water to drink and cook with, we could use only a quart of fresh water to rinse ourselves after a swim or a saltwater bath. Wow! I was determined to be a good sport, so I said nothing. How I was going to miss my twice-a-day showers!

Beachcombing on the Florida Keys is quite different from walking a sand beach on the mainland. All sorts of debris. Large, flat-sided crates in which were the wilted remains of heads of lettuce. Grapefruit, uninjured by the salt water and quite usable. Extremely large coconuts and smaller ones from the area. Bushel baskets, a pint-sized Green River Whiskey bottle nearly a third full, and just what I was looking for, a two-quart jar with its lid.

By this time my legs were really sore and I was ready to sit down. "Let's go home," I said.

"You go. Take the baskets and the grapefruit with you. I'm going up the beach to look for some long planks. We need to build a more solid dock."

I plodded back to the house and got out a book to read, and

woke up when Russ came back. It was now time to make supper. I watched as he lit the stove. Soon I would have to do it myself, but I wasn't in a hurry.

The ice was going fast, so I cooked all the meat. Supper was ready by the time the lantern was lit. We had a delightful meal. Hunger truly does make a delectable sauce.

Russ washed dishes in the ocean by flashlight, brought them in, and rinsed them with a small amount of fresh water. I put the remainder of the food in the freshly washed glass jar. Quickly, we raised the icebox lid and snuggled the jar against the remaining ice and closed the lid.

I wondered if I would ever get used to margarine. Russ had explained that butter wouldn't keep without ice. We kept our margarine in a quart jar. At that time, because of a bicker between the dairy people and the margarine people, margarine could not be sold colored. The capsule or packet of color came with the margarine. If you wanted it colored, you did it yourself. Having it in a jar made it easier.

The food safely stored, we decided to read a bit. Russ was in the armchair with his back to the kitchen, and I was on the bench next to him. I was just thinking how fantastically quiet it was when a movement caught my eye. Just a sort of flicker. Looking more closely at the spot, I saw a large rat peering down at the table from the rafter under the roof. Spilling most of my after-dinner coffee in my lap, I froze. Then, trying to sound nonchalant, in what I firmly believed to be a soft tone of voice I said, "Russ, get your .22. There's a rat on the rafter just above the screen, across from me."

"Just keep on talking, but not so damn loud. I expected it. This house hasn't been lived in for awhile. My .22 is right behind me." He was moving as he said this and slowly brought out the gun.

I continued to talk, more softly now, and among the things I remember I said was that I had never seen such a large rat at such close quarters and I never wanted to see one that close again. My eyes were just glued on the rat and the sound of the shot came as a surprise. I jumped up when the rat fell to the floor after bouncing off the bench on the other side of the table. Funny! I had only intended to stand up. I found that I was standing on the bench.

With a casual remark that he would plug the hole in the roof the next morning, Russ put the gun alongside his chair. Twice more that night he shot and killed a rat. There was only a short time in between. This was the beginning of quite a long feud with rats.

It seemed to me that the biggest problem we were going to have was water. I asked about washing clothes.

"Wash them in salt water. Rinse them in fresh. We'll have that much," Russ said.

I said, "Soap won't make suds in salt water."

"Why do you suppose I brought all that Kirk's Hardwater Soap? We still have clean clothes to wear, so we'll wait a bit." From then on, slightly soiled clothing no longer went into the wash, just dirty.

I suddenly noticed that the wall behind Russ wasn't white anymore. If I had hair on my back, it would have been standing up. The spots seemed to be moving. I thought at first they were palmetto bugs, the kind that leave that bitter odor of almonds when they are crushed, and the liquid burns like fire when you get it on your skin.

"Look, behind you on the wall, palmetto bugs."

"Nope, just flying roaches. Too many to swat, though. I'll have to poison them." As he talked, Russ got a tube of roach paste from the flat-topped partition between him and the kitchen. He dabbed the paste generously on the wall. The roaches, apparently hypnotized by the bright light, didn't move. I actually enjoyed watching them die of that poison, thinking I didn't have to swat them and mess with them.

It was impossible to sit there and try to read. I felt too crawly. It didn't bother Russ, though. He just continued to read as I crawled the ladder to the bedroom. After sitting still for so long, my muscles were again screaming about being abused. I wished that I didn't have to make the effort to get undressed.

Breakfast was the last of our bacon, with some scrambled eggs. Boy, the rats must have been hungry to come out in the daytime. I saw one on the rafter in almost the same place as the night before. While I was softly telling Russ about that one, I saw another on the floor, peering around the corner from the kitchen. It wasn't six feet from me. I put my feet up on the bench and watched that one. The second shot killed it.

After breakfast, Russ got one of the bushel baskets, put the rats in it and said, "I'll get those I threw out last night and throw all of them off the dock. The tide is going out and they aren't apt to drift ashore later. Hey Charlotte, I can't find them. Not one rat here. What do you suppose got them? Raccoons?"

"I wouldn't know."

"I'll throw these in the water and be right back to help you stow the canned goods and scrub the floors."

While stowing the canned goods on the shelves, I saw that roaches (or something) had eaten some of the paper labels. I decided that I had better mark the contents of the cans. I got out my sewing basket and found a piece of Jan's crayon to mark the can tops. If I hadn't, our meals would have been a sort of guessing game. Gee, I was glad that our paper-boxed supplies were in the safe.

Russ wasn't back yet, and I was wondering just how he expected to spare enough fresh water to scrub the floors. I saw him coming up the path from the dock with a wooden bucket in his hand. It didn't have a handle, but it was just what we needed. He went out front and scooped it full of dry sand above the high-tide mark. I watched him when he came in and was startled to see him throw handfuls of sand around on the kitchen floor. When he did the same in the living room, I started to talk.

"Now, now, never mind. This is a good way to clean floors. We won't need soap, and salt water will do it. Now the bucket is empty. Just fill it with ocean water, as much as you can carry, and bring it back in."

I did, sloshing some of it on me. I found him scrubbing the sand around with the heavy-duty broom. He had finished the kitchen by then and instructed me to slosh it against the walls and then rinse it out. I did, and got a little more wet. More buckets, and each time I got wetter. Finally, when I stumbled and spilled a bucketful, he said, "Take the lightweight broom and sweep out the sand and water." I was pushing the sand ahead of me successfully when he came in and vigorously sloshed more water. Then we propped open the front and back doors so the wind could get it. It didn't seem to take long before it was dry. By then, my broom was dry, too, and I swept out the last of the fine sand. The floor looked bleached.

"Russ, we didn't do the walls in the living room."

"Forget it for now. Some of that roach paste is still there."

These new muscles I was making were complaining. My clothes had stopped dripping, and I felt sticky.

"How about hanging your clothes on the line and putting on your swimsuit? We can look for boxes for your dresser."

"Fine."

Later, while walking down the high-tide mark, I caught a sparkle of glass in the bushes. Investigating it, I found that it was a large pear-shaped bottle of dark glass. When I called Russ to come look, he said that it was an old demijohn which would hold more than four gallons. He said, "Wish we could find more." This inspired me to go further into the bushes in spite of the fact that I might run across a snake. He put the bottle just above the high-tide line and said, "Easier to find on our way home. No use carrying it both ways."

"Gee, it is nice to be able to set your possessions down and find them when you return. A new experience."

Watching carefully because of snakes, I soon found two more of these large demijohns. As I carried my finds towards the beach, he was walking towards me with one in each hand. Just as he reached me, he put one bottle down and picked up a square piece of wood and said, "Hah, good! This has been a lucky morning for us."

"What're you so pleased about?"

"This is Spanish cedar. I'll carve some corks for the bottles."

Home with our treasures, we lunched on cold hamburgers and used the last of the ice for ice water. "You look pretty pooped, Charlotte. Sit and read awhile. I'm going to explore a bit. I want to locate the little lime grove that's supposed to be on the pointy end of the key, between the house and the dock. Bill said the entrance was just west of the path."

I sat down in the armchair and woke up when he returned with some orange-sized, brown fruit.

"These are sapodillas. I found two trees near the edge of the grove. The sap of these trees is chicle; that's what they make chewing gum out of. The tree is tapped the same way as the maple tree." While talking, he broke a fruit in half and gave it to me. The fruit also is brown, but lighter than the skin. It is sweet as honey, more like candy than fruit. I saved the rest to put in the safe for later.

"There are some tremendous mangrove snappers in the creek," Russ said, referring to the cut between Elliott and Sands Key. "Let's get some for dinner."

As I followed him to his tackle-box on the back porch, I was thinking it would take me a bit longer to get used to the idea that I couldn't shop for what I wanted. We had nothing in the meat line now but some canned corned beef, and that would have to be saved for emergencies.

Russ gave me two hand lines ready to use, and we went outside.

"Wait for me," he said. "I shouldn't be long. Just going to get a conch for bait." Perhaps ten minutes later he returned, soaking wet. He had a large, spiral shell in one hand.

"Charlotte, do you remember when you were told to put the open pink side to your ear so you could hear the sound of the waves? This is the most common of Florida souvenirs brought home by tourists."

He got his sheath knife and led the way. In answer to my many questions as to how we were to use the thing for bait, he answered, "I can show you better than I can tell you. Wait and learn how while you are watching."

Reaching the water, he turned the conch so that the pointy end was on top. Counting aloud for my benefit, he touched each point. Then with the thick part of the blade, he rapped sharply on the shell between the fourth and fifth points, explaining that the shell there is thin. Then, the knife partially inserted, he gave a sort of half twist and explained that the animal was fastened to the shell and he had to cut it loose. Turning the shell over, he pried with the knife at a banjo-pick shaped, horny substance. It loosened some, and he grabbed it with his fingers and slowly pulled the animal from the shell.

"This thing like a banjo pick is the foot. Those are the eye-

19

stalks, the bump they are on is the head. This is all good firm flesh. This next part is flabby, the stomach and innards. Using the knife, he cut off the head and flabby part and let it drop. I saw many fish dart towards it as it slowly sank in the water. Then he put the remainder of the animal in the broad lip of the shell and scrubbed his hands with sand and water. (The transparent, sticky covering of the conch is a nuisance.) He finally cleaned his hands and the rest of the conch. The cut end of the conch was snow white and covered with a black skin.

Boy, it seemed to me that the thing would be easier to prepare than fish. I had no occasion to learn at the time how much more work it is when a conch is prepared for food.

Russ cut some bait-sized pieces and we started fishing. I had the time of my life. I guess Russ didn't, though. I still had to be taught to take fish off the hook without getting snagged by either the fish or the hook. Russ unhooked the fish for me and threw back two out of three that I caught.

"Why?"

"I have to fillet them, so we'll keep only the big ones."

My next catch was a different variety and small. I was surprised when Russ didn't flip that back into the water.

"This is moonfish—a great delicacy. See if you can catch enough of these for supper."

He was right! Meanwhile, I was catching them and he was too busy helping me to fish himself. Before long I had caught six moonfish and went up to prepare the potatoes and other things, thinking that he could have done just as well without me. I'd better learn to handle fish and hooks myself.

It seemed like only a few minutes when he came running up the path with an almost curtainlike effect around his head. Sand-flies. Boy! Were they wicked tonight! I met him at the back door and took the fish as he grabbed the spray gun and puffed in a circle to kill the bugs.

"The damn things got so bad I couldn't stay to skin the fish. I'll have to do that in the sink."

I hadn't started the stove yet, hoping he would. The look he gave me then encouraged me to try. I mentally rehearsed the way he had done it. Then—success, another hurdle passed. The hardest thing about cooking on the vapor stove was to remember that

20

the fiercely hot flame took only half the time to cook things, compared to electricity. I turned the fire way down, and soon the fish were nicely browned. It was another delectable treat.

Eating by lantern light again, we decided to have our evening meals earlier, before the sandflies got so bad. While we were talking about this, the first rat of the evening appeared. By now I was getting used to them and merely told Russ where it was. He shot it, and two more that night. The patched bullet holes were showing up on the roof like black freckles.

By morning, the rats, which were thrown outside, had all disappeared.

As we headed towards the beach I said, "By the way, Russ, we got bottles instead of boxes yesterday. I still need a convenient place to put our clothes."

"Yeah, I know. This morning you find your boxes and I'll concentrate on any kind of metal container which might have something useful in it. We have to repair that leaky skiff at the dock. When that's done, we can collect the boards we need to repair the dock. While you are looking for boxes, keep your eyes open for creosoted lumber, especially 2 by 6's or bigger. Pull them above the high-tide line. I'll put them higher later."

"What does 'creosoted' mean?"

"If the boards look brownish and smell like tar, it's probably creosoted. I guess I couldn't expect you to know something like that."

I started off towards an apple box at the water line and put it above the high-tide line. Going farther up the beach, I saw a long 2 by 6. It looked brownish and when I smelled it, I decided it was what I'd been told to look for. Pulling it ashore, I got my hands all brown and messy. The next one I found was wider and longer. The outer end was still in the water and I had a hard time with it. Holding the shore end tightly, I heaved back. I sat down hard with the end of the board on my lap and watched a round black container pop out from under the outer end. It floated partly out of water. Remembering what Russ had said about metal containers, I struggled out from under the end of the board and waded out after it. By this time he had caught up with me and carried the can ashore. Prying off the lid, he identified the contents as

Trinidad asphalt.

"Boy, are we lucky! Just what we need for the skiff. I found some caulking cotton down the beach. We have what we need to stop the leaks in the skiff."

I walked up the beach, sort of browsing now, looking for more brown boards and almost hoping I wouldn't see one. My hands sort of burned now from the brown stuff and sand rub I had given them in an effort to get it off. Looking back, I saw Russ, waist deep, going towards a box which was floating with its top level with the water. He steered it ashore and made no effort to pick it up until it had grounded on the sand. From his actions, then, it was apparent that the box was quite heavy. I walked back to look, and he pried one of the top boards off, disclosing heavy waxed paper. When he tore a hole in that, we saw a thick, brownish substance, which I immediately and wrongly identified as ambergris.

"Huh! It doesn't even meet the first test! The smell is not disagreeable. In my opinion it's spar grease. I'll use it instead of paint on the boat bottom."

By now we had more than we could carry in one trip. We decided to share the weight of the spar grease and carried it between us until my fingers gave out. Putting it down, we went back for boxes and other things, including the asphalt. While walking back, Russ spotted another demijohn in the bushes and I found a square, black bottle. It had the raised design of a key on one side. Russ said it was old, so I decided to carry it home in spite of the fact that I was tired.

We finally arrived at the house with our goodies and still had time to fish for supper. Russ got the remainder of the conch from the topside of the shutter where he had placed it the night before for safekeeping. He surprised me when he started to cut pieces from it and said, "I'll put these things away, you catch the fish. Don't keep any runts unless they are moonfish. I'll be down later."

As I slid my feet up the board to the dock, I made up my mind to get a wide, thick board to replace that narrow, springy one. All that walking on the soft sand had stretched a few more of my leg muscles so that I was glad to sit down. I must have dozed off for a few minutes because I suddenly noticed the hand line slipping through my fingers. I clamped down on it, pulled in the line, and found that I had caught a large snapper. When it started to flop around on the dock, I realized that I would have to get the hook out myself. I managed to hold it still with my feet and wiggle the hook out. Success at last. I stood up to toss the fish on shore, saw that it landed near the water's edge. I turned back in time to see my line going into the water. I hadn't tied it. Well, I'd learn. I managed to jump on it. I pulled the line in and found another large snapper and managed to get the hook out without too much damage to my hands. Two fish that size should be enough for supper. I looked at the one that I had thrown on shore and saw that it had flopped part way back into the water. I hurried towards it with the second one and kicked it back from the edge. I could go to the house now. Oops! My line was still on the dock. Returning for it, I decided to try once more. With my line again in the water, I was wishing for something to lean against. I decided to call it a day and wound up the line as I pulled it in. Then I felt a slight tug, less than I had experienced with the smallest fish, however, I continued to pull the line in. In the clear water I saw something, but what? It looked like a large green snake with a dorsal fin. It appeared to be at least four feet long and larger than my upper arm in thickness. I pulled the head end out of water, and the silly thing started to crawl up the line, tying knots in itself. The wicked little eyes seemed to say that I was responsible for its predicament and that it would get even. By now it was part way on the dock. I had really caught a weirdie, and I wanted to show it to Russ. Giving it more line, I flipped it to the shore side of the dock, and going halfway down the plank, I jumped ashore. More line again, and I started dragging it up the path while I called Russ to come see.

I was watching the rocks in the path, rather than the snake, and I noticed that the line felt heavier. "Throw it!" I did—into the bushes on the ocean side.

Russ was furious about my carelessness. I then and there heard a lengthy lecture about moray eels. While they are not poisonous, they are scavengers, and their bites almost always become infected.

"The next time you catch one, cut the line and let him have it!"

This led to Russ giving me a sheath knife to wear on my belt. He had made it many years before when he was serving some time in a steel mill. Then he took a machete and went into the bushes to kill the eel.

Full of adrenaline from my excitement and my narrow escape from injury, I went along to the dock to watch him fillet the fish. I knew I would soon be expected to do that chore myself.

At supper that night, Russ told me that he had oiled and made usable a grindstone that sits outside at the far corner of the house. In the morning he wanted to re-sharpen our sheath knives and his machete. No reading that night. I was too pooped. This was quite a mad pace for a city gal.

Dishes done the next morning, I turned the crank of the grindstone and dripped water on the metal as he sharpened the blades. When we had finished he said, "It's going to be high tide in about an hour and we'll be able to pull the skiff out onto land. Everything we need to repair it is stacked behind you beside the house."

I looked and saw the asphalt can, a scrub brush, and a piece of broken machete alongside the spar grease.

"You carry those things. I'll take the spar grease, it's heavier than the asphalt. I've got the caulking cotton in my pocket. Now don't start asking questions about how we are going to do it. Watch and learn."

I gathered my load together and started for the dock. After I banged the can of asphalt against my shins a few times, I decided to make two trips instead of one. Back for the asphalt, I carried it in my arms. Naturally, then, I couldn't see the rocks in the path and took a header right into the bushes. Fortunately, I struggled up, thinking how glad I was that the lid stayed on and I didn't have the stuff all over me. Just then I heard, "Charlotte, did you hurt yourself?"

I said, "No," as I turned around and saw that Russ was grinning from ear to ear.

"You sure looked funny, diving into those bushes. I'm glad you aren't hurt. Do you want me to carry that?"

"No, thanks, pal, I can manage." I continued slowly down the path.

We put our loads down at the water's edge and Russ went to get the skiff. I wandered into the bushes on the ocean side to see what was there. I saw quite a few bottles, and even though they were a pretty lavender color, I didn't bother to pick them up. Then a bit farther on, I saw a knobby piece of wood with a long rope attached to it. I picked that up and went back to the water's edge. Russ saw what I had and said, "Good, just what we need! Cut the rope off as close to the wood as you can, and then throw me one end of the line." I did this and watched as he tied the rope to the bow, next to the one already there. Getting out of the boat, he waded ashore and we started to pull the boat to the shore. We weren't in a hurry and allowed the rising tide to help us. Soon we had the boat partially above the water and he said "Now we need various lengths of board, from three feet to six. Let's look."

Before long we had what we needed and the work began. Leaning the shortest piece of board against one side of the skiff, we lifted the skiff until the board slipped under the edge of the boat, the gunwale, then the next largest board in the same way, and we soon had the skiff almost but not quite overbalanced. With a bit more bracing, the furry-looking bottom soon became easy to work on.

"You can either go beachcombing or help me scrape." I went beachcombing, but not before seeing some of the miniature sea life that lived in the sea growth on the boat. Small critters, called brittle stars, looked much like skinny octopi. Tiny fish, crabs, and barnacles.

On the beach again I pulled ashore several large boards, among them some with a beautiful grain. Later, I learned to identify these as quarter-sawed oak. Now that I could recognize Spanish cedar, I picked up many small pieces and put them inside my shirt. Later on, the longest of the oak boards was made into two benches. I found the other boxes I needed for my dresser and a really good one for my magazine rack. On my way back to the house with the boxes, I found a three-inch wide paintbrush. And two rather large coconuts–I had coconut custard in mind.

I was making lunch when Russ came to the house. Later on, I went along to the dock to see what he had done. The boat had been caulked with the cotton dipped in asphalt and pushed into the cracks with the broken blade, the bottom had been greased with the spar grease, and it was ready for turning. We were also smeared with spar grease when we reversed the operation and lowered the boat. Now the other side had to be raised. We almost lost our grip on the sides of the boat many times and had to dip our hands in sand. Now we took time to give them a sand wash. Before long, we had the other side in position for scraping. And, at Russ' suggestion, I went to catch our supper.

The rest of the conch had disappeared from the shutter top, so I waded out into the ocean to look for more. Never having seen a conch on the ocean bottom before, I must have passed several before I recognized one by its shape. I had forgotten that they have small sea growths camouflaging them. Shoulder deep by now, I had to swim down to get it. Walking back to shore, I noticed that a tiny fish was swimming in the water above the foot. When I got to the dock and showed it to Russ, he identified it as a cardinal fish, a fish that lives with the conch, mostly inside the shell.

"Russ, why don't we sort of corral these conchs so that we can get them in a hurry if we want to?"

"It's slightly illogical. They need to move around to get their food. Besides—oh, forget it for now. I'll figure out a way. Incidentally, when you go up to the house again, add a crawfish grabber to the want list.

I was just about to ask him to prepare the conch for me when I decided to try it myself. Rapping myself on the knuckles a few times, I finally managed to make the break in the shell necessary to get the critter out. I thought he had been too busy to watch, but I heard him say, "It wasn't too difficult, was it?"

Gosh! That sounded like a compliment. He seemed to believe that if you had seen something done, you should be able to do it. I caught enough fish for supper before the sandflies came, and as he had finished the boat by then, he told me to run up and fix the rest of the supper while he cleaned them. When I hung my wet clothes on the line, I went in and got things ready. I hadn't lit the stove when he came up and handed me the fish.

"Get some clothes on and come give me a hand. I saw the remains of an old kerosene stove down by the little grove. We'll use that for cooking tonight. Our gasoline is getting low, and there is enough breeze out front to keep the sandflies away.

"Just what do we need with the 'remains' of a kerosene stove?"

"Never mind. Just wait and see."

Together we carried the 'remains' to the house and then a bit farther to the top of the ridge which sloped down to the ocean. There, we turned the stove upside down so that the burner holes were resting on the sand and the back and lower shelf formed a back and roof. Russ sent me into the house to get the food in cooking pans. When I returned he had raised the stove a few inches above the sand with boards and had two compact little fires going under the burner holes. I set the pans over the fires and this caused the smoke from the Spanish cedar he was burning to coil around and into the pans. It smelled delightful.

It took quite a while for the food to cook, but it was very pleasant sitting out in the open. The few sandflies seemed to avoid the area of the smoke. I made up my mind that whenever possible I would cook in my kerosene stove, over cedar fires. Soon the wind picked up and the blowing sand made it necessary to move inside to eat. When there, I added mosquito tent to our want list. The food was delightful and the smoky taste was an added sauce. This evening we were eating early enough to finish our food in the twilight.

Later I remarked that I wished I knew something to put on my hands and face to keep the sandflies away.

"Did you try citronella?"

"Yes, and the darn things love it!"

"Well, the next best thing we can use is oil on the screens. Tomorrow, you look for some. We can use the paintbrush you found to apply it. Lordy, I wonder what the old-timers did, when they weren't sitting in the smudge of black mangrove smoke, to avoid the biters. Toughed it out, I guess."

Our lantern attracted the things, and they shriveled up and died when they got near it. There was always a pile of their carcasses under it after it had burned a little while.

High tide came soon after breakfast and we hurried down to the skiff. All that remained to do was to spread the grease and lower the boat. That didn't take long, say about half as long as it took to get the grease off our hands! Kirk's soap finished that process. We now kept a bar stashed at the dock in a tin can.

Russ had carried the oars from the back porch, so we launched the boat and went for a boat ride. He was rowing towards the front of the house. "We are going to take care of corralling the conchs. I figured out a way which will be better than building a fence around them."

"How?"

He removed from his pocket some heavy cord that had gotten packed rather than thrown away, and an ice pick with a bit of wood stuck on the tip. "With these and some rocks which you are going to get. Wait and see. Now, look for conchs."

I looked down into the clear water and finally said, "There's one."

"Go over and get it."

I was fully dressed but getting used to getting wet. The weather was delightful. I got the conch and handed it to Russ. Then I just stayed in the water and hung on the side of the boat spotting the conchs and getting them, mostly around eight or nine feet deep.

By the time we reached the front of the house, I had gathered over a dozen. Now Russ said, "It's time to anchor these. Swim ashore and bring back a fist-sized piece of coral rock for each one."

Wet clothes seem to weigh a ton when you are swimming, and I was glad to wade when the water was shallow enough. Gathering the rocks on shore was no problem, but I had no place to put them except inside my shirt. I did, and clumsily walked into the water to chin height. There I waited for Russ to row in.

I had been hearing pounding noises before that, and now I saw what had caused them. Russ put the thin shell of the conch on the boat seat and, using the ice pick, made a hole in the shell; then he tied a length of string to it. Now that I had brought my rocks, he tied one to each piece of string. He handed me a conch with its attached anchor and told me to drop it. Lowering it knee-high, I dropped and watched that it landed right side down. I had to swim a stroke or two to reach the boat for the next conch. Russ had me drop the conchs far enough apart that each had its own foraging ground.

"They'll wander a bit for feed now."

"Wander? How do they walk?"

"That banjo-pick foot is their only means of moving. Extending it, they pull themselves along to it. In muddy bottom they are really in trouble. They push about a quarter-length of the foot into the bottom and pull themselves along. The extra weight I added should keep them pretty well in the same spot."

It was easier swimming ashore than getting into the boat with my wet clothes. So I did. Russ rowed ashore and beached in front of the house. I sat on the doorstep while he made sandwiches.

"Russ, we had better look for some oil. We have been ignoring the sandflies every day and cussing them every night. Maybe we can find some bug spray."

"People on boats wouldn't use that. By the way, I'd like some conch stew for supper."

"Gosh, I don't know how to make that."

"Never mind, you'll learn. Let's make some first and then talk about it. We need four more conchs."

Russ in the boat again, me in the water again—soon I found the conchs.

"Why don't you swim ashore now and look for oil cans," Russ said, "I'll go around to the dock and fix these for eating."

Getting used to swimming while fully clothed, I swam in, and within a quarter mile had found two screw-top cans with some oil in each. This beach store was fabulous. Almost everything we needed.

I hurried to the dock now. I needed to know how to prepare conch for food. I hadn't even seen a conch with the meat inside until a short time before.

There were a lot of things I hadn't heard of until this sojourn on the Keys.

When I arrived, Russ had already removed the conchs from their shells. Now he cut off the flabby parts and threw them into the water. While he washed the "glue" off the flesh, I watched the many fish nibble on the pieces of conch. Now, putting the washed pieces on a board, he cut off the head bump and the mantle, the thin black skin which covers the entire lip of the shell when the animal extends its body from the shell. Making a full-length slit, he removed a three-eighths inch tube from it. Then he said, "Grab that fat, round piece of teak wood on the dock and take it to the house, we'll need that. I'll be right up. I'll skin these inside and then I won't have sandfly troubles. Oh, the thing that just looks like a piece of wood is a hawsepipe plug. Hush, wait and see."

After I put the plug on the worktable, I took off my wet clothes and hung them on the line. Then, thinking of the sandflies, I got the oil cans out to show Russ. He was coming up the path now.

"Good, just about enough to paint the screens. Get a large bean can out of the burning barrel and wash it in the ocean. These conchs can wait until the screens are ready. Bring the paintbrush in when you come."

When I returned with the things, he bent the can to an oval shape so he could put the brush in. Draining both oil cans into it, he went outside and started his painting. From there, he told me to peel and cube four large onions and four large potatoes. The potatoes were to be boiled and the onions fried in bacon fat. Also, he told me to put pyrethrum powder on the want list. He said the smoke from that would kill sandflies. "Those damn 'flying teeth'!"

"How does it smell?"

"Not disagreeable at all. Something like burning leaves. I'll make a burner for it out of half a coconut shell, saw some slits in it, and make a base for it out of some pumice stone. You can look for that on the beach. It floats in on the tide. Remind me of it. By the way, get the flour ready."

"What do I put it in? How much?"

"Put four heaping tablespoonfuls in the heavy iron skillet, over a low fire, and stir it until it is golden brown. Then turn the fire off. I'll be back in long before that happens. Well, maybe not. I'd better take a saltwater bath before I come in."

I put out a quart of rinse water, hung a towel on the doorknob and went back to my cooking. The flour was done when I heard Russ rinsing himself.

"I need the lead beater from my toolbox, so I'll come in the back way."

"What the hell are you going to do with a lead beater? What is it?"

"Plumbers use it to beat lead pipes. It is a mallet made of the toughest wood known, *lignum vitae*. My Dad and I used it when we installed the plumbing in his house. I am going to use it to tenderize the conch. Wait and see."

Soon he was in the kitchen washing the plug and the lead beater. While they drained, he worked on the conch. Using my dullest kitchen knife to grip, rather than cut, he pulled pieces of the black skin off. It didn't look easy. When most of it was off, he used a sharp knife to thinly slice off the rest. When all four had been peeled, he put the plug on the table, took a piece of conch and the lead beater over and started beating. The plug sort of jumped when he beat, but it stayed on the table. He had left the foot on the conch and was holding it by that. As pieces were beaten off, he said, "Get a gallon-sized kettle, put about three inches of water in it and bring it to me."

The onions were done now so I turned off that fire. When I told him the potatoes were done, he told me to drain the water from them into a small pan and put it outside to cool. What, another pan!

When the conchs had been beaten, he put the pan on the fire.

"Watch that very closely now. When it comes to a foaming boil, take the big wooden spoon and stir it down, the second time also. When it comes to a boil the third time, turn it off. If it cooks too long, you can use it for shoe soles. Drain the water off in another pan and set it out to cool. Then, open a can of green peas and drain the juice off.

"Does that get saved, too?"

"No, throw that away. Just leave the peas in the can for now."

What? No pan for them? Just six so far! Time for a cigarette now. I had just lit up when I saw the foamy boil Russ had told me about. Putting my cigarette in the seashell ashtray, I grabbed the spoon and stirred. It only took a few minutes to boil up again, and the third time I took it off the fire. Draining the water off, I put the pan outside and sat down to finish my cigarette.

When the conch and potato water had cooled, Russ brought the pans inside and I went to watch him. How was he going to use them? I watched as he put the skillet over a low fire and added the conch water to the flour, stirring constantly. Thinning the gravy more with some of the potato water, he finished it. Then he added some celery salt to it and reached into the kettle for a piece of conch. I just couldn't believe it! He had beaten the conch into small pieces and now there were three large chunks of conch. It had to be cut into small pieces again. This done, everything was put into the large kettle except the remains of the potato water. As he stirred the kettle slowly over a low fire, he said, "Better make a note for me to make a dipper out of half a coconut shell. You'll have to beachcomb for a piece of mahogany for the handle. It should be a piece of wood at least two inches thick and at least a foot long. It's ready now, let's eat.

Using a cup, I filled two large soup bowls so full that I was afraid to carry them up the step to the table. I put them on the wide top of the partition between the two rooms and only spilled a little bit. Up the step to the other room, I found it was easy to put the bowls on the table without spilling.

The custodian of the day was pulling the shades again, so Russ lit the lantern. The oil-painted screens kept out the sand-flies, and we were comfortable as we ate the stew. It was marvelous. The flavor was somewhere between that of clam and oyster. Fit for the gods. In spite of the enormous amount we had eaten, half of it was left. How to keep it?

It was time for dishwashing. I reached for Russ' bowl and something caught my eye. I looked around again, and then stared in amazement at the ledge. It was no longer white, but a mixture of black and dark red. Just millions of ants milling around. A good many of them were eating the drips of stew, and the others were just fighting. I called Russ' attention to it, and we watched as the battle raged on. Fair-sized black ants were battling with smaller red ones. They bit off legs, and some cases we saw where they had been bitten apart at the waist. There were so many of these pieces lying around that the ants stumbled over them. We had a close view of it, and it was gory in a minor sort of way. There was no blood visible, though.

"Charlotte, I think the black ones are winning."

"I don't agree. I think there are more black pieces lying around than there are red ones."

A truce area existed only where both kinds of ants were eating the stew. I looked again towards that spot, and the stew was gone. The battle had covered that area. Who won? We don't know. Suddenly it seemed that a truce had been declared. The remaining ants went off in different directions. When all the able-bodied ants had left, there remained on the surface at least two large cups of assorted heads, legs and bodies. As we were standing there talking about how best to clean up the mess, the ants reappeared in force. Not to fight, though. To clear the battlefield. In a short time each of the species had removed all the spare parts of their opponents. They passed each other during this salvaging operation, but the truce held. Soon the ledge was clean again. It looked polished. I had never before seen ants in such numbers. Now I was not only worried about the stew spoiling before tomorrow night, but how to keep the ants away.

Russ must have been thinking of that also. He gathered the dishes and went out to wash them, telling me that he would be right back. Returning, he put everything in the sink except the kettle of stew, one soup plate and a kettle of salt water. He poured some salt water into the soup plate and put it on the table. He told me to get a large can of beans from the shelf and put it in the soup plate. With a little more ocean water, he filled the plate to the brim and balanced the stew kettle on the can of beans. With the lid on the kettle, we hoped it would be safe from ants. And rats. We hadn't seen any of those for a day or so.

I hurried down the ladder the next morning and was pleased to find the stew untouched. It had to be reheated so that it would keep until suppertime. I let it stay over a very low fire while we had breakfast. Then Russ put it back on its pedestal.

Once again at our "store," the beach, we gathered all the boxes visible over half a mile and started taking them to the house. On my third trip back to get more, I found the necessary piece of mahogany for my conch stew dipper.

Now to work. We needed many small nails for my dresser. Russ showed me how to pry apart some of the boxes without bending the nails. I was being useful! Finally got enough to use. When Russ spread two orange crates apart and nailed a long, flat box to the top, I had my dresser. Now for the magazine rack.

Russ sawed an apple box from the edge of the open side to the bottom corner of the other side. This made a triangular trough. Four legs nailed on the sides completed it. Russ took more orange crates apart and inserted the ends into two other orange crates. This gave us shelf space for small items. We now had a medicine cabinet, and a box could be unpacked. We nailed the cabinet to the wall in the kitchen storage space. Things looked more "on purpose" now.

Gosh! It seemed as though I was always thirsty. I couldn't get used to drinking water which had run off a roof, but I knew better than to comment on it. Who had gotten me into this interesting mess, anyway? Me! Thinking of the clear sparkling water in Miami, I suggested to Russ that we look for more demijohns so that we would have enough when we got a chance to haul water from Miami. With only a skiff as transportation, that wouldn't be soon, but it couldn't hurt to be ready for it.

While we waded in the bushes, Russ stayed fairly close to me because of my dislike for snakes. As we went slowly along, we saw many other small bottles, different sizes and shapes. Most of them were lavender, but an occasional one looked black. A closer look showed that they were a dark green. I found a wicker-covered gallon jar which would be fine to take in the boat. By late afternoon we found four large ones. I got more than my share of sunburn that day and especially noticed it when I slapped the sandflies on my way back to the house. I would have left the rinsing of the bottles for another time, but Russ is a do-it-now person. I did go in to our medicine cabinet and looked for still another thing to keep the sandflies off. Vicks salve was the only thing I hadn't tried so I tried that. It hurt my sunburn, but it did keep the sandflies off. When the bottles had been rinsed and put with the others on the porch, they occupied a most impressive space. We had ten of them.

We finished the conch stew that night and it tasted even better than it had the night before.

During breakfast the next morning, Russ said, "I'd like some coconut pancakes. How about gathering some coconuts–six of the largest you can find. I'll go look for something to take the hulls off."

34

It didn't take me long to gather them and I was tossing them towards the house when he called me to give him a hand. I arrived down-beach to find him dragging a large plank with a four-inch spike sticking out of it, near the end.

"Do you need something that big just to take the hulls off?"

"Not exactly, but I do need something with a spike in it. That was the first available."

We carried it to the front of the house. He sat down on the plank, facing the spike. I handed him a coconut. He turned the stem side down and bumped it onto the spike and pulled it towards him. Loosening the hull in this way, all around the nut, he then handed it to me with instructions to pull it off. Sounds easy–I finally managed to get most of it off. He finished working on the last one and turned the board over, sticking the spike into the sand. He then started to pull off husks and I saw how it should be done, if you have enough muscle.

"When we get most of the stuff off all of these we can use the flat side of the grindstone and wear the rest off. Then with some pumice stone we can finish 'sanding' them. That way we can use the shell as well as the meat in it." The first part of the operation didn't seem to take long, but sanding with the pumice to suit him took quite a while. Finished at last, he searched in his toolbox and came up with a large C-clamp. He clamped one of the nuts to the workbench and I held it steady as he sawed it. "Whoa–never mind holding it now–I almost made a bad mistake. Get a glass."

I did and he punched out the soft spot in the end and shook the milk into the glass. We shared it and it was delicious, almost cool. Clamped again to the bench, the coconut didn't take long to saw.

"What do you figure to make out of this one?"

"Don't be so impatient. If we can get the meat out of this one without breaking it, it will be suitable for the dipper. If it cracks, I'll use the next best one."

He scraped off the fuzz from the sawing and pried out some of the meat. He handed it to me. It was very good. We ate coconut meat instead of lunch. After all the nuts were cut, he pried out the meat and I took some in to grate for pudding. With a package of vanilla pudding, I soon had my coconut treat. I set it aside to cool and started to grate more. Russ came in then and told me not to make any for the pancakes. "It will taste better if you do it in the morning–not so dry."

"What are you whittling?"

"I'm making a handle for the dipper. Right now I haven't any idea as to how I will fasten it on."

About a week later, we salvaged the most useful object of all, a radio in a small wooden box with a hinged top. Two of the small bolts in the radio were used to make the dipper complete.

Coconut Shell Items

DIPPER

← HANDLE CARVED FROM MADIERA LIMB.

← SALVAGED BRASS BOLTS.

← 1/2 MATURE COCONUT SHELL RUBBED SMOOTH WITH PUMICE.

WINDPROOF ASH TRAY

side   top view

WIRE TO HOLD CIGARETTE

Bottom is cut
PART OF SHELL WIRED ON.

TRINKET BOX.

← LATCH.

← HINGE SALVAGED

← COCONUT CUT SO LID IS FORMED

← BASE HOLLOWED TO HOLD COCONUT.

BASE – HINGE – AND LATCH SALVAGED
FROM BEACH.

RM-Elliott Key
1934

36

CHAPTER THREE

Sea-water Laundry. Freshwater Problem.
Add a Spring to the Mattress.

By now we had quite an accumulation of washing, including sheets, towels, and pillow cases–two bushel baskets full. I knew it would be a problem, but Russ would have the answer. We were in the position of the pioneers after the invention of Kirk's Hardwater Soap. Fortunately we had a lot of that.

We carried our baskets to the dock with the soap, two new scrub brushes and the wooden bucket. It now had a nice rope handle. Russ dunked a pair of dungarees in the salt water, lay them on the dock in front of me, handed me a bar of soap and a brush, and told me to get started. He watched for a minute, then sloshed more water on them and said, "Bear down on the brush more, you won't get them clean that way."

He started then and soon had washed two garments to my one.

"Why don't you rinse the things we have washed. I'll do the sheets and we'll get through quicker. Take each one separately, lay down, lean over the edge of the dock, swish it around until the water doesn't look milky anymore."

It was easy. I flipped the rinsed garments over me, onto the dock, making no effort to wring them at the time. Soon I had everything all rinsed.

"I'm going to wash the things I have on. Take off your things and I'll wash them, too."

I must have looked startled because he laughed. "Why not? We can hear a boat coming a mile away. Plenty of time to get to

37

the house and put on our swimsuits." I stripped–it was very pleasant lying there in the sun. Russ began to wring the clothes so I started to help. I got my feelings hurt when he snorted at my efforts. Taking something that I had finished, he wrung quite a stream of water from it.

"Take your time making muscles. You don't have enough now to get these things dry enough to rinse in fresh water."

Finished at last, he picked up the heaviest basket and I followed him with the other. As I went down the plank, he was watching. I managed to keep my balance and he beamed approval and started off.

"Why didn't you carry it down? It would have been easier than wringing them out again if I hadn't made it."

"Well, you'll enjoy life more if you aren't so dependent on me for everything."

Arriving at the rainwater tank, Russ put down his basket and went to get the tub on the back porch. Rinsing procedure here was orderly. First our underwear, then the sheets and pillowslips, shirts and then pants. Things weren't rung so dry this time. It would make them too wrinkly. I was able to manage my share.

The clothesline was a real weirdie as far as I was concerned. I didn't try to figure it out for the sheets, just hung them double. They dried quickly and folding them, we studied this patent clothesline. Russ finally figured it out, put corners of clothing between the wires and ran the little slide over them. Somehow it held them. The wind had started to pick up and got so strong that some of the thinner things started to tear. We took them out of the clothesline and put them on the ground. Later I found the fresh water rinse was classified as a luxury. We kept hoping for rain.

After that, we wore clothing to go into the jungle, bathing suits for beachcombing, and nothing at all when we didn't have to. Only under the most unusual circumstances would any of the Conchs ever walk far, and we would hear their boat.

For days now we hadn't seen an airplane, and it was longer since we had heard a boat. The silence was almost overwhelming.

We had a late lunch and discussed a spring for our bed, and what method we could use for getting it into the upstairs room. Three extra beds were unnecessary. We could use one of those springs and put boards under the mattress. The only possible way was to unhook the spring from the frame, both ends and one side, collapse the frame, put it on the roof and through the window space, and reassemble it once inside.

Now to start that. The boards for the bed could wait for another time. It was quite tricky unhooking those wires from the spring. Russ stretched it enough so I could flip the hooks off. He got onto the roof and I hoisted it up; inside I tried to pull it in. It was maddening. Had the partial walls been painted we would have left many signs of our struggle. The screens weren't damaged, but that was not through luck, just plain hard work. We finally got enough of the frame inside so Russ could get in and help me. Straightening out the collapsed spring was simple, but re-hooking it was almost impossible. By putting a hammer handle through the mesh, I could just stretch the spring enough so Russ could re-hook it. From on top of the mattress, of course—there was very little room upstairs.

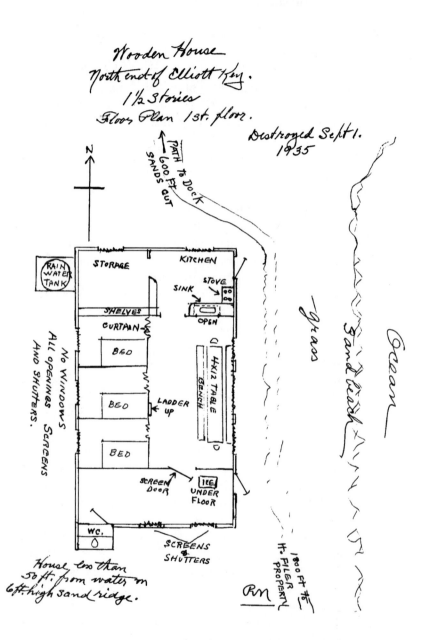

Wooden House
North end of Elliott Key.
1½ Stories
Floor Plan 1st. floor.

Destroyed Sept 1.
1935

N

PATH To Dock
600 Ft.
SANDS CUT

Ocean

Sand Beach

Grass

RAIN
WATER
TANK

STORAGE

KITCHEN

SINK

STOVE

SHELVES

OPEN

CURTAIN

BED

4x12 TABLE
BENCH

BED

LADDER
UP

BED

No WINDOWS
ALL OPENINGS SCREENS
AND SHUTTERS.

SCREEN
DOOR

ICE
UNDER
FLOOR

WC.

SCREENS
&
SHUTTERS

House less than
50 ft. from water on
6 ft. high sand ridge.

1800 FT. ±
Ft. PILE & PROPERTY

RN

40

CHAPTER FOUR

Meet: George Deen, Chester, Mayor A.D.H. Fossey,
Flip and Bertha. Get Re-made Machete.
Bill Frowns on Our Loaned Power Boat.

Time seemed to flow along. We never knew what time it was. We had long since lost track of what day it was. We believed that it was about three weeks since we had arrived when about noon one day, we heard a boat in the cut. It was rather large. We walked down the path, and as we did, we saw it go towards a large black mangrove tree almost opposite us. A small pudgy man got onto the bow and tied the boat to the tree. He then climbed down the tree and went towards the stern of the boat. There, he caught the line the man on the boat threw him and tied it. This was our first sight of George Deen. At this time he owned Sands Key.

The man on shore, we found later, was a hotel clerk who had begged George for the privilege of camping on a deserted island. He handed over the side of the boat the many packages and boxes of his guest. Introductions were made across the expanse of water, and George, as he asked us to call him, said that he would be back in two weeks, if not before. Good-byes were said and when we looked again, his guest was carrying his supplies around front of the ocean side. Had he wanted to talk, we would have stayed. We found out later that he was very bashful.

Our bread and crackers were all gone now, as well as some hardtack Russ had purchased. He gave me further evidence of his cooking ability that night. The corn bread he made tasted like cake to me.

We noticed the next day that the stranger had made a lean-to facing the ocean and the prevailing wind. Russ said he was lucky the weather was nice. If a squall came up, there would be a real mess inside. Fortunately, none did. We often saw him sitting on the muddy bank, fishing in the cut. We wondered what he did about sandflies.

A few days after he arrived, we were going down the path to work in the little lime grove, and we heard George's guest calling, "You, sir, would you please come over to talk!"

"Okay," Russ called to him, and told me to entertain myself until he got back. I walked to the dock with him and then went along the edge of the water to beachcomb. There I found an old machete. The tip end was broken off and the handle had almost rotted off, but the metal was still good. Near it was another glass jar with a lid. Returning to the house some time later, I saw that Russ and the stranger were both there, as well as the stranger's gear; this was on the back porch and made quite an impressive pile. His last name escapes me now, but his first name was Chester, and that's what we called him from then on.

His visibly swollen hands and face showed why he had called Russ. He needed help. Because they required privacy while treating the swellings (remember, I had mentioned previously that he had been sitting on the mud bank), they went into the second bedroom and pulled the curtains. He had muck itch. It is very similar to poison ivy.

I went out front, got a conch and went fishing. Cleaning the moonfish I caught was a recent accomplishment of mine, and in spite of the sandflies, I managed to get it done. They didn't bother me quite as much lately. I wondered why. Much later on, we found that the more sweets we ate the more the sandflies bothered us.

Russ told me later that while I was fishing, he had heated some rainwater so Chester could take a sponge bath. While he was bathing, Russ made up the bed for him with some of Chester's linen. Camping out, with linen!

Our drug supplies were quite complete and Russ got out the remedy for poisonwood–photographer's hypo–and prepared it for application. He dabbed the solution on all the affected areas. The strategic area was treated by wetting Chester's shorts with the solution. Waxed paper from my kitchen supplies helped keep the sheet and mattress dry.

Supper ready now, Russ took the straight back chair into the bedroom and placed Chester's supper on it. He managed to slip to the edge of the bed and eat. Russ renewed the solution afterward and got up twice during the night to help our new friend.

As Russ went down the ladder the next morning, Chester called and suggested that we break into his supplies. He'd like some canned sausages for breakfast and wanted to share them. I prepared these things while Russ attended to Chester. Awake, he did not complain. It was only in his sleep that he made the soft moans that let us know just how uncomfortable he was.

After our luscious breakfast–with MEAT–I listened to Chester's praises of my cooking. But could anyone fail to cook scrambled eggs properly? I deduced he must have overcooked or undercooked his.

When Russ said that he intended to stick around the house and take care of Chester, I got out the broken machete I had found the day before.

"This isn't too bad! I can make a short one of this. You can handle it better than the regular size."

I got a tin can of water and went out back. He oiled the grindstone. I turned the crank, first with one arm and then with the other. My arms hadn't quite given out when he had ground down the broken part and formed a sloping point. Now he ground the rust off the rest of the blade and sharpened the edge. Then he said that it was time to take care of Chester, and I gratefully sat down and lit a cigarette.

Thinking then of the handle, I remembered a square piece of Spanish cedar which just might do, but I couldn't imagine what he would use to fasten the wood to the metal part of the handle.

"I had to wake the poor guy up to put on more of the mix," Russ said.

"I think I have the right piece of wood for the handle!"

He agreed, and started to carve it out. Time after time he asked me to grasp it, and finally he was satisfied. Now he sawed it in half lengthwise. Between the C-clamp and me, it held steady. Carving a light recess for the metal, he drilled some holes through it and got ready to fasten the handle to the blade. This

43

he accomplished by using pieces of heavy copper wire. He used short pieces of wire to rivet the handle to the metal.

I had a most pleasant sensation, then, knowing that I was to be trusted with this weapon. It was eight inches shorter than a standard machete and I could handle it easily.

Naturally, I went out to try it. I went back of the house to the jungle there and started slashing my way into it. I was so pleased with the results and sort of drunk with power that I might have continued if there had not been suddenly the sharp sound of breaking glass. I had smashed a lovely demijohn which lay among the tangled vines and bushes. Enough for one day! Walking back towards the house I saw a huge black snake. It was bigger around that the calf of my leg, and it looked ten feet long. As it slithered towards the water tank, I ran towards the back door, went in and told Russ about it. He went out to look and I stayed inside, watching.

"Here it is, under the water tank. It's only six and a half feet long. Maybe a few inches more."

Again inside he said, "It's a harmless snake. It won't bother you if you don't bother it. That accounts for the missing rats. He ate them. He can be a big help to us. Leave him alone."

Gosh, he almost sounded as though he thought I was going to pursue and attack the nasty thing!

By now Chester had dressed and came out of his bedroom.

"I've never seen a snake that big, except in a circus. Show me, Russ!"

They went out and looked. From what I heard Chester say, he agreed with my estimate of the snake. "Boy, it is huge. I wish I had a camera! The boys won't believe me when I tell them this!"

Back inside, Chester eased himself down into the chair. I asked him just how he had decided to camp out on Sands Key.

"I'm a desk clerk in one of the large hotels on Miami Beach. When I draw the night shift, I have plenty of time to read. One of the boys subscribes to adventure stories. I got interested in them. Dammit! My first night wasn't too bad. I was totally exhausted by the time I lugged all my equipment to the front of the island and set up my lean-to. After struggling with the little gasoline stove I had bought, I finally got it going. My food wasn't scorched too much and I managed to eat it. I was between the sheets before dark, and pulled the sheets over my head when the sandflies came.

"The next morning I itched all over and had a couple of big welts on my bottom. When I made my bed, I found out where the welts came from. Two four-inch scorpions were in it. Dead, of course. I must have rolled on them. Boy, they hurt when they sting. I sat sideways most of that day. "Fishing was good and I caught a lot. I stopped counting after forty-five. The way I did it, I knew I could only eat one, so when I caught the second one, I put the smallest one back. I kept doing that all the time I was fishing–for bragging purposes, for when I get back to the hotel."

"What did I use for bait? Oh, a jar of some rind-like things they sold me at the same store where I bought my fishing rod. I napped that afternoon, so I had trouble getting to sleep that night. Every so often I would lift up the sheet and look for scorpions with my flashlight. I slapped four more with my shoe. They take a lot of killing, don't they?

"When I woke up yesterday morning I itched more that ever. I don't know what I would have done if you hadn't come within hearing distance. Do you realize it was just torture for me, and I spent most of my time watching for one of you to get within yelling distance, so I could ask for help. Most of the time I hurt too much to sit."

"Chester, Mr. Deen said that he would be back in two weeks."

"I wouldn't have lasted that long! I hope you both realize how grateful I am."

"My wife and I have only been here about three weeks ourselves. We haven't seen anyone to talk to until you came. Sorry you had to get muck itch in order to get acquainted, but glad to have you with us."

More of Chester's supplies that night provided us with the easiest meal we had prepared for a long time. Just heated some beef stew and green peas.

At noon Chester had on bedroom slippers, but that night he appeared at the table fully dressed. He had on black socks and his dress shoes were unlaced, his feet swelling over the tops.

"Chester, take off those shoes and socks!" Russ said. "That black dye could get into those raw places on your feet. I'll find something for you." He returned with a new pair of white cotton socks and his spare tennis shoes. Fortunately, his feet were about the same size as Chester's. The softer tennis shoes gave Chester's feet a bit more room. Right after supper, he excused himself and went to bed.

The next morning when Russ got downstairs, he found that Chester had quietly set the table and gotten his sausages and eggs out. He found him in the kitchen, staring in a frustrated manner at the stove. "I thought I would start breakfast, but this stove is a new one on me."

"Charlotte is still afraid of it."

Russ lit it and Chester made breakfast. His hands were only slightly round now and he handled things more naturally. He remarked about "feeling almost human" again and how comfortable the tennis shoes were. Then he went for a short walk. Before long, he was back for another treatment.

Just before noon we heard a boat and went to see who it was. Then we had the pleasure of meeting the owner of the property, Mr. A.D.H. Fossey, the mayor of Miami at the time. [Fossey would *become* mayor, for a 1935-1937 term. At this time, he is a highly successful land developer—ed.] Russ stayed to talk a bit and I went up to the house to tell Chester who the visitors were.

When Russ returned he was reading a letter which Mr. Fossey had brought from his sister, Katherine. The both families were worried about us being isolated on the island, and her husband offered the use of his Dodge speedboat for as long as Russ wanted to borrow it. Thoughtful, heart-warming, Heaven sent, what are the words for a gesture like that?

Chester interrupted my thoughts when he said, "Russ, would you please ask Mayor Fossey if he has room aboard? I'd love to go back to Miami with him. I'd like to get back to civilization. Reading those corny stories got me into this!"

When Russ asked the Fosseys if they were staying overnight, they were surprised. "Today is Sunday! Didn't you know?"

Well, we had lost another day. We thought it was Saturday.

"Plenty of room aboard," was Mr. Fossey's answer to Chester's request. We helped him carry his equipment aboard and were happy to accept when he offered us his remaining food supplies. They were a welcome change.

We worked in the little grove each day. Russ cut down the weeds and I pulled up the vines which threatened to strangle the lime trees. While pulling the vines from the trees I noticed that many small limes and blossoms were torn loose when I did this, so from then on I just pulled up the roots so the things would die. From a tangled mess, the little three-acre grove was beginning to emerge as an orderly group of trees. It's worth working when you can see that you are accomplishing something.

In the afternoons we went beachcombing. Every day we added more usable lumber to our supply, and I was getting used to the idea that we could leave things and find them when we returned.

One morning, using the skiff, we gathered a large load of lumber within two city blocks of the house. It looked most impressive until we unloaded it on the shore near the dock and counted those boards which needed replacing.

I stubbed my toe on an old, rust-encrusted file by the stacked lumber. I expected a little sympathy, but Russ was jubilant. I couldn't imagine why until he said, "Come on up. We'll make a nice fish knife out of that and I won't have to get my sheath knife salty all the time."

Thinning one side to a tapered edge, grinding the rust off the rest of the file, he then pounded and sort of mushroomed the end. Another piece of Spanish cedar was whittled to make a handle. It was riveted together with copper wire.

"How abut some crawfish for supper?"

"I haven't had any for ages. Can I help?"

"Nope! You get the wooden bucket, go out front and get it about a third full of ocean water. I'll need it when I get back. I shouldn't be long."

When he returned carrying two large crawfish tails, I asked how he caught them.

"With my hand, silly."

He put them into a rather large kettle, covered them with salt water and said, "I'll cook these. If they overcook, they get tough. I know just what shade of red they should be." On the hot fire they didn't take long. He dumped them in the sink and left them to cool a bit. Then he cracked the shells and peeled them. I had had crawfish many times before–these were different. Fresh out of the ocean with a semi-scorched margarine-lime juice sauce. This magnified their flavor. They were a real gourmet dish. Too tired to read, I put my complaining muscles to bed.

Just at daybreak we heard a motor in the cut. From the sounds of the voices, several people. Russ dressed more quickly than I and was at the door when they arrived. It was Flip and his girl friend Bertha and another couple, an oldish, dignified looking man and a teen-age girl. They appeared very tired and announced that they were hungry.

The dignified looking man muttered, "It was a damn shame that we got lost on our way down here last night. We had intended to spend the night with you."

Bertha had competently started breakfast with food they had brought along and we were their guests. It was a bit surprising to me when they announced, right after breakfast, that they had to get back to Miami that morning. I thought it was too bad they had gotten lost in the bay the night before and wandered on the edge of the flats all night!

Later, many times, the same thing occurred. Whenever Flip had another couple with him (who weren't married–to each other), he would start from Miami for Elliott Key about five in the afternoon, get lost, fumble his way through the channels in the dark and spend the entire night roaming, then show up in time for an early breakfast. (Before he was arrested for rum running, he had used Sands Key Cut and the cut in Hawk Channel for every run. Strange, all this concern for other people's morality, in view of the fact that he and his girl friend weren't married.)

Flip was very thoughtful and a successful rum runner. He had managed to avoid capture for almost two years. Shortly before he was captured, he was thoughtful enough to invest his profits in some gilt-edged bonds, take them to a lawyer and have an agreement drawn up; it required both his signature and that of Bertha. In exchange for handling the money which accrued from the stock, the use of his car, house and savings account, she was to provide him with all necessary food, clean comfortable living quarters, cigarettes and a minimum of six bottles of beer a day. In case he died before she did, she inherited all his possessions.

When he told us of this agreement one day, he said, "Had it done proper. I felt *hot*. The Mon was really breathin' down my neck." Only a few weeks later he was caught rum running. He served his two-years-and-a-day in the Atlanta pen. Bertha drove to Atlanta to pick him up and brought him back to Miami. He retired then. Flip said that he couldn't prove it but he thought Bill had turned him in. It had only been a fun thing and an easy way to get a stake.

One day while visiting him in his home, we were shown his most prized possessions. His first purchase after returning to Miami was a diploma frame. This was hanging on the wall over his other most cherished possession. It was a very large piece of pumice stone, for which he bought a pedestal, after receiving a letter, attached to it, from Robert "Believe-It-Or-Not" Ripley, thanking Flip for his entry of a ten-pound, floating rock in Ripley's contest. The framed diploma stated that Thomas P. Flynn, having served two years and a day for rum running, had paid his debt to society. In full.

Now, back to the breakfast table. I told Bertha to leave the dishes. I would do them.

"Flip do you have room in the boat for one more?" Russ asked. "I have to go to Lauderdale to pick up a boat."

Flip just beamed at Russ and said, "Sure thing!"

Russ had always said that Flip was a nice fellow, but somehow I got the impression that Russ had done him a favor. Some time later, I found out that he just about worshiped Russ. This proved to be a most fortunate thing for Russ and me. More about that later...

We had talked our situation over and decided to give up the apartment, and using the car, take our remaining possessions to Lauderdale for storage. This was a sudden decision. I couldn't be a clinging vine at this stage of the game, so I said nothing.

It didn't take Russ long to get into city clothes. He got the want list and carried the bottles outside. Flip and his friends helped carry them to the boat. I watched them load up, waved when they left and went back to the house. I had managed to seem nonchalant and told Russ I didn't mind being left alone, but, gee, the house seemed empty.

I decided to get some crawfish for my supper. In my bathing suit and sneakers I went to the dock again. I didn't know just what area they could be found in. I did remember seeing some on the ocean side of the cut. I waded out slowly so as not to disturb them and seeing some large feelers, I reached over and grabbed them tight enough to hold them, partially. The feelers tore my skin as the thing pulled backwards. I gripped more firmly and found myself the proud possessor of a pair of crawfish feelers. Another try netted me another pair of feelers. I was glad no one was watching. This, I wouldn't brag about.

Returning to shore, I started to read, and leftovers were good enough for supper. All this time for reading was a terrific treat. I heard the boat and went down with a flashlight to help Russ with the groceries and the ice.

Over breakfast the next morning, Russ said that he had had a fast trip to Miami and didn't delay to visit. Getting the car, he loaded in the bottles, then went to the apartment and gathered the few things we had left. The landlady wasn't home so he dropped the key in the mailbox with a note telling of our decision to give up the apartment.

Reaching Fort Lauderdale, he phoned Katherine and told her that he would really like to take up John's offer and borrow the boat until we could buy one of our own.

"Oh, I'm so glad," she said. "We were all so worried about you and Charlotte. Come on over and have lunch."

"Could I make it in about an hour?" he asked. "I have to go to the folks and get some things there. I need to get back to the island by dark, if I can."

"Fine. I expect John home any minute. He has the boat keys for you."

At his parents' home he stored some few things and filled part of our want list from things there. After a short visit, he was back at Katherine's. John greeted him saying, "Glad you came after the boat. Now you won't be such a Robinson Crusoe."

"It isn't that bad—but close."

"Here's the key. Keep the boat as long as you want. We haven't been using it."

"John, I wonder if you would keep your eyes open for a boat for me. I have in mind something solid, like a Coast Guard surf boat. I also would need a small motor to install in it. I hope I can get it for around seventy-five dollars. Oh, and John, I wonder if you can sell my car? I'll leave it with you."

"Glad to take care of that. Lots of boats being advertised right now, and as for the car—that won't be a problem. I'll write you in care of Fossey when I have news for you."

"My car is loaded right now with stuff to put in the boat. I wonder if, on the way there, you could show me a place to buy extra gas cans."

They both went with him so one of them could drive his car back. They put extra gas cans in their car. The boat was soon loaded and Russ was on his way to Miami.

At Everett's he had the water and gasoline containers filled while he took a cab to the grocery store. He was settling the bill when Bill came along, looking startled and not too pleased. He said, "Where did you get that boat? How'd you get up here?"

"Flip brought me—I borrowed this boat."

"Russ, I'll be down to see you right soon. Good-bye now."

CHAPTER FIVE

Break Demijohn. Meet Border Patrolmen, Happy and Al.
Captain William Reno Russell and Son, Reno.
Old Tree. Find Big Grove.

Talking about the day before, Russ said, "It seemed to gripe Bill that I had a boat. He didn't like it. I sure wonder what's cooking!"

Having been told by Mr. Fossey that he owned another grove about three miles down on the bay side, opposite the Conch settlement on the ocean side, we decided to look for it. First, it would be necessary to unload all that lovely water and the other supplies. It was a tiring chore, and I was glad we were only going into the jungle to look for the grove. It sounded easy.

With a gallon jug of water, we started into the jungle on the partial path I had started the day I got my machete, and continued on from there. As Russ was doing the path clearing, I offered to carry the water jug. He had been carrying it on one finger, but it was too heavy for me that way, so I decided to carry it on my rope belt. By adjusting my steps to the bumping swing of it, I managed quite well. Russ was doing only the necessary cutting for a path, and I found that it helped my progress if I cut some, too. I was getting a great deal of pleasure cutting branches. As I cut one that was a partial bar to the path, I got overly enthusiastic. My half circle swing took off the bottom of the jug, very neatly, and jarred the machete out of my hand.

When I yelled "Dammit," Russ came trotting back to see what had happened. I got a real lecture out of that episode and the frightening information that if the jug had not been there to

53

absorb the blow, I would have had a bad gash in my leg. Boy, how lucky can you get! I was very pleased when he said, "That's enough for today. Let's go home." He sounded a bit shaken, too!

There was no conversation on the return trip, and in an effort to relieve the tension when we got back to the house, I jokingly made a muscle for him. Surprise! You could actually see a little bump where my biceps were supposed to be.

It was shortly after noon now and we heard "Hello" from the dock area. We looked down the path and saw two uniformed men getting off a speedboat. They had come in so silently that we didn't hear them. Russ told me to stay in the house, "See their hands? They are holster high!" Then he went to meet them.

They stood and waited as Russ waved a hand and went towards them. Soon I heard him say, "Oh, we've been here over a month. Come on up and meet my wife."

We had met some new friends, border patrolmen. I made a pot of coffee. We sat down to drink it and get acquainted. They said they were investigating the area and had been suspicious of John's pretty little Dodge speedboat. They told us that this particular spot was a favorite of rum runners and smugglers, and they had been ready for trouble when they saw the boat. Al Hood and Happy Bjornass said that they were very pleased that we were going to live there, and they would stop in to see us when they were in the area. "Can we bring you anything when we come down this way?"

"I'd love some reading material. Any outdated magazine would be new to us."

"We will," Al said, as they walked down the path. Now, both at once, they said, "Thanks for the coffee."

They hadn't been gone too long when we got our second visitors of the day. We saw a round-bottomed skiff at the dock. It was sculled by an upright, elderly man. There was a younger man in the boat with him. Getting onto the dock, they each brought with them two demijohns. Now, approaching the house, they very properly called, "Hello, the house!" Russ went out to meet them.

They introduced themselves as Captain William Reno Russell and his son Reno, "Sponge fishermen, out of Key West. Come by for water."

"Help yourself."

"Son, go look in the tank and see if they can spare any."

Lifting the lid, Reno peered in and said, "About a third full, Papa."

"I'll thank you for ten gallons. We can get the rest of what we need from the family that lives down-key from here. They have a cistern. Same name, but no kin."

He was surprised when Russ said, "We haven't met them yet."

I invited them in for coffee. The fact that they didn't take seconds didn't register until later. Russ told me the strong kind they preferred and I realized that my kind seemed terribly thin to them. Our friendship with Captain Russell and his son dated from that day and it was a warm one. He apologized before he left, saying, "No one has lived in this house and we have used the water as our own. Please forgive it."

"We'll always be happy to share with you."

Once again we had lost track of the days and were returning from beachcombing well loaded with our finds when we heard a boat in the cut. We had a large wooden box filled with incidental goodies. And we had pushed two bamboo poles between the slats. I had the ends of the poles, leading the way, and Russ was following with the other ends on his shoulders. Our swimsuits were draped around our necks.

What? Saturday again? What a mad scramble as we set the things down and got into our suits. Russ ran down to the dock to let our boat drift back. No room for two boats at that dock. It was Mayor Fossey and his family. When I got there, I saw that the aftercockpit of the boat was simply loaded with a variety of things. He said, with a smile, "Your friend Chester asked me if I would deliver these for him. Here is a letter he sent you."

Russ read it aloud, "Sending a few things to thank you for your nursing and your hospitality. Chester."

We were really amazed at the thoughtfulness of the gifts. A pair of Muscovy ducks in a small cage, a mother duck and six little ones in a crate, a miniature-sized feeder and a large one, fifty pounds of duck food and fifty pounds of special food for the little ones. This was only part of it. Personal gifts–a dozen pair of white cotton socks (to replace one pair), a gross of Bull Durham tobacco sacks, cigarette wrappers to go with them, as well as a large cast-iron Dutch oven. There was also a small wire fish trap and the artificial bait to go with it. And, some Esquire magazines. (Chester had been very impressed when we gave him one to read.)

The Fosseys helped carry all that loot up to the house. We decided to leave the ducks in their pens overnight and release them the next morning so that they would have all day to get used to their new surroundings. We left their cages near the back door of the house. Russ had absolute faith in the huge black snake. It was justified.

"How would you like to have some crawfish for lunch, Mr. Fossey?" Russ asked.

"That would be fine."

"I've got a crawfish grabber." (Illegal now.)

"What in the world is that?"

"A real goodie. You don't have to go into the water after them."

They got into the skiff. Major Fossey immediately commented, "There's no water in it for a change! Did you bail it just before we came?"

"No, I caulked it with some Trinidad asphalt and some caulking cotton I found. Not having any paint, I smeared some of the spar grease I found on it. I got that on the beach, too."

Mr. Fossey merely said, "Ingenious," with a smile. (At that time we weren't aware that he had been a master of a deep-sea sailing vessel running between England and Australia).

They rowed the boat out midstream and let it drift until they saw a crawfish. Russ grabbed it. By this time, they saw another. When they pulled this one in, Mr. Fossey said, "Let me try it." He quickly learned the trick. Russ rowed the boat and Mr. Fossey did the grabbing.

Back at the dock, Russ prepared the crawfish for cooking. He twisted off the tails, threw the heads in the wooden bucket, broke off one of the feelers, and used it for deveining. He inserted it into the vent, giving it a half-twist and withdrawing it. The tube came with it. From the exclamations I heard, this was a new method for the Fosseys. The tails were put in the wooden bucket with ocean water and taken to the house. The head ends were put into a box and thrown out in the water in front of the house. Russ said that if they had been put in the cut, the live crawfish would have left that area.

The crawfish were soon ready and were served with some food that Mrs. Fossey had prepared. She asked for Russ' recipe for the sauce. After lunch, the Fosseys went fishing, and we went to the little grove to gather limes for them.

Supper was fish, among other things. The Fosseys had caught a great many fish and put them into their large fish well in the center of the cockpit.

During supper, Ralph, the Fosseys' son, said, "I wonder what happened to 'Cuz' and his friend. They should have been here by now. The sailboat they rented at Dinner Key had an outboard on it, and they left before we did."

"I wouldn't worry about it," his father said. "If they had motor trouble, they could always row. They'll get here."

Supper over, the children went down to the boat to fish, saying that they would spend the night on the boat.

We played bridge for a time and then went to bed.

Breakfast was a leisurely affair. Mrs. Fossey prepared ham and eggs for all of us, and Russ made coconut pancakes. Everybody loved them. Cuz and his friend arrived, but said they were too tired to eat. Just took off their shoes and lay down on the Fosseys' bed.

Lunch was ready and they were still sleeping. Ralph said that he would wake up Cuz. He cut an onion in half and put it right under his cousin's nose. A few seconds of nose wiggling and muttering, then his cousin sat up, wide awake, his eyes watering.

We heard the story of their trip down-bay during lunch. When the wind dropped out, they lowered the sail and started the outboard. The outboard ran until they were close to Soldiers Key, and then quit. Neither of them knew how to adjust or repair it, so they were forced to row against an outgoing tide. Dark found them on the ocean side of A Key. "Then the tide changed and we saw Fowey Rock Light from every angle until we saw Elliott Key in the first light of daybreak. My hands were less blistered than his, so I rowed us in."

The Fosseys left right after lunch, towing the sailboat.

57

On their next trip down, we heard an amusing story of their trip back to Miami. When they were a bit more than halfway home, Ralph expressed concern about the small leak he had discovered on the way down. As his father steered the boat, Ralph lifted the hatch over the fish well and said, "Ohmigosh, look! Get the pump!"

Cuz, in his innocence, did so, and they let him pump for almost an hour before they let him in on the joke. His hands were a sorry mess!

On our way to work in the big grove the next morning, we took four jelly coconuts. I carried these in a burlap bag over my left shoulder. I had my machete, but I used it sparingly and cautiously. I remembered with a shudder how dangerous the thing could be.

Towards noon, according to the sun, we came to a partial clearing caused by an unusual tree. It looked to be twenty feet tall, and the trunk was about three feet through at the base. The branches rose, curved down, and up again. The bottom branches had a low bend and were large enough to make a comfortable seat. I sat down and watched Russ prepare our lunch. He cut off one end of a coconut, deep enough to remove the top of the shell. He handed it to me and cut off two narrow slices from the green covering of another one and handed them to me. He fixed his in the same manner. I handed him one of the slices, and watched. Making believe I knew all the time that these were spoon substitutes, I ate with mine. While eating my second coconut, I asked Russ how he knew we were going towards the bay side. Then I got some instructions about navigating by the sun.

On our way again, it wasn't long before we reached our first lime tree. Russ turned sharply right, and we were soon at the water's edge. Back again into the grove. It was just one big, tangled mess, except for a path we found. The path ran towards the ocean side. This grove, according to Mr. Fossey, was fourteen acres.

I sat down on a large stump, which Russ identified as buttonwood. It was so much larger than any tree we saw, and still growing, that it was amazing. It was four feet across the top of the stump. The wood had a lovely, curly grain, and when I heard that the wood is blond in color, I wistfully said how nice it would be to have a slice of it polished for a tabletop. Russ reminded me that all he had in the saw line was a 26-inch handsaw.

We explored and found that there were quite a few ripe limes on the trees. We picked the burlap bag full, and then looked around. Most of the original trees were surrounded by small volunteers. These could be pulled up and sold. All the trees were covered with vines, including one which Russ called the "haulback vine." Naturally, I found it. The entire thing was covered with curved hooks, including the leaves. I got into one and it seemed each little leaf hooked onto my clothing. It was impossible to back out. All the finer branches and leaves seemed to leap forward to grab clothing and skin. I finally gave up and called Russ. Laughing at my predicament, he told me to stand still. Cutting the vines, he unhooked them from me. Some ten minutes later, I was in the clear again. I hadn't ripped my shirt.

"Lots of work clearing this grove. We'll need help."

That was music to my ears.

To save gasoline, we walked to the big grove each day and did a bit more pulling up the roots of the vines. Russ put up a marker on the water edge of the grove so that we could find it from the water. Each day we picked more ripe limes. These we carried into a patch of haul-back until we could get them by boat.

The Muscovy Ducks Multiplied!

CHAPTER SIX

Meet a Rum Runner, Mugs Gillette. Pants Repair. Conch Horn.

One morning as we were getting ready to go to the big grove, we heard a boat at the dock. We went down and watched as the big boat nosed forward past the dock, until the bow was on the shore. The man in the boat, whom Russ greeted as Mugs, threw the anchor on shore, cut his motor, dropped over the side and walked towards us.

Mugs had a jovial expression. He looked like a beardless Santa Claus with brown eyes and hair. He casually announced, "I've got some time to kill." By way of explanation he pointed out towards the Gulf Stream. Off shore in Hawk Channel, we could see two rather large vessels, a 45-foot Coast Guard boat and, a half-mile south of it, a 75-foot Coast Guard cutter, just sort of sitting there waiting. I couldn't imagine why the presence of the Coast Guard boats would cause him to have time to kill. Boy, was I naïve! I must have looked puzzled. Mugs said, "I'm on my way over for a load and they are in my way."

Until then I had only read and heard about rum runners, with the exception of Bill. Flip was the past tense. His career had been over when I met him. Here was a real, live, active one!

During the ensuing conversation, we learned that Mugs had sort of drifted down-bay with a large fishing pole visible. When he saw one of the small speedboats operated by the Border Patrol come near, he stopped to fish. He remained there fishing until they were out of sight again, then continued on his way to our cut.

Off shore there was a cut through Hawk Channel Reef,

through which a smallish vessel could go without danger. On seeing the "Mon," he had decided to stop and visit us. Of course, the Miami grapevine had informed everyone that we were now on the north end of Elliot Key.

Mugs explained to us that capture on his way over was not disastrous. He was carrying no contraband, but if he was stopped and searched he would have to eat the paper on which his list was written.

"I had to eat my list twice! The first time was real rough on me. I wrote it on regular paper. That's hard to chew and swallow. Now I write it on the thinnest paper I can buy. No law against having money," he said as he pulled at a roll of money that was so large he had trouble getting it out of his hip pocket. He further explained that he usually brought in custom orders and that involved a great many boxes of fancy liquors.

I asked why he kept his list in his unbuttoned shirt pocket. He grinned. "Saves time if I have to eat it. Time is important."

We invited Mugs to lunch and he said that he had his mouth set for conch stew. I went up to fix the potatoes and other things while they got the conchs. Three of us working together made short work of it.

During lunch, Mugs remarked that he had an extra boat and as he could only use one at a time, he thought we might like to borrow it. He put it in a way that we would be doing him a big favor if we used it.

"As a matter of fact, Russ, I think I'll use the other boat next time over. Charge the battery. I'll tow this one down and leave it for you."

I couldn't understand why he was so generous to a casual acquaintance, but if it was all right with Russ, it was all right with me.

Russ said, "It would be a real pleasure to run a work boat. We've got to be so darn careful about the mahogany on John's boat. By the way, Mugs, I am going to need help in clearing the big grove."

Mugs grinned again and patted Russ on the shoulder. "Forget that for now. I'll take care of that for ya. Just don't question anything odd you find in your boat the next time up, at least until you are down-bay a bit."

The smaller Coast Guard boat took off in a northerly direction about then and Mugs said, "I'll be on my way now. That cutter seems to be heading south."

I put the dishes in the pan at the water's edge and secured the stew, then hurried down to the dock after them. I saw that Mugs was aboard and pulling his anchor. Backing off the bank, he went out the cut. His trolling rod was fixed and he zigzagged as fishermen do. It was quite exciting to watch as he got near Hawk Channel. When he was about two-thirds of the way to the cut in the reef, the 75-footer turned around and got underway to intersect his path. Their bow wave showed that they were going very fast. Mugs put on full power and darted ahead. He was through the cut and out the other side before the other vessel got near him. Thrilling sport for a gambling man! Now I could understand why some people ran rum.

We picked the limes in the small grove and graded them. The small ones, we called them the "A & P limes," would buy our groceries. Tired, we didn't mind going to bed in the daylight, so Russ could get up at two in the morning. Our alarm clock was set for the first time since we had arrived on the key.

Quick breakfast over, he was on his way with the water jugs. He went around to the big grove and got those bags that we had left there.

His trip was uneventful. Market was just opening when he arrived. Large limes sold, he walked to a grocery store and traded the small limes for groceries. He got a cent a piece for the limes at that time. In a taxi, then, he got the ice, and went back to the boat. The empty gas and water containers filled, he was on his way. He arrived home just before the sandflies made their nightly appearance. After we carried up the ice, groceries and one bottle of water, he decided to leave the rest for morning.

Steak for supper, fresh fruit, cake!

After breakfast we brought up the water bottles and stored the gasoline cans on shore. As we handled these things, I was thinking that I never could have carried a bottle of water the first day I arrived. I was pleased with myself. Hey, no aching muscles for some time now! I noticed then that there was a fish line dangling off the stern. I mentioned it.

"Oh, yeah. I bought some bandanna handkerchiefs and towed them in the salt water to set their color."

It did, too. Even when they were worn out and being used for rags, they still retained the original color.

Up at the house we decided to go for a swim. We were ready when we heard a boat. We jumped into our swimsuits and looked out the kitchen screen. Some strangers were coming up the path, carrying demijohns on their shoulders. The third one in line looked odd. It seemed as though the front of his pants was missing. I told Russ I was going upstairs–he looked and said, "It's all right. It's just black pants with white cloth mending." We greeted them and asked them in for coffee. They introduced themselves as sponge fishermen from the sponge boat *Gertrude*, which was in the lee of the island about a mile down. They had, like Captain Russell, been "using the water as their own," and were surprised to find us living there.

They preferred to stay in the kitchen to drink their coffee, and after standing a minute took up the usual squatting position of the Conchs. Trying not to be too obvious about it, I looked at the repair job. Large, galloping stitches and safety pins secured the cloth on the top and both sides. The lower six inches hung free, giving the appearance of a loincloth. The word "PILLS" was on part of it.

Because of the water Russ brought from Miami, we could spare them the rainwater they needed. Suddenly, again, I felt "water poor." They left after filling their jugs, and we were alone again.

I had found a large empty horse conch the day before. Russ saw it, "Good, just what we need for a boat horn." Taking it to the back porch, he sawed some of the pointed end off, rounding the edges of the cut on the grinding wheel. Only took a few minutes. And, he blew a loud note on the shell. It is a vibrating and penetrating noise. Later, when he was returning from Miami, he always blew it when he reached Soldier Key, twelve miles from us. With this notice that he was on his way, I would start supper.

CHAPTER SEVEN

Bill Responsible for Buzzards. Threatens Russ. Threatens Me.
Flip Saves Russ' Life. Flip Almost Killed by Bill
and Stooge, Saved by Bertha. Russ Buys Life Insurance.
Meet Gary and Shad.

Early the next morning Bill arrived in Flip's boat, with a girl friend. We heard the boat and watched as they got out of it. Russ turned to me and said softly, "Don't say a thing. He looks ornery as hell. Just be polite."

After introducing us to his girl friend, Bill stayed just long enough to smoke a cigarette. Then he said, "Come on, Russ, let's get some fish for lunch."

When they returned a couple of hours later, with fish, Bill looked sort of grim and Russ looked nerve-bitten. There was very little talking during lunch except for Bill's girl friend. She wanted to spend the night. They left right after lunch. Russ walked down to the dock with them while I took the dishes outside to wash.

He was just furious when he returned. He probably had been upset all during lunch. He said, "That son of a bitch! Do you know, all the time we were fishing he kept after me. First he suggested, then he requested, then he demanded that I stash liquor and small packages for him. Probably dope! I finally convinced the bastard that I wouldn't have any part of anything like that. Then he said, 'Russ, did you notice the buzzards at the north end of Sands Key right after you got here?' I said, 'Yes.' He said, 'They are there because that guy refused to cooperate with me.' It was a threat–that was very plain. Then he said, 'Let's go eat lunch.' I guess, though, he thought that if he gave me enough time, I'd get scared and change my mind. The miserable bastard. He probably had this in mind all the time he was telling us about this island. He is really far out. A couple of weeks ago he bragged to me about being the father of his neighbor's triplets. From now on, we both wear sheath knives at all times, *and don't forget it!*"

Shortly afterwards, we met two of our neighbors, a Captain Russell and his oldest son—no relation to Captain *Reno* Russell. They had come in by powerboat and as they came up the path called, "Hello, the house."

When Russ met them just outside the door they introduced themselves saying that they had been in Key West visiting relatives or they would have been to see us sooner.

From first hearing our names, they called us Mr. and Mrs. Russ. We served the usual coffee and cookies, then visited for a time.

I listened rather than joined the conversation. It seemed that there was some contest of wits going on. They asked so many questions as to whether we both left at the same time, where we went and how long we were usually gone. Russ sort of slithered around some of the questions to ask some of his own. Shortly before they left, they invited us to visit them at their home. Russ told them we would probably go down that way in a few days.

After they left, he said, "This is a usual thing for *some* of the Conchs. You saw them looking around. They want what we have. Give them an opportunity and they will take our things. The word 'steal' isn't in their vocabulary. They 'borrow' things and hide them. Mostly in their storm houses in the groves and jungle. It's a sort of game they play. If you find the 'borrowed' items, you can take any of their possessions at the same time. When asked about any lost or stolen article, they get insulted. According to the unwritten rules of the game, you must find it yourself."

Visiting rum runners became a usual thing, but we no longer went to the dock to meet a boat. We made coffee for them, as well as for the Border Patrol, when they came to see us.

A few days later, because I was under the weather, Russ left for the big grove alone. I had just finished my housework when I heard a boat. I went to the kitchen window and looked down the path. It was Bill in what looked like Flip's boat. There was a man in the boat, and the motor was still running.

I quickly put on my belt with the sheath knife and unstrapped the little strap that contained the handle when the knife wasn't in use. Remembering his threat to Russ, I was tense. I didn't want him in the house and met him just outside the door. He came very close and I had to look up into his eyes because he was a foot taller than Russ or I.

"What do you want, Bill?"

He pushed his right hand towards me, uncurled his fingers and displayed a pretty little pearl-handled gun. "I'm going to kill you and then him."

I had expected trouble and when he started to talk, I already had my sheath knife poking in above his belt. He looked very startled when he peered down at my shiny knife.

"I could still hurt you!"

Bill backed off, surprised and still angry. Then he said, "You damn people have spoiled everything for me. I'll get you both."

With that, he turned and ran down the dock to the boat.

I waited until I saw the boat leave. Then I locked the door and started down the path to the big grove with my machete in my hand. As I ran and walked, by spurts, through the path, I was thinking that Bill knew that Russ went to the big grove and might look for him there. I had no hopes of running that three miles before he could get there by boat, but I tried. I kidded myself that I had brought my machete as a weapon against snakes. Guess I was already classifying Bill as a snake.

There just aren't proper words to explain how I felt when I reached the grove and saw Russ casually preparing to return home. My imagination had worked overtime on the long way there. I was exhausted, physically and mentally. When I finally got my breath, I told Russ what had happened. Then he said that he had heard a boat stop and after a few minutes start up again, but he was busy and didn't pay any attention to it. "Wow! Could have been–I don't know. Let's go home."

"From now on we stay together at all times. If it is not feasible for some reason, you go into the jungle when you hear a boat.

If it isn't Bill, it will be all right to come out again. Let whoever it is identify themselves before you show yourself. In the jungle no one can find you if you keep quiet."

I was still under the weather when he left a few days later to sell the limes and replenish our supplies. Containers in the boat the night before, he was ready to go at two in the morning. I promised to go into the jungle at the first sound of a boat, and he was on his way. I wanted to stay awake and alert, so I read by lantern light until morning. Had a snack, packed a lunch and got ready to go into the jungle if necessary. I filled a gallon jug with water and carried it in a ways, just in case!

I heard about Russ' experiences when he returned.

"I got to the market in time to get a good price for the limes and tied up at Everett's place soon after. While tying up, I heard a car. Sneaking a look, I saw it was Bill. I didn't let on to him that I knew he was there, but just straightened some things in the boat before I went up the ladder to street level. The ladder was actually six boards nailed to the dock. Apparently, Bill made an early morning patrol to watch the rum runners come up the river at that sleepy time when things were slowest. They usually came in at that time of the morning to unload.

"There was Bill, waiting for me about two steps away. All of a sudden, Bill pushed that pretty little gun you told me about into my stomach. I was ready for him because I suspected something and knew now that he had a vicious temper. By the time the gun was in my belly, I had pushed the point of my sheath knife into his stomach about the belt. He didn't bleed much!

"Like most people, Bill had more fear of a knife than a gun. He just froze and didn't say anything.

"'Go ahead and shoot,' I said. 'I'll still have time to rip you wide open.'

"Charlotte, we'll never know just how Bill happened to be there. He might have known that the produce market only ran on Tuesdays and Thursdays. In the future, to try and avoid trouble, I'll make it on alternate days."

"Get back to it, Russ—"

"Well, Bill is apparently one of those people who can dish it out but can't take it. He wouldn't mind killing someone if he didn't get hurt in any way. He hadn't bargained for the fact that I would stand up to him. He started cussing, and yelling. Among the things he yelled was, 'I'll kill you yet. You people have spoiled everything for me. I had a lot of plans and they've all gone wrong.' He backed away far enough so I couldn't reach him with my knife, turned and ran for his car. Still shouting all kinds of curses and threats, he drove away. Kind of stupid of him. Except for the very early hour, there could have been a lot of witnesses. Later, I found that there had been one, Bertha!

"It shook me pretty much. I just stood there for a few minutes. I had been expecting trouble, but strangely enough, nothing like that. When Bill was out of sight I thought I had better get updated on the activities of the underworld along the river there. I walked the short distance to Flip's house. It was just a short block away and as a man who had served time in the pen for rum running, Flip should know what was going on.

"In spite of the early hour—it was just after five in the morning—Bertha met me at the door, fully dressed. She had heard Bill shouting. She signaled me to be very quiet. I supposed that Flip had had a rough night and was sleeping it off. She closed the door to the other part of the house. Then, with her accent, she said in a very confidential tone of voice, 'He's some better. He's not feeling so goot yet. He still hurts!'

"I didn't know what she was talking about and I told her so. She was real surprised to find that out. Of course, she didn't think about us being on the Keys. She told me this story:"

Bertha told Russ that a few days before, Bill had approached Flip with the suggestion that he would pay for the gas if Flip would use his boat and go down to Elliott Key. Naturally, Flip said yes. He was looking forward to seeing Russ again. Bertha said that Bill gave him a funny look. Then they left.

Flip told her about the trip when he got back. They had gone right to our dock and then Bill told Flip to stay in the boat and keep the motor running. Flip didn't like the idea very much, but the long silent trip had led him to expect something. Knowing that Bill wore a gun in a shoulder holster, he decided to obey. Bill had jumped out of the boat before Flip could say anything. It was only a few minutes later that he came raging down the path and ordered Flip to go to the big grove on the bay side. He didn't like it, but he did as he was told.

When they got near the shore side of the big grove several miles down, Bill whispered to Flip to cut the motor. He did and the boat drifted towards shore. When it stopped, Bill whispered again, telling Flip to stay in the boat. By then they had stopped drifting near shore and Bill eased the anchor into the water. Stepping over into the water, he quietly waded ashore while removing the gun from the holster.

Flip now knew what Bill planned to do and he eased over the side. Because Flip had obeyed before when told to stay in the boat, Bill wouldn't expect any interference. Flip told Bertha he could hear by the noises in the jungle, just about where Russ was. He sneaked up on Bill just as he was aiming his gun at those noises and said in his ear, "You keel him, and I keel you!"

Bill was startled and turned around just furious. Flip was holding a blackjack close to his ear. When he saw that, he acted scared and slowly put his gun away. They went back in silence. When they got there, Bill said, "Let's go home." Flip felt sort of safe. He knew Bill wouldn't kill him now because too many people knew he was out with him in the boat. They had been friends and were now enemies because Flip had saved Russ' life. The two-hour boat ride back to Miami was silent. When they arrived in Miami and tied the boat, Bill didn't say anything at all. He just left.

Bertha continued. When Flip got home he was real disturbed as he told her all about that. Then he had a couple of beers, ate some lunch, drank several more beers and took a nap. She didn't think anything about that because Flip quite often drank eight or ten beers in a day and had been "damaged" in the past. He would sleep it off.

That night after dark Bill drove up in a car and called in a matter he had often done in the past, "Come on, Flip, let's get a brew."

In the past Flip had always gone along with Bill. There was a tavern nearby that illegally sold beer and other drinks. Some of the stuff they had was really wicked–beer spiked with ether. In spite of Bertha's protest, Flip went out to the car. Bertha saw that there was another man with Bill. She stood there listening and in a minute heard Flip yelling for help.

She had been prepared for trouble and, under the guise of having just finished raking her garden, she put the short-pronged steel rake by the door. Now she grabbed it and with a lunge got Bill with some of the prongs. She had "to yank it loose" before she could hit again. Bill yelled and his stooge ran to the car. Bill limped there with Bertha wielding her weapon, trying for another good hit. She only managed to hit the door as he closed it and took off.

Now she ran back to where Flip lay unconscious. He had been beaten very badly and she knew that she couldn't carry him into the house, so she ran in and called the police. Returning to Flip, she sat down and put his head on her lap. He became conscious and made her promise not to tell the police who had beaten him because he knew they would ask questions. Bertha didn't want to promise, but Flip finally convinced her that he would be beaten again, and she would, too, if word got out about what she had done. When he said, "Maybe they even keel us," she was convinced. They couldn't afford to have any witnesses in the dangerous game they were playing. Flip knew that Bill was involved with dope and aliens. (We were stupid enough to believe that Bill was only a rum runner!)

The police took Flip to the hospital in their car. They didn't even wait for the ambulance.

Flip told Bertha that he acted real stupid and said he couldn't figure out who did it. Said he acted as though he was punch drunk and told them he never had any enemies and couldn't understand why someone would do that to him.

After the police took Flip to the hospital, they came back to Bertha, saying that he had been beaten with brass knuckles and perhaps a piece of pipe. "He is real bad," they said. When they started questioning Bertha, she told them, "How could I see who it was? It was dark and there ain't no street lights here." (At that time, that portion of Miami, down along the river, was completely unlighted. The only lights were a few night lights on a marina. This was only two blocks from the Miami Avenue Bridge.)

The next morning, Flip called Bertha from the hospital and insisted she come after him. He wanted to go home. She didn't argue with him and drove over. She had quite a time at the hospital. She demanded bills up to the minute so she could pay them. The doctor said he wouldn't let Flip leave; he was in no condition to. Bertha told them she didn't care what they wanted; it was her husband's wishes that guided her. They finally helped her put Flip in the car even though it was quite difficult and very painful to Flip.

Mr. Everett saw them when they returned and helped to get Flip into bed. He was told the same story as the police. "In fact," Bertha said to Russ, "you are the only one to know. Keep quiet about it, except for Charlotte, will ya?" Flip told Bertha that he was afraid that if he stayed in the hospital, Bill would get in and finish him off.

"We just sat and looked at each other," Russ said. "Then I told Bertha what had happened to you the day Bill came to the house and how your quick reactions with the knife had probably saved your life. I also told her how you had run to the grove in an effort to warn me. That was really a narrow escape. I wouldn't have had any warning and Bill could have shot me. I told her what she had missed that morning when Bill was at the dock to meet me with the gun. When she asked why he had run away, I told her I had stuck my knife far enough into him to make him bleed. She laughed then and made coffee.

"Some of the tenseness was gone now, and we drank our coffee without talking. I told her then that I had things to do and would come back to let her know how everything turned out.

"I walked over the Miami Avenue Bridge towards the business district, up Miami Avenue, and had a nice breakfast at a place we used to eat quite often. It cost me nineteen cents; and for another dime, I had all the trimmings. This included eggs, bacon, grits, toast, coffee and grapefruit. They even furnished jam for the toast." In those days, it was NRA, Roosevelt's Blue Eagle situation. [The public was urged to boycott businesses unless they displayed the National Recovery Act's Blue Eagle emblem–ed.]

"During breakfast, I finished my plans. I decided to go to a business office I knew of. I don't like to fight. If someone pushes me into a corner–look out–but if there is another way, I'll try it. I'd rather be peaceful and look at things from that viewpoint.

"I went to the office of a major, nationally known insurance company," Russ said, "and I waited for it to open." (This was during the Depression, and insurance salesmen were hard pushed to make a living selling insurance. The company is still well known, so I don't want to say the name.)

"It wasn't too long before a man came along and opened the door while asking if there was anything he could do for me. I said, 'Yeah, as a matter of fact, I'd like to buy some life insurance. A good policy, perhaps ten thousand dollars' worth.' Boy, you should have seen the guy's reaction, then! It was really beautiful. He went behind the desk and opened a memo pad. With his finger on a number, he started dialing before he sat down. He got a response from the other end of the line and asked for Dr. Morrow. He listened a minute, then said, 'Tell him to call me as soon as he is finished.' Giving his name, he hung up.

"I was a bit more relieved now, and my tiredness finally hit me. I sat down in the chair opposite the insurance man. He got out some forms and started to ask questions. I interrupted him and told him that it was only fair to tell him that the time it took to get the policy was important because I had to leave for home in a couple of hours, by noon, if possible. I let him know that there were several other companies in the same area I could go to if he couldn't accommodate me. I had decided to wait a few minutes if the doctor didn't call.

"Just then the phone rang and the appointment was made for a half hour later at an office that was in the same building. I answered questions for the insurance man until the time was up, and he went along to the doctor's office with me. Everything worked out fine. He asked more questions during the physical and was convinced that everything was okay. Back in the insurance office, he drew up the policy, and the doctor called to say that I had passed all tests.

"When all the paperwork was finished, he asked how I wanted to make my payments. I paid three months in advance."

(In those days of short money, that made the insurance man happy. Most policies were paid by the week. The insurance man had to make collection rounds and mark off the ten-cent or twenty-five-cent premium payments on a card.)

"I stood up and put the receipt for the cash payment in my wallet, then went to the door. There, I turned around and said,

'Oh, by the way, if I don't show up to make the next payment, you can look for a fellow by the name of Bill K. I'd rather not tell you his last name because of his connections. He tried to kill me twice, and he also tried to kill my wife.' Now the guy was really shook. He stammered for a minute, then made a motion for me to go back to the desk. This was just a little too much for him. He finally could talk again and he started asking questions. I told him Bill's real name and address. He made notes all the time I talked. He wanted a complete physical description and a fully detailed description of the occasions when he had tried to kill us. There was an insurance man with a ten thousand-dollar policy which they might have to suddenly pay off with only a minimum premium payment! When I finally left the office, the agent wished me good luck. I knew he really meant it.

"I bought our groceries and called a taxi to take the things back to the boat. Somehow I wasn't worried about seeing Bill again this morning. Getting the gas and water containers filled, I went back to Flip's house.

"Flip had just finished breakfast. He was wrapped up like a mummy. He talked through the corner of his mouth. It was really swollen where they had beaten him. Of course, he had that speech impediment and with his swollen mouth, it was almost impossible to understand him, but I gathered that Flip was happy to see me safe and sound. Bertha told me that she had told Flip about our experience.

"I told him how sorry I was that his actions in saving my life had almost cost him his. He refused to think he had done anything unusual, and in his typical fashion said, 'Hoppy to! Hoppy to! Any time, Mon!'

"Then I told Flip and Bertha what I had done after I left that morning. When I got to the part about telling the insurance man–after I was insured–of Bill's attempt to kill me, Flip really grinned until he winced with pain. He nodded his head in agreement, though, that the insurance company would protect their investment in me. He said, 'That was a powerful idea!' It seemed to pep him up some.

"He mumbled, 'I'm not afraid of Bill as long as I have my old pal here,' meaning Bertha. He had his arm around her as she sat on the bed next to him. 'She fought them off with a rake!' That seemed almost unbelievable to Flip. A rake is considered a woman's weapon. Don't ever underrate either of those things, a rake or a woman.

"I shook Flip's uninjured left hand and patted him on the unbandaged shoulder and said, 'Good-bye, I'll see you both soon.'

"I found out later that the insurance company really took the threats seriously. Everywhere Bill went he was up for investigation. That really was good life insurance."

We went to bed that night with the loaded gun alongside the bed. Matter of fact, we took it with us when we left the house. We never met a strange boat at the dock again. We knew Bill could no longer borrow Flip's boat, and we were afraid he would come in another boat.

In the morning we heard one, and waited to see who would appear. It was two strange men, and only after they had introduced themselves as Gary and Shad, new neighbors come to call, did Russ put down the gun and invite them in. They had an old commercial fish boat made out of 2 by 4's and had made arrangements to rent an empty house down-key from us next to John Russell's place. It was a two-story place and belonged to the Sweetings. They said that they had come in to be neighborly and would like us to visit them because all the peace and quiet was driving them nuts. "We are city guys and not used to such quiet." They laughed when they told us what the owner had said he would have to ask eight dollars a month for that house and cistern. "It's only going to be headquarters for us while we get enough fish to make a trip to Miami. We're going to build some furniture. In the meantime, we'll just put some mattresses we brought along on the floor."

Russ asked them if they knew Bill and told them of our experiences. Both of them said that they had heard of him. He had the reputation of being a rough character in the dark and a coward in the daylight. Then Russ mentioned that he was thinking of renting a boat. Gary gave him an address on the river and said that although it would cost eight dollars a month, the owner would keep the motor in repair.

After they left, Russ said, "We will leave before daylight,

75

return John's boat, and get a rental boat." Both of us? Goody. Packing a small bag with our town clothes, we went to bed–with the gun, of course.

CHAPTER EIGHT

Return Loaned Boat, Rent One.
Flip Brings Little Augie–without Leon. Skeleton on Sands Key.
Meet Bob Craig. Cool off Boat. Hire Help.

Breakfast was made by lantern light. Russ fed the ducks by flashlight. Now he was on the back porch looking for something.

"What do you need?"

"I found it. This wide motorcycle belt."

"What possible use could you have for that?"

"On the way home the last time, the motor sounded slightly ragged. Sounded like bearing trouble. I can use this to make a bearing."

It was not long before we were on our way. Sure enough. We were about halfway to Miami when the motor started clanking. Russ shut it down and threw out the anchor. After allowing the motor to cool for a while, he started to work. I helped as much as I could, that is, did what he told me to do. Soon he had the motor apart and it was a bad bearing. He cut a leather bearing, reassembled it, and we were on our way once more.

It was a long boat ride for me, but an interesting one after we got into the Inland Waterway. Sixty miles from home we were in Fort Lauderdale. It was after noon when Russ telephoned Katherine. She and John drove down to the dock. We thanked them for the use of the boat and told them that we were going to rent a work boat. Russ also told them about the leather bearing he had installed. (John told us that it was still running on the leather belt when he sold it a year later.)

77

John said, "I got a nice price for the car, but as yet I haven't located the kind of motor you want. When I locate it, I'll let you know. Do you need the car money?"

"Thanks, no, keep it for the boat and motor."

"John, this time please send the letter to Mayor Fossey and a copy in care of the Border Patrol. Mayor Fossey doesn't come down every week, but they do."

Not wanting to worry anyone, we didn't mention anything of the exciting events. We were afraid that they would insist on our coming back to civilization. Loading our bit of luggage in her car, Katherine took me to my parents' home to visit and then took Russ to their parents' home.

During my visit with my folks and Jan, it was difficult to picture returning to the isolation of the island, but, I had asked for it. I spent so much time in the shower that Mom rapped on the door and asked if something was wrong.

"Nope, I'm just making up for some hot showers I missed on the Keys."

Next morning, in Dad's car, on the way to pick up Russ, Mom asked if I regretted my decision. I was very definite when I told her I didn't. Still, I'm not sure that I convinced her. We had experienced a real rough introduction into how the other half lived. It might have shown in my tone of voice.

Getting a few more things from storage in Russ' folks' house, we got in the car, ready to catch the bus to Miami. As we said good-bye now, it wasn't difficult to see that his parents didn't approve either.

Only had to walk a few blocks from the bus station in Miami to arrive at the address Gary had given us and were surprised to find that the man expected us and had a 22-foot boat all ready gassed up for us. Russ paid for that and the first month's rent in advance. Then the man offered to take us in his car to a nearby grocery. We took advantage of this lucky break. On the way he told us that Gary and Shad had appeared with a load of fish the day before and told him to expect us.

Going down-river to Mr. Everett's dock, I noticed a variety of odors I had never noticed before. I wondered if my sense of smell was becoming more acute. While we were topping off the gas tank, Mr. Everett said Flip and Bertha had told him about our experiences with Bill, and he was just waiting for a chance to run him off the property. "He hasn't been around."

We visited with Flip and Bertha before leaving. Flip was much improved and said he, or they, would be down in a few days. Nothing exciting had happened since Russ' last visit.

During our short stay in town we had filled up with ice cream, cake and other goodies. We paid for it as usual when we arrived at the dock. The sandflies just mobbed us. While fussing about that, I remarked how smelly the Miami air was. Breathing the clean air of the Keys had spoiled the Miami air for me.

During a late breakfast we heard Mr. Fossey's motor. Pretty funny–we had been in town and didn't know what day it was. We were so used to losing track of days, it no longer bothered us. We went to the dock to drop our boat back.

During that day, Russ told Mr. Fossey about our experiences with Bill. Then Mr. Fossey told Russ that Bill was a most casual acquaintance of his. He had been most insistent that Mr. Fossey allow the use of the house for clearing the lime groves. He had thought it strange that he didn't even meet us before we moved to his place, but inasmuch as he benefited by it, found no reason to refuse. Now, he said that he saw it as we did–Bill wanted us there so we would be custodians of his smuggled things.

Then he said, "It was most fortunate that Bill was such a poor judge of character. Had he found someone who would cooperate with him, the island could very well have become a smuggler's nest."

We were visiting at the dock when a small boat with an outboard came into the cut. The man shut off his motor, dropped his anchor, and began to fish. The first thing he caught was a moray eel. Not checking what was on his line, he just yanked it into the boat. Immediately, it started slithering towards him. With a horrified expression he yelled, "Kill it, somebody, I can't swim!" With that, he jumped overboard. He grabbed the side of the boat when he came up and just continued to yell. He moved around the boat by changing his hand position, and the moray followed him. In the meantime, Russ had grabbed the machete from the powerboat and got out the skiff. He went over, jumped into the man's boat with his bow line in his hand and killed the moray. He made quite a slice in the man's boat doing it. As Russ flipped the still wiggling thing over the side, the man climbed aboard to get away from it. In a very shaky voice, he said, "Thank you."

He started to pull his anchor as Russ got aboard our skiff. Saying, "I've had it," the man started his motor and left towards the bay. He had twelve miles to go—if he had come from Princeton—a long trip for a few minutes' fishing.

The Fosseys left around three that afternoon. Alone again. A nice peaceful day.

We were in the little grove the next day when Russ said, "I hear Flip's motor. I can't imagine him loaning it to Bill again, but hand me the gun." He went out to look. It was Flip coming up the path and he introduced us to "my friend, Little Augie." He told us that they had been friends since before his rum running days.

Little Augie stepped forward to shake hands and said, "I'm pretty *hot* right now, but I figure I can still make a dozen trips before they catch me."

They had brought enough lunch for all of us and I made coffee. After lunch, they sat Conch-style on their heels and started reminiscing about the good old days. Three pals, Leon (pronounced Le-own), Flip and Little Augie had pooled their money and started business with one boat. They soon had enough money to buy two more boats and each went into business for himself.

Trips were described as "free" or "real close." Real close was when they had to throw the liquor overboard to destroy the evidence or hide their boat in the mangroves to avoid being captured by the Border Patrol or the Coast Guard. From my viewpoint this was odd, law-breaking discussed as though it was ordinary business.

It was still early afternoon when Flip said they had to go. He hadn't completely recovered and tired easily. He told us that Bill hadn't been around the service station and he hadn't had any news of him.

The most important thing in the next few days was the hatching of a bunch of little fluffy ducks.

One morning we heard three horn blasts. Russ judged the sound to be coming from the bay side. With the gun, we went out in the boat to look. It was George Deen, owner of Sands Key, aground on the flat. With our boat, Russ pulled the much larger boat off and received the first of many verbal thanks he was to receive for the same favor.

George had brought quite a lot of lumber as well as a carpenter, Bob Craig. He tied his boat securely to a mangrove on his key and the unloading got under way.

When things were unloaded, George came to visit with us. He said that the carpenter was going to build him a weekend cottage, and he hoped it wouldn't take too long as he hoped to bring several guests in the not too distant future. (Poor George, it didn't get finished before the Labor Day hurricane. That we know.) George told us that he had been told there was a brass cannon in the jungle on his island and he would go halves with us if we found it. He had no idea of its location. Some raccoon hunters had told him about it.

Then he said, "Oh, yes. According to the newspaper, some fisherman found a male skeleton on my key next to a lean-to on the north end."

I started to say something. Russ shook his head "no," so I kept still. George left soon after saying that he would be back the following week.

Instead of walking, we went to the big grove by boat the next day and noticed that the carpenter had put up a canvas lean-to. When we returned to the house around three that afternoon, he hailed us. Russ dropped me at the dock and went over to see what he wanted.

I went up to start the cooking and was busy peeling potatoes when they came up. Russ had invited Bob to supper, and he brought up enough cleaned fish for all of us. He said that his problem was that he had neglected to bring any grits or potatoes from town. He wanted the loan of some.

We ate and then visited until quite late. Instead of going back to his camp, he asked if he could spend the night. We had plenty of room and he was pleasant company, so, of course, it was okay.

Russ made pancakes for breakfast. I set the table and put on margarine, syrup, and jam to go with them. The jam happened to be closer to Bob, and I watched amazed as he wrapped his fingers around the jar and proceeded to eat *all* of it before he touched a pancake. In the future, I only put syrup and margarine on the table when he ate with us.

Afterwards we dropped Bob with a package of grits on Sands Key and left for the big grove. The problem that faced us was not the usual one. It had been a good many years since this one had been cleared, and it was a foot-tripping mess. There were a great many young volunteer lime trees. Russ said that he had decided to ask George if there was a market for the little trees. If so, we could hire help and let them earn their own keep.

George arrived a few days later bringing more lumber and some groceries for Bob. After checking the progress of his cottage, he came to see us. When Russ asked about the lime trees, he told of a man named McCarthy who had contacted him in an attempt to buy some. He had offered ten cents a tree and his tree nursery was on the south side of the Princeton Canal. This was the answer to our problem!

The next time in Miami, Russ met Mr. McCarthy. He introduced him, over the phone, to his foreman, Mr. Weeks. He told him how he wanted the trees prepared for delivery and said that he would provide the burlap bags to put them in. Mr. McCarthy said that he could sell all we could provide him with. The Japanese nurserymen on Miami Beach were begging for the trees to use as hedges. Besides prickly protection, they had fruit.

The following day Russ left for Princeton to hire help to clean the grove. At the colored settlement he hired two men at a dollar and a half a day and a place to stay. Walking with them the mile back to the dock, he told them that he would advance them the necessary grocery money, and they could supplement their food with fish.

He advanced about four dollars to each of them and bought our groceries. Then from the store he called Mr. Weeks. Getting instructions as to the location of the dock, he went there. Mr. Weeks met him with a supply of burlap bags.

Back to the island now, Russ took the men to the small frame house in the grove. It had a large mattress and boxes on the walls for supplies. He showed them where they were to cook outdoors.

He came to the house for cooking pans, plates and other necessities. Adding two fishing lines to the pile, he went back to the grove. He showed the men the chitons on the rock and how to get them off. Then he showed them how to scoop the bit of meat for bait. They settled down to fish with the other supplies next to them.

Returning in the morning he found them eating some fish, quite pleased with themselves. Because of the hot weather, they started work early in the morning and quit around three, if not before. Russ had a frum pole and showed them how to use it. One end of the pole was tied to the lower base and exposed roots of the little trees, and levering it over a support eased the trees out. Then he showed them how to prune and prepare the trees for packing. By three o'clock they had prepared quite a few, wrapped them, stored them in a shady place, and watered them with the water from the boat jug. He gave the men our alarm clock and told them to set it for 5 A.M. so they could have an early breakfast and get a good start.

A few days later, during which all the bundled trees were wet every day, there were several bundles ready in addition to one skiff load. In the calm weather, Russ made the trip to Princeton very quickly and was surprised to see Mr. Weeks at the dock waiting for him. He was just as anxious to get the trees as we were to get rid of them. There were only enough trees to pay one man's salary for a week, plus the gas to deliver them, but Russ was willing to gamble that the work would go more smoothly as the men learned their jobs.

When Russ returned the next morning around nine o'clock, the men were fishing. Exasperated, he told them that they had to earn their own salaries. No work getting trees, no pay! They worked much better from then on.

A few days later, the men had enough trees so another trip was necessary. Then the men told him they were willing to work an extra week and gave him a list of supplies needed.

He brought them a bonus, a pint of "shine" he had bought from a colored boy who approached him as he was leaving the store. He told me they acted like happy children.

These trips to Princeton meant that we could have fresh

meat very frequently. It was a real welcome change.

We had adopted the Conch term for middle afternoon to dark, now, so I'll say it was Monday "evening" when we heard a boat. As usual, Russ got out the gun before he went out to look. It was Mugs. He was in a different boat and had the double-ender in tow. Russ hurried down to help him. When he got there, Mugs was holding the boat in place with the motor against the incoming tide. He untied the bow line of the double-ender and tossed it to Russ who tied it to the end of the dock. The stern was tied to the mangrove on shore. By that time, Mugs had put his bow ashore as before, tossed his anchor and greeted us. Then, he started calling loudly, "E.C. Oh, E.C." It startled me. When Russ asked who he was calling, Mugs grinned. "Grapevine tells me that you hired my unloading man to work in the grove. I want him to fix some conch stew for us. He's a damn good cook. He was trained in a parsonage in the Bahamas."

There was silence for a minute as we digested this strange information, and Mugs laughed uproariously. Then he said, "Whereabouts is he?"

Russ told him that the men were in the grove on the bay side, but he wasn't aware that one was E.C. They had given their names as Bob and Earnest.

"Let's take the old double-ender around there and you can see if it runs well enough so you want to borrow it," Mugs said. We all got into the boat then. It was a fast, smooth ride and I loved it.

"I will really enjoy using this boat," I said. "It's fast."

Sure enough, when we got to the grove, one of the men came trotting out in answer to Mugs' call. He greeted Mr. Mugs happily. The other man didn't want to be left alone, so we brought them both back to the house. Russ showed E.C. where we had anchored the conchs and we went on up to the house to visit.

At that time, we didn't even think about it. Later, when friends asked us about what liquor gifts we had received, we realized that Mugs had never had a drink in our presence and no mention was ever made about a bottle.

It wasn't too long before the men came to the house with eight prepared conchs and said they were ready to make the stew.

Russ showed E.C. were the necessary ingredients were and when he asked for the meat grinder, showed him the plug and the lead beater and told him how to use it.

Mugs said, "I'm real pleased you like the boat. Don't like it to be idle. Runs better if it's used a lot." He seemed to think we were doing him a favor.

E.C. set the table nicely. He had even located my table napkins and folded them in an unusual manner. It was nice being waited on. His stew was a different from ours, more highly seasoned, but delicious. He had made an enormous quantity, but when we had all finished eating, there was surprisingly little left. The men took it along when Russ and Mugs took them back to the grove.

They filled both boats with the extra cans of gas Mugs had brought with him and then came up to the house to visit. Mugs talked about many things in general and one thing in particular.

"I'm still trying to find out who the son of a bitch was who hijacked a load of liquor from me a while back. After I had it in my car ashore, I went back to my boat, and that's when it happened. He got away with twenty sacks of unclarified rye, a special order. By the time I got back from hoisting my boat up out of sight in the shipyard, it was gone."

I hope my face showed only interest. I was afraid of showing anything. We both remembered hiding that amount under our bed. Mugs stood up then, and I was glad to change the subject. "Leaving now?"

"Let's go look. If the boats are gone, I'll go."

At the dock again, I thanked him for his thoughtfulness in letting us use the boat. He was always chuckling, so I didn't think anything of it when he laughed heartily as he waved good-bye.

The next load of trees was soon ready and we both went on the delivery trip. There was plenty of room and we didn't have to tow the skiff. The boat was very fast and we were a third of the way across when we saw a small, fast boat approaching. Russ slowed down a little, and I waved, thinking it was our friends, the Border Patrol.

It was the Border Patrol all right, but not our friends, and not very friendly, as their drawn guns demonstrated.

We halted when ordered to do so. Tying their boat alongside ours, they proceeded to search, that is, one of them did. The other was facing us with his gun at all times. The man made a very thorough search and often got stuck by the lime thorns as he moved the trees around.

I was very indignant and I said, "Why did you stop us. What are you looking for? We have to deliver these trees and you're delaying us." All the time I was talking until the search finished, they were quiet. I saw many red marks on the face and hands of the searching man and thought, "Good. Red ants."

Finished, both men got back in their boat and said, "You're clean. You can go."

We waited until they untied their boat from ours and left, furiously scratching. Once again on our way, I told Russ that it was a darn shame that they couldn't tell the difference between an honest citizen and a rum runner. I became even more upset when Russ started to laugh.

He finally managed to stop laughing and then he said, "Just how naïve can you get? Didn't you realize that Mugs loaned us this boat because it was hot? He wanted us to cool it off for him, using it legally. I thought it would be better if I didn't tell you in advance. Your innocent reactions helped convince the Border Patrol that we didn't know anything." Then he laughed some more.

There was no answer to that line of reasoning, but I was full of injured dignity and I didn't like to be laughed at either! The rest of the trip was smooth, and Russ again pocketed the receipt for the trees for collection from Mr. McCarthy.

During the return trip, Russ remarked about how pleased he was that I had kept my mouth shut when Mugs told us about being hijacked. He went on to say, "We are on the fence! We can't tell on anyone. When it is something serious like aliens or dope, we'll go to the proper authority."

The men had been cleaning the jungle in rows, and when they said they had reached the last tree in line, Russ went a bit further, and there found a box. According to the label, it was "slow" dynamite, or 40 per-cent dynamite. He saw under the heavy waxed paper that it was almost full. It was standard size and looked in good condition. Discussing this find later, Russ and Mr. Fossey decided that the Civilian Conservation Corps had used the dynamite to crack the hard-pan rock in the bottoms of water holes to drain them to get rid of mosquitoes. They finally found out that this wasn't the way to do it. The water did not drain away; it just made a larger home for more mosquitoes. Eventually the CCC reverted to the old Conch custom of filling burlap bags with wood chips, soaking them in barrels of old engine oil and hanging them over the water hole to drip. The film killed the mosquito larvae.

For almost a month now, we had been stopped and searched whenever we left the dock in the double-ender. The last two times, the Border Patrol merely came close enough to see who it was, then turned and left.

To our friends, Happy and Al, I explained that a new friend of ours had loaned us the double-ender because our rental boat was too small to haul lime trees. This time I *acted* naïve, I could tell by their expression that they found it hard to believe, but they didn't say anything.

CHAPTER NINE

My First Solo by Boat.

During our trips to Miami and Princeton, Russ had explained his method of navigating these "short" distances. Judging the wind drift "upstairs," he picked a cloud to steer by. After a period of time–indefinite, we carried no watch–he picked another cloud of the same level, more northern or southern, depending on the wind "upstairs." Now, in this manner, you can get from point A to point B. While you are doing this, you also find it necessary to watch the color of the water so you don't run aground.

Now Russ seemed to feel that I was fully instructed and ready to make a solo trip. It was necessary that he work with the men that day.

I was proud and pleased at the thought of being on my own. Told him that I didn't mind at all. I was more familiar with the rental boat and thought I could handle it better than the double-ender in which I had had such humiliating experiences. Two skiffs were available now that the found one had been repaired. They were full of trees and waiting at the grove when we arrived.

I was to make a triangular trip; twelve miles due west to Princeton; north to Miami and then back to Elliott, east south-east from Miami. I dressed in Russell's sailor whites that morning and was ready. As the demijohns were carried to the cabin, Russ gave me the due bills for McCarthy and some expense money.

It was a beautiful sunny morning as I took the boat towards the big grove. Russ told me to go to the house when I returned as he intended to walk there that afternoon.

We had been having some trouble with a clogged fuel line in the rental boat, not too often, because it was a short run to the little grove. Russ reminded me of it. I told him that I was sure I could fix it because I had often watched as he freed it up. I recited brightly:

"I remove the cap of the gas tank. Put my mouth against the tank opening–tightly, so the expelled air won't blow my face away while I am blowing in. Inhale through the nose. Blow through the mouth until it's too difficult to get more air in. Release my mouth and the pressure."

Russ said, "Do it just that way and you'll be all right."

(We found out later that some slob had put a glazed-surface business card in the tank.)

I let the motor idle while Russ tied the two skiffs to the stern cleats with different lengths of line. He explained that he had to do this to keep the boats from bumping into each other. Also, I was to avoid splashing any salt water on the trees. It might kill them.

Just as I was ready to leave, the men brought out ten additional bundles of trees and put them in the cockpit. They had hidden them out to surprise us.

The clouds "upstairs" were marching north now, head winds and a following sea down where I was. It was a bit rough, but I attempted to be nonchalant and went on my first boat trip alone!

Because of the following sea, it soon became necessary to tack like a sailboat in order to keep the skiffs from riding up and ramming the stern. Then, of course, the fuel line needed attention. I slowed the motor and memorized my cloud. I hurried below, cleared the line and returned to the wheel just in time to tack again and avoid being hit by the skiffs.

I increased the speed and located my cloud. Time to pick another one. I was just too busy to be worried about missing the narrow canal entrance at Princeton. If I did miss it, I would waste a lot of time locating it. The entrance could only be seen from off shore.

Four different times during this leg of the trip, I had to slow down and clear the fuel line. I was a mighty proud gal when I saw the rock-edged extension of the Princeton Canal. I had gone twelve miles by cloud navigation and reached a spot just twelve feet wide.

The next part was easy. Reaching Mr. Weeks' dock, I tied up and walked half a mile to his house. He was in the field and his wife sent her young brother for him. He soon arrived in a large truck; there were four men standing in the back. I rode in the cab with him on the way to the boat.

His men unloaded the trees and he gave me the due bill. I put it with the others in my wallet. Ready to leave now, I decided to leave the skiffs. They had been so annoying on the first part of the trip that I didn't want to be bothered with them.

I felt that the worst part of the trip was over. Going out a way beyond the rock edge of the canal, I turned towards Miami. Then I realized that I hadn't been to Miami along the shoreline before and would have to watch the color of the water for depth.

The waves weren't as much of a problem as I expected, but the fuel line seemed to clog more often and was difficult to clear. Watching the water now, with an occasional glance toward the shore so I could stay away from it had a sort of hypnotic effect. My face was getting quite sore from the work of clearing the fuel line.

I believe that at least two hours had passed when I heard voices. Startled, I looked up. Around me, I saw many small sailboats darting close to me and then tacking away. All of them were handled by children. Looking down at the water again, I saw that it was much shallower. I reached over to slow the motor, and I was aground.

What to do now. Russ had taught me all I knew about boats, and he never went aground.

It was a pretty silly situation. The kids in the sailboats didn't make me feel any better when they called, "Want a tow?"

I tried to back off, but the bow was fast in the mud.

I sat there for quite a few minutes making my plans. First, the anchor. I threw that from the stern of the boat into the deeper water to the starboard side. With my mighty muscles, it went all of ten feet. I would have to get out and push, and then get back in. Since the bow was quite high, I tied a loop in the bow line so I could step in it to climb up. Now, with the motor in slow reverse, I was ready, except for the fact that I still had to go into the business district in Miami in the clothes I was wearing. Fortunately, I had worn a pair of Russell's boxer shorts, and they were modest. I took off my white pants, rolled up the bottom of the jacket a ways and was ready.

Then I picked a time when the majority of the sailboats had made another tack to avoid hitting me. I climbed onto the cabin and went down the rope at the bow. I had tied double knots in my shoelaces so they wouldn't pull off. Never thought of going barefoot.

Now I was standing in the mud almost to my knees. Putting my shoulder against the boat, I started to push. That didn't work. I simply sank deeper in the mud. Then I lunged at the boat. This seemed to move it a little. Using my body weight, all 110 pounds of it, I finally moved the boat enough so I needed to take a step forward. I had gone deeper into the mud with each lunge and push, all the time holding onto the bow line. Now I had to pull myself from the mud without pulling the boat back. I finally managed, and lunging again, got the boat off the flat. Hanging onto the rope, I turned and sat on it to help me out of the mud. Even with the motor in slow reverse, this pulled the boat forward again. Almost onto the flat.

My tennis shoes seemed to be anchoring me, and the laces hurt. Under the strain, as the rope tightened, the top button of my shorts popped off, and I knew the remaining bottom button wouldn't hold them up. Finally free of the mud, I had no choice, so I put my foot in the loop and climbed to the bow. Almost, but not quite, losing my shorts in the process.

All the little people clapped and cheered. For that I could forgive them their offer of a tow. I belly-crawled forward clutching my shorts, finally reached the instrument panel, and leaning over, shut the motor off.

I lay there panting on the hot cabin roof a few minutes, modestly awaiting an opportunity to go into the cabin for my long pants. The little people were having a ball seeing who could come the closest to the boat without hitting it. When most of them tacked away, I quickly slipped over the edge and went into the cabin.

The knots in my shoes were really tight. I finally got them off, and then my socks. I used my shorts to wipe off the sticky,

92

stinky mud from myself. Using a fairly clean engine rag, I sponged down with the drinking water, and still damp, put on my white pants and rolled down my jacket.

Going topside, I pulled in the anchor and then saw that all the larger boats were about a quarter mile out from where I was.

When I started the motor, all the little people cheered. I grinned and waved as I left. I went slowly and watched the water depth and was finally in the channel. Going up the Miami River soon afterwards was quite easy after that ridiculous experience.

When I pulled into Mr. Everett's dock, he was standing there, so I threw my sheath knife into the cabin. It was illegal to wear it in town, and Bill wouldn't be apt to try anything with other people around. Mr. Everett caught the bow line and secured it for me while I tied the stern. He just stood there staring. I looked up and he started to laugh. My feelings were a bit tender now and I wondered what was so funny. He finally stopped laughing and could talk.

"What happened to you? How did you manage to get all that fresh mud aboard? What made your face so dirty and red?"

When I told him about the mud flat episode, he laughed again and said, "Come on up and look in the mirror. You will see why I laughed."

Looking in his mirror, I was shook. I even looked funny to myself. The dirty red ring under my mouth extended to the under part of my nose—it had been rubbed raw. There was a blister on my upper lip. The mess on my face was a mixture of red, black grease, and dirt. That fuel line hadn't given me any assist in the beauty line. He handed me a clean cloth dipped in oil and I used that in a more or less painful removal of the dirt. The rest of it came off with soap and water. My face looked ridiculous and was puffing up a bit.

I had to travel by bus into the business district to collect the money for the lime trees from Mr. McCarthy. I put on my still wet shoes and got instructions from Mr. Everett.

The attention I got on the bus made me glad that I wasn't dressed as a female. I also had to face the office staff before I could present my bill to Mr. McCarthy. From their glances, I realized my face was still a mess.

He wrote out a check for me and told me to cash it at his

bank in the same block. I tried to act casual as I walked into the bank and was grateful that I knew no one there. I managed to ignore the stares, and after cashing the check, I got to the door in time to catch a cab that was discharging a passenger.

I went to the grocery. I got a good number of the day's specials in addition to other items, and with them, caught another cab. On the way to the boat, I could see the driver occasionally looking at me in the rear-vision mirror.

Mr. Everett helped me load my groceries and handed down the hose so I could fill the water jugs. Then he said, "I'll get your ice while the boys fill the cans and top your gas tank."

When the ice was stowed, I went to the office to pay him. He took the money and said, "Just a minute, now. Stand still." Then he put a very soothing ointment on my face. It was hurting a bit more now. I thanked him and asked if I could buy the rest of it. He handed it to me, saying, "I bought it for you—be my guest."

Thanking him again, I went to see Flip and Bertha for a few minutes. They laughed, not at me but with me, as I told my story. Then they said, "But you do look s-o-o-o funny."

Russ had heard the motor and met me. He caught the bow line and tied the stern. I didn't offer any explanation for my appearance. While we were unloading, he didn't ask for any, but I noticed the funny look on his face when he went into the cabin for the water jugs and saw my muddy shorts there.

After we finished the stowing, he said, "Just sit down and rest. I'll finish supper." Shortly after, he handed me a glass of ice water and asked, "Have any trouble?"

"Boy! That isn't half of it. You can see what clearing the gas line did to my face. With the following waves . . . ." I told him the long story.

He didn't laugh, just sort of snorted. He was most amused when I got to the part when I had to wait until I could go into the cabin. Then he said, "I saw your muddy shorts there. I figured you ran aground somewhere. Good thing you got off when you did. If you had waited much longer, you'd still be aground waiting for high tide. Tying that knot in the line so you could get back aboard was most ingenious. Now, let me look at your shoulder. You probably bruised it when you lunged at the boat.

"It's not bad. Sort of pretty with those blue and purple

marks. It's going to be sore in the morning, though. Hold still. I'll clean up your face with this Oil of Sol. It will help you heal."

He was gentle, but I couldn't help wince. I hadn't known what he would say when I told him about leaving the skiffs in Princeton. It was pleasant to hear him say that it had been a good idea. He intended to tell me to do it and had forgotten.

"By the way," he said, "we won't have to carry water to the grove to wet the trees anymore. At quitting time, I used a stick of dynamite to blow a saucer-shaped hole in the rocks and it's full of sweet water."

"What's sweet water?"

"I thought you knew. It's the rainwater in the soil partly mixed with some salt water that comes up. It will work very well on the trees."

I fell asleep during supper and he sent me to bed.

CHAPTER TEN

Big Erskine Comes to Island to "Cool Off."

There followed a few uneventful days during which my face began to heal. The men were working very well now and Russ could leave them without supervision.

We had quite a few crates of limes and he decided to leave shortly before ten o'clock to sell them. I was to stay home and be prepared to take to the jungle if Bill showed up.

Russ told me later that after selling the limes, he tied up at Everett's and walked to our favorite little restaurant for breakfast. Later he went to the grocery, and with our supplies took a taxi to the boat.

When he started to load the things aboard, he got a shock. In the bow was a large mound of burlap bags. Then he remembered what Mugs had said the last time he was at the island. "Don't question any supplies you find in your boat. Ignore them. Time enough to check them when you get down-bay."

The mound of bags was not only in the bow but extended down along one side of the motor, and putting the groceries on the other side balanced the boat.

About an hour after Russ left the dock, there was a sudden upheaval of the bags and from them appeared a smiling dark brown face. The man said, "Mr. Russ, Mr. Mugs said that you would take care of me for a while. I'll be your house-boy and help in the grove. Mr. Mugs said you could use some help getting the other boys in line. They are pretty uppity. Especially that E.C. I know him! I brought a cot and some extra food along. My name is Erskine Ferguson, but you just call me Big Erskine like everybody else does."

During the time he was with us, he made many changes in the way the men worked and did all my cooking chores for me. His cot was set up on the screened back porch. He always walked to and from the big grove as he said he didn't want to be seen in a boat.

Erskine was six foot four and weighed about 350 pounds, but he moved as silently as a cat. I hadn't heard him return from the grove so I was startled to see him wading in from the ocean with two conchs in each hand the first afternoon of his stay.

"You just sit still, Miss Charlotte. I'm going to fix us some stew."

It was real nice being waited on again.

While preparing the food, he said, "Mr. Mugs told me all about Bill. Don't you worry about him while I'm around! I can take care of him and anybody else that might trouble you!"

It was most fortunate that Erskine went to the grove by the path because the border patrolmen, Happy and Al, showed up for a visit.

With Big Erskine in the grove, Russ could stay with me. The output there almost doubled now. He was right about knowing how to make the other men work. He set the pace and they tried to keep up with him.

Erskine was a "Bahama boy" and had a college education. During a conversation with Russ one evening he said, "I almost got captured by the Mon. I was unloading man for Mr. Manning at the time. We saw them coming. We were only about a quarter of a mile from shore at the time, so I put my shark knife between my teeth, took a sack of liquor in each hand, and jumped overboard. That way I saved two cases of liquor for Mr. Manning. It wouldn't have helped him any if I had stayed in his boat and gotten caught."

One day, when we were preparing to go to Princeton to make a lime tree delivery and reclaim the skiffs, Russ asked Big Erskine to stay at the house and watch things for us.

He called Russ aside. I continued to the boat. Once we were out in the bay, Russ told me of the conversation they had:

Erskine said, "Mr. Russ, don't you leave any liquor in the

house! That was my downfall once and I might get tempted again. A high yellow gal found out how much I liked my liquor and she took me! She really did! She got my house, my boat, my car and everything else I had. I had to start all over again, work for someone else, and make another stake.

"That was quite a while back and I have quite a lot of money saved up again. I made it unloading for other people. Just as soon as I cool off, I'm going to buy a boat and get back in the business.

"Mr. Russ, after I swam ashore from Mr. Manning's boat I went to my hideout. Some friends of mine that worked for Mr. Mugs told him about me. He fixed it for me to get in your boat and come down here to help you while I cool off."

"There isn't any liquor in the house," Russ said, "so you won't be tempted. Just sit around and read if you want to. I don't expect the Border Patrol today, but if they come, here's the padlock and key. You'll recognize the sound of the motor and have time enough to lock up and go into the jungle."

We delivered the trees, got the due bill, groceries, and towing the skiffs, had a pleasant trip back. Big Erskine met us and said that he had a nice crawfish dinner ready.

Mugs must have judged the cooling off time of the double-ender. At any rate, the last time over, we hadn't even seen the Mon. Mugs arrived a few days later with several cans of spare gasoline in his boat. After docking in his usual manner, he asked, "How about swapping boats now? I'll top this tank off for you, and after we fill the double-ender, you can have what's left in the cans. I didn't see any sight of the Mon in the ocean, so I'll get along over. Give me a hand, will ya?"

While they were filling the boats, I was fussing at Mugs and telling him how humiliating it had been to be stopped and searched all the time. He just roared with laughter and Russ joined him. Russ then told him about the first time and how I had stormed at the Border Patrol.

Mugs said, "That's the funniest damn thing I ever heard! I purely wish that I could have seen that man get stuck by the thorns when he moved those trees looking for liquor. That part about the red ants pleasures me a lot."

By now both boats had been filled and he said, "Well, now you are used to having the Mon stop you, maybe you won't mind cooling this boat for me."

What can you say to a guy like that? I grinned back at him and said, "Okay. Russ seemed to enjoy it so much."

We waved and wished him good luck on what proved to be his last trip.

Mugs had told us often that he considered rum running as a lucrative fun-game and expected to get caught some day. "My house and boats are paid for. I've got a real nice bank account and I can afford to take my vacation and retire if I have to."

He was caught with a full load on his way back from the Bahamas. Just a few more blocks to his dock, when the Border Patrol stopped him. Flip brought us that news on his next trip down. He also said, "No sign of Bill."

The following morning brought a letter from Katherine, delivered by the Border Patrol. The news was that John had made a down payment on a Coast Guard surf boat and had also located a possible motor.

When Big Erskine came back to the house that afternoon, Russ said, "I'm making a trip to Miami in the morning. If you feel cool enough, I'll take you along."

"Mr. Russ, I might be pushing things a bit, but I want to get my own boat and get back in business. I don't think there is any need to tell the boys in the grove about it though. That day I stayed at the house they got a lot done. They just about bust a gut trying to show me up."

In the morning I promised to go into the jungle if I heard a boat. It wasn't necessary and I had a pleasant day.

On his return, Russ told me that Big Erskine had asked to be put ashore on the south side near the river entrance. "When I told him that I had to collect for the trees before I could pay him, he laughed. 'I'll be down to the Keys real soon. See you then.'"

After seeing McCarthy, Russ went to Lauderdale and called Katherine. She picked him up and they went to see the boat. He was delighted with it. He also bought the motor. It was a two-cylinder, two-cycle Ferro in good condition. The boat and motor cost him $50. (Hush, remember this was during the Depression.)

He made arrangements to have them delivered to John's dock so he could work on them later, then to the bus station and Miami bound.

Russ visited Flip and Bertha. "No sign of Bill," they said. They had heard that he was working in West Palm Beach. It just seemed as though he couldn't keep a job. Flip grinned when he said that. Boy! That sounded good. Peace of mind *and* a boat of our own.

Russ returned before six that night and the next day took the men to Princeton and was back around noon. After lunch, we went to our lumber store, the beach, and gathered material for a crawfish car.

That was finished around noon the next day, and ready to store crawfish.

CHAPTER ELEVEN

Big Erskine–Back in Business–Avoids Border Patrol. Alderman
Case. Smugglers' Boats Build Bahia Mar in
Fort Lauderdale. Hair Cut. Borrow Jan.
Captain John Russell's Lightering Stories.

We heard a powerful motor in the cut the next day. Russ looked and said, "There are two colored men in the boat. One of them looks like Big Erskine."

Soon Erskine appeared on the path with another man. He had a five-gallon jug in his hand, swinging it as though it were quart size. He had come for drinking water and his wages. After he had filled his jug, Russ called me and we walked to the boat with him. It was an open, streamlined boat with more than the usual beam, a Wollard-built boat. Most of the better fast boats were built by Lee Wollard in Miami.

Erskine said, "I've been waiting a long time to buy my boat and I've been studying things. Most all the boats that have been caught were cabin boats. I don't want any high cabin to make a silhouette and call attention to me."

He was pleased when Russ told him he had one of the best hulls available at the time. He left soon but not before asking politely, "Do you mind if we get some conchs down-key?"

Russ laughed, "It's God's ocean. Help yourself. By the way, Erskine, your motor sounds more powerful than the one the Border Patrol has."

"I figured it that way. I plan to run away from the Mon. I won't argue with them." Looking east, we saw a large Coast Guard boat was slowly cruising in Hawk Channel. Erskine waved good-bye and sailed. He went around the front of the key.

From the house we could see that he had stopped about two blocks down, and was using a sponge hook to pick up the conchs. He moved the boat south and towards shore. I noticed that the boat's dull, camouflaged paint job seemed to change its shape and blend it with the water. After he threw his anchor, the other man got out and waded ashore to a box. He threw some wet sand into it from the edge of the water and then, further up-shore, he got dry sand and another box and carried it towards the boat.

Russ explained it to me, an old island trick. The wet sand would protect the boat from the fire they would soon build in the dry sand to cook their food on board.

It was lucky Big Erskine had left when he did. We suddenly noticed activity on his boat. It circled slowly and fish poles appeared. It moved slowly away from the shore and they stopped.

It was then that we heard the sound of a motor in the cut. Apparently he had heard it first and assumed the camouflage of a fisherman.

Russ ran towards the dock saying, "That sounds like the Border Patrol. I'll try to delay them a little. I just hope Erskine doesn't panic." This was one time we weren't so pleased to see Happy and Al. No telling what their presence here might mean to Big Erskine. I followed Russ to the dock and we talked there for a while. Russ told them about an airplane that, curiously, had almost buzzed us some days before. When he saw the plane coming from the west side of the island, they were going slow and he had fully expected them to wave. Instead of that, they circled and retraced their path again moving over the house and towards the grove. Happy laughed and said, "That's one of the reasons we are here. They asked us to investigate what they said appeared to be a newly made path to the bayside, possibly for rum running or smuggling. What do you know about it?"

"That's been there for quite a while now. We cut it before we had a powerboat and use it sometimes now to save gas. It leads to the big lime grove down-key."

Then, reaching into the cockpit of his boat, Happy brought out a bag and said, "I brought something to go with the coffee." They were welcome things. Fresh fruit, cookies, and magazines.

When we reached the house, I set the table and Russ made the coffee. I hoped Russ would grab his chair. That was the one that Happy preferred and always used when he could. It faced towards Erskine's boat. No luck. Happy eased himself into it as I finished setting out the dishes. Soon we were drinking coffee and nibbling cookies.

Suddenly Happy put down his cup and said, "Al, if I didn't know better, I'd say that was Big Erskine on that boat way down there. He's hiding out now."

Al had to lean forward to see, and said, "Yeah, it does sort of look like him. Maybe not as big, though."

"Who is Big Erskine?"

Happy grinned. Shaking his head, he said, "He's quite a man. If you get close enough to tell him to stop, he will. Never a hostile motion of any kind. Do you know what he did when we caught Manning? He was a real slick runner. He fooled us quite a while. Big Erskine was on the boat with Manning, no mistaking that boy. He just put his shark knife between his teeth, grabbed a sack of liquor in each hand, jumped over and swam ashore. It was more than two hundred yards and in one of the roughest seas we have ever been out in. Had we gone after him, we would have lost Manning and that big load of liquor he had. Manning was a real good loser. Not like some we hear about," he added with a grimace.

"When we got him, he just said, 'Well, you finally caught me. Now I'll take my vacation and retire.' You know, most of those guys do quit. Seems like getting caught ends the fun of the game. Hey, Al, do you remember the time Big Erskine was running down that path. He was carrying one sack under each arm, one in each hand and one balanced on his head, just loping along. I yelled 'Stop' and he did, without juggling that sack off his head."

Then he turned to me and continued, "Do you realize he was carrying five dozen bottles of liquor the way an ordinary man would carry five loaves of bread?"

Russ said, "Let me tell it. I know some Coast Guard men who were in on it. Jody Hollingsworth and his brother were on routine patrol from the Coast Guard base then located on the beach at Fort Lauderdale, across from what is now known as the

Bahia Mar yacht basin. They spotted a long, sleek-looking boat running without lights. The Coast Guard cutter pursued and caught up with it and fired a shot across the bow. The other boat came to a stop and the cutter went alongside, preparatory for searching for contraband.

"Most of the crew lined the rail watching as two of their number took lines to tie to the smaller boat. After apparent surrender, Alderman, the owner and skipper of the boat, grabbed a submachine gun from its position alongside the wheel, and finger on the trigger, swung it in an arc, hitting most of the men along the rail of the Coast Guard boat. Some died instantly. Many others were injured.

"Then Alderman climbed aboard the cutter and sloshed his spare can of gas on the men on the deck. Fortunately, when he tried to light it, the gas didn't catch. He had tried to destroy the boat and crew so there would be no witnesses to the murders. The radioman on board, though injured, crawled into the radio room and sent out a 'Mayday' asking for help from all other law enforcement agencies.

"While the radioman was doing this, Jody Hollingsworth secured a gun and shot Alderman. He wounded him in such a manner that he was temporarily down. Three other men with Alderman were still aboard the smaller boat and had taken no part in this violence. They now raised their hands in surrender. By this time, many small, fast boats arrived on the scene–just a few miles east of Fort Lauderdale. They boarded the smuggler and handcuffed the three men. In the meantime, Alderman had been captured on the deck of the cutter.

"Placing all the smugglers in restraint on their vessel, the Coast Guard proceeded at full speed to their base in Fort Lauderdale, where they were met by ambulances that were summoned by one of the vessels that came to their assistance. Alderman was taken to the hospital along with the seamen he had injured. During his stay there, he was under heavy guard at all times. When he had recovered sufficiently, he was placed in maximum security in the Dade County Jail in Miami.

"A minister visited Alderman, who got religion like so many other hardened criminals about to pay the penalty for their crimes. He seemed to think that society should forgive him all the acts of violence before he got religion. He claimed that he was beyond the U.S. limits, and the government had no right to stop him.

"He was put on trial in federal court in Miami and found guilty of murder on two counts and sentenced to be hanged. The place chosen was on the inside of the seaplane hanger at the base near the old New River inlet, which no longer exists. The time was to be at eleven o'clock on a certain set date.

"At the trial, his three companions who had taken no part in the violence were given the regular prison sentences set for smugglers.

"When the day of the hanging arrived, Alderman was brought to Fort Lauderdale in the center of a well-armed convoy. When they entered the Coast Guard base, all members of the convoy entered with him and all gates were locked. Newspapermen were kept outside the gates but after the hanging, they were notified that Alderman was dead.

"Some of the Coast Guardsmen were so seriously injured that they were retired and received permanent pensions. A few of them are still alive today.

"Alderman's boat was added to a pile of some three hundred others on a sand spit between the Coast Guard base and Las Olas Sound.

"In those days, the law said that any equipment seized had to be safely stored and later sold to the highest bidder at auction. This put the Coast Guard at a big disadvantage because it allowed the syndicate to use supposedly innocent third parties to re-purchase their equipment. With minor repairs, the boats were soon out at sea again. This gave the Coast Guard and other law enforcement agencies a king-sized headache. They tried unsuccessfully to fight this completely crazy law. There had been rumors that the law would be changed and allow the Coast Guard to destroy the captured equipment. Unfortunately, this change in the law hadn't taken place at this time. Most of the smugglers' boats were more high-powered than the government boats. Unofficially, some of the best smugglers' boats were 'lost at sea' while being towed from one base to another. Later on, this same equipment, completely overhauled, disguised by changes in the superstructure, and bearing Coast Guard numbers—of a small size–were used to run down and capture many of the smugglers.

"During this particular period, the Coast Guard had no more room on the small sandbar they were using to store the captured boats and took a bulldozer to push them closer together. It was more than possible that Alderman's boat had been captured and resold. That possibly caused the destruction of all the boats on the sand spit at that time.

"The true story has never been revealed, but someone in command left a directive rather than an official order. At any rate, the personnel at the base treated the citizens of Fort Lauderdale with a tremendous Fourth of July spectacle when these boats were burned. They chopped holes in the gas tanks to avoid explosions, ran a gasoline trail over and through the boats and set them afire. There was no official notice–that was an impossibility under the circumstances. Everyone seemed to know that it was going to take place at low tide. Standing room was at a premium along Las Olas Sound. Opposite this place, many of us stood on our car tops to see the spectacle.

"After that, the once small sandbar was considerably built up by successive layers of smugglers' boats with their motors, set afire, every time the Coast Guard lacked room for more. This is the foundation for the solid land that is now known as the Bahia Mar yacht basin in Fort Lauderdale.

"With the death of Alderman and the destruction of most of the equipment of the syndicate, their operations dropped off sharply. This left the sportsman type, like those who operated on the Keys. The few who ran their tiny (by comparison) boats from Fort Lauderdale and who continued to bring in their small loads of fancy liquors. Entirely different from the northern gangster type of rum runner, this type of operator depended on skill to outwit rather than fight the government agencies. They very seldom carried guns and would surrender immediately on call. They were aware that they could be released on bond in a matter of a few hours."

Both Happy and Al had been spellbound while Russ was telling them this story. Then Happy said that he had never heard all of the details of the episode before.

Al sort of shuddered and remarked that in the places where

he had been stationed, nothing of the kind ever happened.

The coffee was *all*, now, and Happy stood up to go. He said, "Al, Erskine doesn't own a boat and both of those in that boat are colored. They're probably fishermen."

Much to our relief, Al agreed. "Could just be fishermen. Big Erskine wouldn't hang around here. Everyone knows we visit here a lot. Russ, we'll tell the Coast Guard about your path to the grove. We'll have to leave now."

We went along to their boat and watched as they turned around and headed into the bay.

"Boy! That was a close one, Charlotte! If they had investigated, Big Erskine might have thought we told on him. It's nerve-wracking, sitting on the fence!"

Russ got out the powerboat and we went to tell Erskine about our visitors. He smiled as he said, "Guess you saw how I moved my boat out some, so I could see who came up the path. I recognized the motor. They visited longer than usual, didn't they?"

"They couldn't quite decide whether it was you or not, and finally decided it was just a couple of fishermen. I told them about the Alderman case and used up all their spare time."

"I guess that means that I can be on my way over. Thanks, Mr. Russ, for all you did for me."

"Good luck, Erskine."

We decided to visit our neighbors, the Russells. Their boat was there so we knew they were home. We had tea and cakes with them. During the visit they said they were going to Miami around noon the next day. I was a bit lonesome for family and thought this was a good opportunity to visit Jan and my parents. I wanted to see if my parents were right about the key being no place for a little girl–except for a short visit. I asked Captain Russell if he had room for me, and then both Jan and me on the way back. He said there was plenty of room in the boat, and they would stop at our dock to pick me up on their way.

I had noticed a pitcher pump alongside the sink and asked about it. Mrs. Russell told me that it was convenient for pumping water from the cistern. We went out to look and I saw that the cistern was covered with a roof and had two small screened windows in it. Peering in, I saw a small log floating there. I asked about it and was told that sometimes during dry weather a raccoon would break in and, if the water was low, the log enabled the raccoon to avoid drowning.

I remarked, "How thoughtful!"

"Thoughtful, huh. If it wasn't there, he'd drown and spoil our drinking water!"

Before leaving that area, we went next door for our first visit with Gary and Shad. They had mentioned renting an empty house. It wasn't empty now! It was most impressive! They had made furniture from large-diameter bamboo found on the beach. Chairs, a table, bookcase and bed frames. On the table was an odd-looking block of stuff, and when I asked was told it was sulphur to put in the cistern to keep the water fresh. We didn't stay there long, as we had to catch our supper before we could eat it.

Towards sundown, we heard Big Erskine's motor roar and saw him going off towards the Bahamas for liquor.

I was dressed for town in Russ's sailor whites when the neighbors appeared at the dock the next day. I carried no luggage, as I had some city clothes at my parent's home. Russ walked down with me to say "hello" to the Russells. The two boys were sitting on the cabin top towards the bow. As I got aboard with the captain and his wife, she handed me an apple box chair. Standing it on end I managed to be almost comfortable.

It was a pleasant trip, and quite warm. I got rather sleepy before we reached our destination quite far up the river. We pulled in at a small wooden dock. There was quite a pile of burlap bags there when we arrived. Captain Russell casually tossed them into the cabin of his boat, saying, "We'll just borrow these." It was the first time I had ever seen anything like that, but I had enough sense not to say anything.

On shore now, Mrs. Russell said, "Come along up the street to our dry cleaners. You can get his address and write it down with his phone number. We will be back there about noon tomorrow. You leave word if you want to ride back with us." While we walked along, she explained that their town clothes were waiting for them at the dry cleaners.

"What we do is leave our key clothes there and put on the city clothes they cleaned for us the last time we were up. Tomorrow, our cleaned key clothes will be waiting for us. We change there. Makes it convenient."

She introduced us and the dry cleaner gave me his business card. I asked him to recommend a nearby barber. I was real shaggy looking now and didn't want to visit my parents in that condition. Russell refused to try to cut my hair. During the long time we had been on the key, I had made several false starts and finally managed to give him a rather acceptable haircut with ordinary scissors. Then I learned he kept his hat on whenever anyone was around. Eventually his hair grew out enough and I trimmed out the steps I had left the last time.

Going to the recommended barbershop, I saw that I had picked a very busy time. I grabbed the last waiting chair before a man behind me could get it. I was pretty sleepy from the long ride and just did manage to stay awake–not enough, though! When it finally was my turn, I got into the chair without telling the barber how I wanted my hair cut, in a boyish bob. I woke up with a real c-o-o-l feeling. Looking in the mirror, then, I saw that I had received a real summer haircut. I was just about scalped! When I fussed at the barber in my naturally low voice, he just looked surprised and said, "That's the way all the boys are wearing their hair!"

I blurted out that I was in town to visit and didn't own a *female* hat, which could be worn with that haircut. He was startled and said, "You should have told me you aren't a boy."

Then I noticed how interested and amused the other customers were in our conversation and I shut up, paid him, and got the sailor hat, and set it on my head. Now it rested on my ears! I was anxious to get out away from the snickers. Vanity was something I had left on the mainland when I went to the Keys, but this situation was a little too much. I got onto the first bus that pulled up in front of the barbershop. Naturally it was going in the wrong direction, and I had to transfer, but I had left the snickers behind.

Finally on the Greyhound bus I read a newspaper someone had left–the first in a long time on the day it was printed. From the station in Lauderdale I took a city bus to within a few blocks of my parents' home.

It was a happy reunion. Jan seemed to have missed me, but being very young, soon went outside to play with her friends. I took that opportunity to change into my feminine clothing after a marvelous shower. My haircut had distressed me. What it did to my folks was disastrous. In my whites, I looked acceptable. In a dress, it called too much attention to my head, and I looked almost indecent.

They asked how long I was staying. I told them that I was there for the night and part of the following morning. When I said I thought I would take Jan back with me, their reactions were a bit startling.

"Well-well, we'll let you borrow her but you bring her back when she gets lonesome for us!"

I sort of understood. I guess after you have raised nine children, you get lonesome for a little one around the house.

When Dad offered me the car that night to go over to Russ' parents, I found myself strangely reluctant. After moving slowly in a boat, in a wide-open space of the water, I hesitated to get into the crowded, speeding traffic.

He drove me over to Russ' parents, and as I got a few more things from storage, I gave them, as I had my parents, an account of the busy but placid life we had on the island.

"Always?"

"Well, mostly."

Of necessity then, I changed the subject. "Russ told me to get some of his long underwear. It's getting a little cooler."

After a nice breakfast the next morning, we were ready to go–almost. I unpacked all the toys and new dresses Jan had packed and replaced them with a few toys and older clothes. Dressed now in my sailor whites, I felt comfortable.

Phoning the dry cleaner in Miami, I left word that I would be there about noon. The bus trip was pleasant. Jan was so interested in everything. We made an odd-looking pair–me in my whites, half-scalped and Jan in a pretty fluffy dress. She was a beautiful child and attracted quite a bit of attention. This bounced off me, especially when she called me "Mama."

In Miami, we made the two bus transfers, and I was elated. At last I could get out of the public eye and avoid comment. We only had a few minutes wait at the dry cleaners before Captain Russell and his family arrived.

I had bought some fresh fruit and cookies for lunch, and Jan shared it with the boys as all three sat on the cabin roof.

Her interest in the boat trip and her comments made it enjoyable for everyone. She babbled happily most of the way to the island.

When we arrived at our dock, Russ was waiting and invited Captain Russell and his family ashore for an early supper. It was ready. In this way, he thanked them.

Supper was interesting. He is an excellent cook, and his Spanish omelet was wonderful, something new to the Russell family. There was just one bit left. Someone had been polite. Not me!

The conversation during and after supper was way out. These Conchs told a story about the days of their parents when the wreckers had reigned supreme. There was a period of over two years when everyone wore silk, from the skin out. They had *lightered* bolts of fabulous silk, plain colors and some with beautiful patterns.

"How did he get it? (Of course, I was the one who asked that stupid question.)

"Lightered it," she said. "From a vessel on the reef. When one got stranded there we had to take stuff off, making it lighter, so it could float off. You saw our china–that's very expensive stuff. Captain, my husband, lightered a very large set from a sailing vessel some time back."

To top that story, they told us that the piano in their home had also been lightered–by her uncle. None of them could play it, but, "Isn't it a real elegant possession?" It seemed that the first one on a grounded vessel got first choice.

Just before leaving, they told us about a happening during the captain's childhood. They were all in church after a stormy weekend. A stiff breeze was blowing in through the church door, which faced the ocean. The minister stepped into the pulpit, folded his hands devoutly, stood a minute looking out towards the ocean and said, "Today's message is 'The Lord helps those who help themselves.'" He ran down the aisle towards his boat. He had seen a vessel with torn sail drifting onto the reef, and he was the first man aboard.

The Russells left before dark as they didn't like to travel on the water after sundown. They were firm believers in Uncle Billy

Brook's theory. He was their sometimes minister. He taught that God had given the Devil control of the sea, "All the waters of the Earth."

Jan was pretty small to be left alone downstairs, so we made a bed for her next to ours, two pillows.

After breakfast, we asked her what she wanted to do. When she said, "fish," we took the five-gallon bucket and went to the dock. She kept us both busy baiting the hook and unhooking fish. She caught two for every one we got. It didn't take long to fill the bucket and add several extra large fish for dinner.

We did some beachcombing that afternoon and had a very pleasant day.

When the ducks' fish was done, Russ poured off the salt water and put the fish into their trough. They stood around and made dry passes over it until it cooled. It was really funny. It didn't seem long before they were finished and the trough was full of fish bones and scales.

We had an enjoyable week before Jan got bored and said, "I want to go home and see Gramma and Grandpop."

During supper that night, Russ promised to take her the next day and told me that he considered it a good time to install the motor in our boat. This, according to him, would take at least two full days and part of the third, if not all of it. He planned to return the evening of the third day, regardless of the time.

Because of the ducks, I would have to stay. We had quite a number of ducks now, in spite of eating most of their eggs. We found all the nests they tried to hide out. We weren't so worried about Bill now, but I continued to wear my sheath knife. I didn't really mind being left alone, but I intended to be very cautious.

Around five the next morning, breakfast by lantern light, Jan was very excited about the boat trip and our good-byes were painless. She waved at me for a few minutes and then got interested in something she saw in the water.

I went back to the house to do the dishes, just in time to foil the ever-ready ants. While doing the dishes, I planned how to occupy my time during Russ' absence.

CHAPTER TWELVE

Alone for Three Days! Trouble Comes in Threes.
Fall through the Sand. U–Dump–It. Aliens.

I thought I would spend the day quietly reading, hadn't done too much of that lately. Tomorrow I would take the skiff over and beachcomb on Sands Key. Neither Russ nor I had gone there, perhaps because of the episode of the buzzards. Bob had left the day before, and we didn't expect him back for a time. Even thinking of the half-interest he had been offered in the brass canon, I wasn't tempted to go into the jungle after it. Russ was too far away. Something might happen.

Before I started to read, I decided to try the trap and artificial bait that Chester had gifted us with. At the dock I followed the instructions, then lowered the trap into the water, and lay down on the dock. Some of the larger snappers went near it but didn't stay. Soon many pretty little fish swam around it, and one, a blue angel with yellow fin, found the entrance. One bite was all it got, as the bait had almost dissolved. As it tried to get out and join the beau gregories and sergeant majors and other little pretties, I felt ashamed of myself. I pulled the trap up enough to open the door and ease the little thing into the water. I never used the trap again.

After reading most of the day, I had snacks for supper and went to bed early.

I had a lonely breakfast the next day, and rowed the skiff to Sands Key. The tide was slack and it was easy. Tying it to a red mangrove, I got to the tree and so to land. I hadn't gone more than ten feet when I saw a raccoon. It suddenly appeared from the jungle growth at my left and walked straight towards the high-tide line. Following this raccoon was one a bit smaller and three little ones.

Now a statement Russ had made proved out. "Clothes freshly washed in salt water have no human odor. If necessary, you can go quite close to a wild animal."

The raccoons passed me with scarcely a glance and I stood still for a time, watching as they turned over the seaweed in their search for edible goodies. I saw them get sargasso fish with their arm-like fins and other things that ride on seaweed and live in it.

Now to go on with my kind of beachcombing, I moved slowly past them and walked along the bushes on the shoreline among the higher hurricane-tide debris. Soon I found a nice thin mahogany board. Standing it up against the bushes so I could see it on my return, I went on. There was the usual debris. Coconuts, sprouted and otherwise, a broken demijohn against a rock, and a great many boards. Some boards were creosoted and could be used for our dock.

I suddenly lost my balance, and my foot fell through. My right leg was out of sight to the knee. As I fell, I threw myself towards higher land, sideways. This had put a strain on my leg. It was badly scratched—my leg looked like it ended at the knee, and I saw the dry sand pouring into the space around it. From the slope of the sand, I thought it was at least two inches deep on top of the broken board. I lay quite still for a time thinking of my predicament. There were shooting pains in my knee now. I didn't want to move in spite of that and was feeling very sorry for myself. Would I have to stay here until Russ got back?

Enough of these thoughts. I eased over into a normal position in relation to my knee and moved it easily. Nothing was broken, but it hurt. Waiting for the pain to ease off a bit, I tried to picture what had trapped me. Naturally, I had read of all the ships that had been wrecked in the area, known as the Spanish Main. I thought it more than possible that a ship had been wrecked so long ago that it had been incorporated into the island. Some of the red mangroves, the island builders, were upshore from me as well as all along the water's edge. Those upshore had firm craggy bark, showing age.

Now I swung my leg again. Nothing under it nor around it.

I raised up and watched more sand trickling down the hole. Afraid now to put too much weight on one spot, I lay there and finally, in spite of the pain, managed to wiggle my leg out. I was very pleased to be on shore again.

My curiosity got the best of me. Slowly sliding around and forward, I watched as more sand fell through. The sun was overhead now–I had been there a lot longer than I realized. It was just possible to see the bottom of the hole. The spot of sunlight looked to be between six and eight feet away. It was hard to judge. Later I wished I had marked the spot. Hindsight is always better than foresight.

I went towards the bushes up-shore and crawled between them before I tried to stand up. I finally managed that by pulling on the bushes. Enough beachcombing for one day! I was only hurt and scratched up a bit. I would be able to go home and sleep safely in bed. Sleep? I didn't know just how little I was to get that night!

I limped towards where I had put the boat and picked up my little mahogany board. I traversed every foot with care! That ship's deck could be large. My lips were well bitten by the time I got back to the boat. Rowing against the tide, I finally made it to our dock. Walking the plank to the shoreline was again difficult.

Remembering what Russ had said about the healing qualities of salt water, I limped around front and went towards the house. I had decided to stay in the house until Russ got home the next day. That way I wouldn't get into any more trouble.

Circumstances changed that some. Russ had always serviced our bathroom facility, and in preparing for the trip, had forgotten it. My turn to do it! Thinking over how he managed, I propped open the outside door and carried out the bucket. While my leg wasn't really injured, I found it quite painful and I studied the situation so as to avoid any traps.

The wind wasn't too bad and the waves were small. A bit of deep breathing away from the thing and I was ready to carry it to the water. The tide was going out now, fortunately. I decided that I would roll up my pants' legs and walk some ten feet into the water to compensate for my lack of strength. Arriving there, I tried to remember how Russ had done it, and threw it–right into an oncoming wave, a big one. I threw the bucket towards shore, as well as my cigarettes and lighter, still dry in my shirt pocket. I went swimming after limping off shore into deeper water. I swam for at least a half hour during which time I gave my hair several soapless shampoos. I felt clean again and went to shore. I found my cigarettes and lighter near the water's edge.

Home again, I stripped, hung my clothes on the line to dry, and put on dry things. It wasn't my lucky day. I was brooding a bit now about what the third event might be. I was really getting very superstitious now and decided to beat the jinx by quietly reading.

Time went surprisingly fast after that. Towards dark, I got my supper and lit the Coleman so I could continue to read. It was about ten o'clock when I checked the hook-locks on the doors, turned off the Coleman, and climbed the ladder to the bedroom. Part way up now, I returned and got the lead beater. Closing the trap door on my return, I pulled the spring with the mattress on it onto the trap door so that anyone trying to move it would awaken me. Then with the flashlight I checked the clip in the .22. Seeing that it was full of bullets, I put the gun on Russ' side of the bed with the lead beater, a box of bullets, and my belt with its ever-present sheath knife. Now I was prepared! I couldn't make up my mind to undress as usual, so I merely removed my tennis shoes and dungarees and shirt.

My knee hurt, but it must have eased off because I went to sleep.

I suddenly awoke and then heard the sound of low or distant voices. No words were distinguishable. I sat up and quietly put on my shirt, pants, tennis shoes and belt, and prepared to go off the roof into the bushes if necessary. I took the gun with me as I moved the few feet forward to look out the front window. Before going to bed I had thought I was emotionally exhausted. Now my mind was going ninety miles an hour. Was it someone running dope? Or aliens? Rum runners? Should I shoot, or–

Both of the house doors faced the path, which angled towards what we call the front door, the one into the kitchen. Anyone arriving there would be under the edge of the roof. Then it would be too late to shoot.

The voices were louder now, but I still couldn't see much. It sounded sort of singsong and garbled as a foreign language does to most of us Americans. When I then leaned away from the window, I was sort of surprised. I had felt frozen. My leg gave me fits as I crawled over, unbuttoned the little window on the jungle side of the house and set it to one side on the floor. Now I was ready to slide off the roof and drop the eight feet to the ground and go into the bushes if I had to. I wouldn't leave unless someone tried to get inside. If that started to happen, I intended to shoot a few times through the screen and the thin wooden floor to slow them up while I was making my getaway.

I sneaked back to the front window and saw some people walking towards the house. Putting the muzzle to the gun against the screen, I froze again. I put some spare bullets in my pocket then and sat quietly listening to the thunder of my heartbeat in my eardrums.

While it seemed to take forever, eventually all the people had passed quietly by the house without making any attempt to enter. They went down the path to the dock. As the last one passed the front window, I slid towards the side window and watched. Minutes seemed elastic about then. It seemed hours before I heard the roar of a loud motor in the cut. It came from the bayside. The talking got louder and I thought I heard an American-sounding voice telling them to hurry. The motor off now, I heard voices and the clanking sound of metal. It was quite some time later before the motor started and I heard the boat return in the direction from which it had come.

I sat and quivered in the silence now. I realized that it had been a group of aliens shepherded by Americans. [Asians were smuggled by way of Cuba, which had no immigration quotas—ed.] I remembered a recent conversation with the Border Patrol during which they had told us of having captured some smugglers with aliens aboard their boat. This had been only a few weeks before.

"All the alien smugglers had rebuilt boats of wide beam. Under the wide overhang of the sides, there were small doors. One of us opened the doors and the other stood guard over the smugglers. Each locker, for that's what they were, held one alien. The aliens had first been placed in canvas bags, and, at the bottom of each bag, there was a smaller bag filled with scrap metal. The drawstrings were pulled rather tight against the aliens' necks, and tied."

When I asked them about the bag of scrap metal, Happy told me that in the past they had pursued large boats, and when they got close to them, they saw large objects thrown into the water. The men handling these bulky objects moved quickly. There was nothing to be seen when the Border Patrol reached the place the objects were dumped. Whatever it was had apparently sunk immediately. When the Border Patrol reached the boat and searched, nothing illegal was aboard. Rope for crawfish traps and a few old engine parts were lying on deck. The men on board claimed to be fishermen and said the metal was used as ballast for crawfish traps. Boats of this type were used in the crawfish business, but these had no bait aboard or anything else to be used for crawfishing. Still, nothing could be proved. The evidence had been destroyed. Thinking of this didn't help my nerves, and I knew I wouldn't be able to sleep any more that night.

I decided to go down and make coffee. Pulling the spring back off the trap door enough so I could get it open, I went down the ladder with the flashlight in my pocket. The butt of the gun on the toes of my right foot made it a bit tricky. I was fully prepared for any excitement and I left the trap door open for a quick retreat.

Putting both gun and flashlight on the table, I felt my way to the kitchen and lit the stove. The kitchen shutter was down and I didn't think the light would be seen outside. I stood there until the coffee was done and turned off the fire.

At the table now, I sat and sipped my coffee and listened for any unusual noise. Before I realized it, I had finished the last in the six-cup pot. The sky was getting lighter and I hoped daylight would come soon. I would be safer then—a matter of degree, but important.

It was just daylight when I heard another powerful motor. In spite of the stiffness of my knee, I swarmed up the ladder with the gun. Try it sometime. You need three hands. I scrambled across the bed to look down the path. What a lovely sight—Border Patrol uniforms. I was never so glad to see anyone in my life. Resting the gun on my toe again, I started down the ladder. I hadn't gotten over the thought that I might need it. I did have second thoughts about meeting them with it and left it standing near the foot of the ladder.

I quickly started another pot of coffee and went to meet them. After I greeted them, I told of the night's happenings. That carried us through the first cup of coffee and they refused seconds, saying that it was more than possible they would find the boat in the Miami River and they didn't dare waste time.

I wanted to sit and talk now that I felt safe, but they told me that alien smugglers never put aliens ashore on an island in daylight, so I would be safe. Russ would be home that night, alien smugglers might not come, but now I was worried about Bill. I couldn't talk about that now; they were on the way out.

They walked quickly, I had to run to catch up. At the dock they skipped the usual short period of warming the motor and went swiftly out the cut on their way to Miami.

A few days later when they returned to the island, they told us that because I had told them of my experience, they had been fast enough to get to Miami and capture eighteen aliens. Seventeen men and one woman. By that time the boat had been disguised as a crawfish boat. Many traps and other gear were aboard. It was impossible for them to discharge their passengers in the daylight, and they were caught while waiting for dark.

I got a great deal of pleasure out of hearing them tell Russ that I had saved my life by acting intelligently.

CHAPTER THIRTEEN

Brother Julien Visits. Gives Us Fiddler. Find Rare Book.

Arriving in Fort Lauderdale, Russ had taken Jan right to my parents' home. There he told them about returning the rental boat and his plans for fixing our boat. Dad took him to John's dock so he could get to work. He intended to work as long as he could, so not much visiting got done then. He worked industriously and when he launched the boat on the third morning, was pleased to see that all the fittings were tight. His parents had driven him there that morning, and while they said they were as pleased with the boat, they still didn't approve of our island living.

Just before Russ left, he called to say good-bye to my parents and Jan. Dode (my brother Julien) answered the phone and said that he would like to spend some time on the Keys with us. Arrangements were made that he would ride his motorcycle to Miami and they would meet at Mr. Everett's dock. He had to arrange for someone to take over his very large paper route while he was gone.

When Russ got to Miami and parked the boat so he could do his shopping, he visited Flip and Bertha for a short time, then with a cab, got his groceries and ice. Returning, he found Dode waiting for him. He made arrangements for Mr. Everett to store the motorcycle; then Dode removed his saddlebags from it and took them aboard the boat.

After helping Russ with our supplies, he picked up the saddlebags, and jiggled them a bit as he did so. He heard a little whimpering sound. With a disturbed expression, Dode opened one of the bags. In it was a little four-pound black and white puppy with a very large bandage on one foot. He told Russ that while making a delivery at a dog kennel in Hollywood, he arrived just in time to keep the owner from shooting the puppy, they said, "to put it out of its misery."

This man at the kennel raised both German pointers and fox terriers. One fox terrier bitch was a house dog, who was fiercely jealous of all other dogs. That morning, as he opened one of the kennels, she darted past him and had almost ruined the pup before he could catch her. The owner was a veterinarian. He said the leg was so mangled it could not be repaired.

Dode told how he had pleaded with the owner not to shoot the pup, saying that he could get it a wonderful home. The man didn't listen to him until he took off his shirt and asked the man to wrap the puppy in it. Then the pup's owner changed his mind and said, "Take it." Dode ripped off the sleeves and wrapped them around the leg. Making a sort of nest of the rest of the shirt, he eased the pup into the saddlebag. Without being asked, then, the owner said the dog had an excellent pedigree, but he wouldn't give anyone the papers without the $50 he had intended asking for the dog. That was a fierce price during the Depression—the pup was of superior pointer stock. (Fiddler proved it.)

Again thanking the man, Dode went to finish his route. On arriving home he had washed and bandaged the pup's leg. Russell's phone call had come just as he finished.

I had heard the strange sound of a put-put motor before they entered the cut, but I wouldn't move until I could see who it was. I was still feeling a bit timid and my leg bothered me.

Russ blew the conch horn, then, and I went down, as fast as I could. I was thrilled to see one of my favorite brothers and was pleased when he handed the little pup to me. The pup had a bewildered expression on its face from so many strange things and people. I carried it up to the house—after admiring *our own boat*.

We carried the supplies up and stowed only the ice and fresh meat before Russ prepared for attending to the dog's injuries. He put newspapers on the kitchen floor, scalded the wash basin, put Clorox in the boiled water, then going to our medicine cabinet, he got out bandages and Oil of Sol. He and Dode sat down on the floor and I handed over the pup. I watched for a few minutes as Russ started to unwrap the leg. Coming to a part where the cloth was stuck to the wound, he dribbled Clorox water on it, and I left. I didn't want to see any more!

I got a book to read, hoping it would take my mind off what they were doing. Soon (it seemed soon) Russ asked me to look into the sewing box and see if I had some white silk thread. I did have some pale yellow and returning with it, asked what he was going to do.

"First I am going to dip it in Oil of Sol, and then we are going to try to tie some of these torn ligaments together." During this time the pup occasionally whimpered and yipped, but they said he was surprisingly good.

Some time later, they announced that part of the job was done and the rest would be easy. Just wrap the leg and find a way to immobilize it, so the pup wouldn't damage the repair job. Before long, I was holding the bandaged pup as it slurped up a mixture of canned milk and water. Dode had bought the milk just before getting to the shipyard.

The pup cried when I moved and soon Russ had a padded box prepared with Dode's shirt. I put the pup in, and by then, it was time to put the supplies away. Russ did that after lighting the Coleman and Dode helped me get supper.

I had waited until they asked me to hold the pup before I started my story of my two exciting days. I wanted their full attention. I got it! In fact the only interruptions were when they asked me to slow down or talk louder. When I had finished telling them about the aliens, Dode picked up one of the papers that had been on the floor, the Miami *Daily News*, and looked at it. He checked the rest and soon found the article.

It was short–about ten lines. It told how the Border Patrol had called the city police and asked them to stand by on call with their paddy wagon, until they gave them an address to go to. When the Border Patrol had located the suspected boat, they phoned in the address. The police arrived soon afterwards and they closed in. While the police stood guard over the smugglers, the patrolmen pulled the Chinese from the side lockers of the boat. Then the smugglers were locked in the wagon with a policeman on guard and the other policemen helped the patrolmen unbag the Chinese. It required two patrol wagons to transport the entire group. (I'm sorry I lost that newspaper item.)

When I sat down then, Russ said, "Things do surely happen to you when I'm not around." He chuckled then and I knew it wasn't about the aliens, but the previous day's happenings.

We visited during supper and after making Dode promise not to tell the folks, Russ told him about Bill and a few other things.

The pup's box was put by Dode's bed and we went to sleep.

After a pancake breakfast, the boys dressed the pup's wound. Russ said that the foot was turned around backwards because of the time between when the ligaments were torn and repaired, and he hoped to cure that condition after the wounds had healed more and he could massage the leg. After they fastened the leg with bandages to the pup's body, they took him to the sand beach in front of the house. He learned to manage all right on three legs, but he sort of hop-darted instead of running. Because of this resemblance to the fiddler crab, we named him Fiddler. He was soon tired out so we put him to bed and went beachcombing.

We found nothing of special interest except for a very thick, water-soaked book without a hard cover or a title page. No use trying to look it over in that condition, so Russ carried it to the house and set it on a slant to allow the water to run off.

Fishing for duck food was next on the schedule and we soon had a bucket cooking over a slow fire. Then with the crawfish grabber, the boys went to get our supper. They got quite a few and the surplus were put in the crawfish car.

I checked the condition of the book, found it to be drying nicely and put it on the slanting shutter outside the kitchen. I turned a few partially dried pages and went in to get the rest of the supper ready. I fed the pup and sat down to read.

The boys returned and cooked the crawfish. Then, taking the pup into the sunlight outside, they checked the leg. The little fellow seemed to understand they were trying to help him. He whimpered, but he didn't move. When they finished, they let him run a bit, then put him to bed before they went to look at the book.

A good many pages could be turned without tearing now.

This book was a compilation of reports of federal correction institutions, entitled, SEX LIFE IN PRISON–"issued to authorized persons only. Limited edition, 48 copies." One copy each for the then forty-eight states. It covered a period of years in penal institutions, both state and federal. The entire and sole subject was sex life in prison. It dealt in all matters pertaining to males, females, homosexuals, no matter how erotic. Some of the situations seemed almost impossible to believe. The book made it quite obvious that the prisoners of either sex would go to inconceivable limits, both physical and mechanical, to obtain contact with the opposite sex or their own kind. It was a book that many medical doctors would have found difficult to believe. The report had no illustrations, but some of the subterfuges and devices were described in such minute detail they left nothing to the imagination. There were over five hundred pages of it. It was intended solely for the guidance of prison wardens. How a copy of this very limited edition could have been thrown into the ocean will always remain a mystery. Because of the very unorthodox information contained in it, we later destroyed it by burning. Several years later we were severely criticized and told that it had been a very valuable collectors' item, even in its damaged condition.

I finally got the boys to come in before supper got too cold. They brought the book in with them and put it on the back porch for safekeeping. Bedtime was early as they planned to leave for Miami around two in the morning.

We had breakfast by lantern light, and they were on their way. I went back to bed to finish my sleep, and the whimpering pup woke me up. I fed him and went to do the dishes. By then, it was too late to do them easily. The darn bugs had found them. I put the buggy dishes in the dishpan and submerged the pan in the water out front. Standing back so the many swimming ants and roaches couldn't get on me, I watched as many tiny fish appeared and made an end of them. I gave the dishes a saltwater wash then and took them inside.

Russ returned before noon, and, telling of a visit with Flip and Bertha, quoted Flip, "No one heard nothin' about Bill. He's still gone."

Russ had brought along a ham and more ice. Now we were

rich as far as ice was concerned. Seems as though ice water made our food taste better.

Fiddler managed to stay awake longer each day. He spent more time on the beach, actively playing with everything from a baby raccoon to a grasshopper. His wounds were healing, but his foot was still turned around backwards. Russ massaged it several times a day and stretched the muscles in the direction he wanted the foot to go.

CHAPTER FOURTEEN

Leon is Murdered. Make Sculling Oar. It Tosses Me.
Little Augie Brags about Hi-jacking Leon
and Throwing Him Overboard.

We planned on spending several hours in the big grove, so we put Fiddler in his box with a partial lid and took him along.

About an hour after we arrived, we heard a motor. The boat seemed to be heading for the grove. Taking his machete with him, Russ ran to the grove entrance, saying, "He's going too fast. Almost out of control." I followed and was in time to see Flip switch off his motor close to the rocky shore. The boat bounced back off the rock. Quite a piece was taken out when it hit. He had made no effort to make a good landing and the scar on the bow was the only one on the boat. When the boat stopped, he threw out the anchor and got into the water, waist deep, and came ashore.

He was unashamedly crying, and drunk. Not too drunk, though, to tell us why he was so unhappy. Once on shore he cried out his story. A body had been found in Biscayne Bay that morning and had been identified as his friend, Leon. Flip told us that Leon couldn't swim but had always worn a life jacket while on a boat. The body had been found without one.

Flip said, "I know some son-of-a-beech done pushed him over the side and hijacked his load." He was right! We heard about it later!

When the Border Patrol found the boat some time later, they termed it hijacking and murder. The large gas tanks in the boat were almost empty, denoting a long run. Aboard the boat was one life jacket. The straps had been cut. There were also some straw jackets from the liquor bottles that had been aboard.

It was difficult reaching him, but we talked to Flip for quite a while. Russ finally got him into our boat and then kept him quietly in one spot by giving him the puppy to hold. Russ explained why it was bandaged and Flip seemed interested. At least it took his mind off his friend for a few minutes at a time. We took his boat in tow and went back to the dock. He had a spare bottle of liquor in the boat and although he nibbled at it from time to time, it didn't seem to add to his condition. Russ saw to it that he ate a good supper and gave him the job of hand-feeding the pup. He did manage to get Flip to spend the night with us.

During breakfast, Flip didn't talk. Afterwards he said, "Those coconut chocolate pancakes were the best thing I tasted in a long time. Thanks, and good-bye now. I got to get back and start lookin' for the bastard that done that to Leon."

Some of the things he said were hard to understand because of his speech impediment, but boiled down, he said he was going to use all of his time from then on to find someone who knew something. He had no doubts about getting the information. It might take a while, "but when I find heem, I will knife-keel heem, real slow-like. It won't be a quick way, like drownin'." With a "be seein' ya," he waved and gunned his boat towards Miami.

We didn't discuss any of this that day. I was doing dishes when Russ came in from the back porch with some pieces of string, saying, "I'm going to make a sculling oar so we can conserve our gasoline. While our boat weighs close to a ton, it is designed so it can be sculled easily. I'll bet I can scull it, with the proper oar, almost as fast as it goes with the motor!"

He handed me one of the loops of string, put the other in his pocket and said, "Let's go." As we walked down the beach, he explained. I spotted a board and measured it.

"I want fresh pine, pitch pine, at least two by six," he said.

I told him I thought there was one on Sands and we went to look. On the way I suggested we see what was under the board I had stepped through. The only definite thing that I remembered was the narrow band of sand below the bushes. Traces of my passing had been blown from the sand by the high wind. We even checked the bushes looking for broken twigs. We finally gave up, and I have always thought we quit too soon.

We looked, each in a different direction, and Russ soon called that he had found the right board. I helped carry it to the boat. Arriving at the dock, we put it lengthwise. He handed me a folding rule from his pocket and told me to measure up four feet from one end and mark the line across the width. I was to divide the rest of the board lengthwise into three equal pieces. He went to the house for the saw and some kerosene.

No pencil available, but I looked on shore and soon found a piece of broken glass to mark with. I was almost through with this chore when he returned. He made some minute changes and said, "Good." Pulling the board forward a bit, he started his cuts. I anchored the board by sitting down. Sawing about a foot, he decided to change the position of the board so as to use the wide spaces between the boards on the dock. With the end towards shore resting on a box on the gangplank, he sawed some more as I anchored it. Using the kerosene to lubricate the saw helped keep the pitch off it. It wasn't too sharp and I was told to add a saw-file to our want list the next time up to the house. The next thing was to cut one of these 2 by 2 pieces into four-foot lengths. Goody, he was finally going to trust me with the saw.

While I was doing this, he went to get his hand drill and some twenty penny nails that had been in the house when we arrived. Returning, he placed the two pieces next to each other and made marks for the holes he wanted to drill. When I asked what they were for, he patiently explained that it would take a wide blade to scull the heavy boat and he was adding these to the six-inch width left unsawed.

Of course, I jiggled them while he was drilling and broke two of his special drills. He exploded then, "I've only got one drill left! For God's sake, don't jiggle again or we'll have to go to Miami for more. If I try to nail without drilling, the wood will split and we'll have to start all over again."

I held my breath while he drilled the rest of the holes.

Now, I held the piece that would be the oar on edge, against

131

an upright, and he nailed the little pieces on. These were set with a nail punch.

Anticipating my question, he answered it, "Because if I don't I'll hit them when I taper the edges." Now it was just a squareish oar.

We had sort of eliminated lunch now; it cut into our days. If we had an early supper we didn't miss it. It was early evening now so I went up to make supper.

We ate and I went to bed leaving him with his usual task of massaging Fiddler's leg.

In his usual fashion, Russ had studied out the answer to the next problem. Taking a piece of an oar found on the beach that morning, he sawed a six-inch slot in it lengthwise. Inserting his large sheath knife with the thick side against the unsawed part, he now had a drawknife, a very good substitute for a plane.

Again I anchored the oar while he worked on it. The next step was to round the handle and then taper the blade. I wasn't allowed to use the drawknife, but I was a handy vise to hold things. When he reached the more nit-picking part of smoothing small places, he told me to get thick pieces of glass. They could be used for the ragged parts. I went back of the house and got bottom pieces of the lovely demijohn I had broken with my brand new machete.

I found that by holding the glass at an angle I could scrape the splintered areas quite smooth. After getting nicked up, I got a rag to hold the glass. Now, anchoring the board so Russ could work, and sitting with my legs outstretched so I could work, I was discovering muscles I didn't know were there. When the pain made me careless, I quit for the day and went up to bandage my finger.

It was another day that I was too tired to read after dishes were done.

Off to the beach store in the morning for pieces of pumice stone for sanding. It comes in all sizes, including the ten-pound piece Flip was so proud of.

We had done a good job! *We?* It took three days, but we had a fine sculling oar. The rest of the day went into making a sculling lock, which Russ fastened to the transom of the powerboat with large nails.

We tried it out the next morning. I do mean we! To make the oar work more freely in the lock, Russ added a handful of our spar grease. A 16-foot boat and about a sixteen-foot oar. A big tail to wag the dog. It looked so easy when Russ moved his arm in that laying down figure-eight motion. We went speeding along. I watched for a while and saw the slight twist he gave his wrist to turn the blade. I decided it was easy.

"Let me try."

"Stand close to me, and put your hand on the handle so you can take over in the middle of a stroke." Moving it back and forth several times, I had the rhythm. Russ released his grip without notice. I tried to take control of the oar and was flipped out of the boat.

As I came to the surface, I could hear him laughing gleefully. I gave him an accusing glance before swimming after the oar, and he laughed harder than ever. I captured the oar and towed it back. He was still laughing as he took the oar and then helped me aboard. I sputtered a bit and finally forgave him. I must have looked quite silly flying out of the boat like that. He just wouldn't admit that he knew what would happen when he released the oar, but I knew better. He couldn't help grinning.

Back at the dock he got some crawfish for supper. He was going to bring them to the house when he heard a motor, so he put them in the car and went into the bushes.

It was Little Augie and he was alone, so Russ went to the dock. Trading on his being a friend of Flip's, he said, "I'm going to spend the night. I brought some ice and steaks." After cooking them, we shared one and Little Augie ate the other. He ate in a chair, but resumed his usual squatting position against the bedroom partition, facing Russ. I had to turn a bit to face him.

This previously silent man began to talk in a southern drawl. He told us that he had made a real good deal. He was all gassed up and on his way down-bay to go over to the Bahamas. He saw a boat without lights coming towards him in the dark. He steered real close to it and talked to the man in the boat. While he was telling this, he hesitated a few times and switched a word or two around. We got the impression that he was friendly with the man he was telling us about.

He said the man bragged about the load he had and said he would soon be living high and free. "I let my boat drift right up close to him and when I was right up to him, I jumped on his boat with my anchor in my hand. I grabbed him, knifed off his life jacket, and pushed him overboard. Seems like he couldn't swim. It was too late to matter when I noticed that though.

"He sure had a real good load, just like he said. I got purely pooped, just changing it from his boat to mine. On my way back to Miami I went slow-like. You know how the Mon is always watching."

I remember sort of freezing as I sat there listening. I wanted to shudder and then I was glad I couldn't. I realized then just what type of person we were listening to. A murderer! He had drowned Leon, and was bragging about it. I suddenly remembered he and Flip squatting there side by side while Flip told us about how he, Leon, and Little Augie had had to pool their money to start in business.

I made an effort to retain the interested expression that I knew had been on my face. I realized that Little Augie, who had admitted to cold-bloodedly killing his friend, would do the same to us if he thought we considered his story more than a brag.

Russ had more control than I. Quite casually he asked Little Augie about the trip back to Miami and how he had gotten rid of the liquor.

"When I got in the shipyard, I called my receiver and told him how much I had and wanted cash when he came to pick up. Told him to hurry. When he got there and counted the load, he paid me. I took off. Wasn't taking any more chances. Got the money banked now. I'm safe!"

When Little Augie turned to me, then, and said, "What do you think?" I had had plenty of time to gain control and gave an imitation of a yawn, then said, "It was very interesting, but I'm so sleepy." I said, "Goodnight," and climbed the ladder.

I heard Russ ask about Bill, and Little Augie said that he hadn't seen him for a while. Then Russ made up a bed for him, turned out the lantern, and came upstairs. Once up there, he closed the hatch and did some unnecessary walking about. In the process of doing so, he put a box on the edge of the trap door, softly, and the gun next to the bed. No talking that night. The floors were too thin. In spite of the fact that I knew I wouldn't sleep, I finally did.

Breakfast was a bit difficult. What could we talk about to a man who had bragged about murder? Fiddler soon caused a bit of welcome distraction. A large raccoon walked out of the bushes and little Fiddler yipped and darted towards him on three legs. The raccoon stopped, acted surprised, and growled, and then left. Fiddler was so proud of himself. He followed it to the edge of the cut weeds. He didn't want that thing trespassing.

Knowing how tense I was, Russ used this chance to get Little Augie outside. Russ patted the pup and told him how brave he was, tackling something so much bigger than he. There was a really tremendous difference in the size of the two animals.

Russ then said that he had to work in the little grove. I was happy to see Little Augie follow him. Before long his boat left and I started to relax again.

On his return, Russ said that Little Augie just had to talk to someone about it and felt safe in talking to us. We had already established a reputation of keeping our mouths shut. In one way, it wasn't hard to keep quiet about our knowledge. We knew Flip meant to kill the man responsible for his friend's death. We weren't interested in saving Little Augie's life, just in saving Flip from the consequences of his actions if he knew.

Some time later–months–we heard that Little Augie's body had been found in Biscayne Bay with the concrete overshoes the underworld used at that time to punish their own kind. The body had been badly mutilated.

Sculling Oar.
14'-6" made from
Salvaged 2" X 6" X 16'-0 pine.

CROSS SECTION OF BLADE
ABOUT 9" AFTER FINISHED.

ADDED FROM HANDLE to MAKE WIDE BLADE
BLADE IS 5 FEET LONG.

THICKER to HAVE STRENGTH.

CUT OFF to MAKE 2" ⭕ HANDLE

finished oar is
rubbed with spar
grease found on beach

Elliott Key
1934

RN

CHAPTER FIFTEEN

Doc and Marty. Whip Ray Almost Catches Doc.
Build Make-do Fish Traps. My Fabulous Bargain
Unappreciated. Trip to Miami through Cloudburst.
Doc Corrects Story after Forty Years.
Rare Sea Worms. Learn to Scull.

We relaxed and attended to our daily chores. The crawfish season was about to start, and we needed help. Doc had told us to call on him. It was decided that Russ would go in the morning and return as soon as he could. I was to stay, take care of our animals, and make an extra large batch of conch stew for supper–also, time permitting, gather large softwood boxes.

I wasn't worried about Bill coming around as we now had an elderly colored man hired to work in the little grove. His cot was on the back porch where Big Erskine's had been. Russ had told him about Bill. Sam assured him he would be alert for any trouble. His work required a machete, and he carried it at all times.

Russ told me about the trip later.

Reaching Miami, he had phoned Doc, who said he would be there as soon as his car could make it, if he could bring his friend Marty with him. Russ said, "Fine. Meet me at Everett's dock."

After breakfast, Russ bought lots of groceries and rope for the traps, then he took a cab for the boat. He never forgot ice. He was reading the morning *Herald* when the boys arrived. When Mr. Everett said "just leave it there–no one will steal *that* car," they did.

It was cool when they started down the bay, but the sun was

bright. It didn't take much sun to turn Marty's Philadelphia pallor to pink on his first boat trip. Going down-bay, they saw that a squall was making. The boys were sitting on the middle seat with long legs stretched out by the motor. The waves got larger and Russ slowed down. Now they were in the squall. The rain and salt spray watered the boat in equal amounts. Fortunately, the motor cover was over the groceries and clothing in the bow. It was necessary now to bail. Bailing was clumsy, done by the boys from behind. They spilled as much as they threw out. They thought it was sort of hilarious for a while; then it got tedious. Now the salt spray was on the motor and everything. In moving, the boys occasionally made a perfect contact and got a shock.

Relaxing when it wasn't necessary to bail, Doc leaned on the side of the boat. Contact! He went to the bow and lay down. We ate some odd-shaped pieces of bread for a week. Bow heavy, now, meant more spray. Doc went back to the seat. It was nice that he had such a good sense of humor because sitting down, he got a shock.

Rain again! Another squall right behind the first. Now it was quite cold and dark. Electric sparks were visible when they jumped around. Like Doc said, "Fat little blue worms." Bailing again. Moving became a game. Cautious–maybe a shock, maybe none–but carelessness might cause two shocks.

Russ said, "I knew I had been on my way long enough to be at the island, so I took a chance of going aground and headed east. It wasn't long before I reached the shoreline of Elliott and I ran until I recognized a landmark. I moved away from the island a bit. I was lucky when I got to the cut–a cruise ship, fully lighted was in the Gulf Stream, and I saw the profile of the dock.

As for me, that day Gary and Shad had dropped by for coffee and cookies and presented me with some guava wine they had made. When they left, I gathered more boxes. My stew was already made. I waited and then ate some. It was quite late then. I was waiting for the sound of the conch horn. Finally, I had given up expecting Russ that night. I was preparing for bed when I heard a motor. I didn't recognize it and quickly put my shoes back on. Flashlight and gun with me, I went down the ladder calling to Sam. Then we heard unfamiliar voices.

"Don't you worry, Mrs. Russ, I'm ready, I won't let no one in here."

With the light, I saw Sam by the back door with the machete upraised. The door shook then and a voice called, "Let me in."

Sam called out, "You all stay out. I'm armed. You ain't about to get in here!"

Then a hoarse sounding voice said, "Damn it, Charlotte, let me in. It's Russ!"

Motioning Sam to stand aside, I started to unhook the door.

Sam said, "Don't you do that, Miss Charlotte. That don't sound like Mr. Russ."

I said, "I've got the gun, and I'll put the light on so we can see." Only then did Sam move a little. I opened the door, and pointing the gun with the flashlight under it, I shined the light on Russ' face. Sam was convinced and let them in.

They entered and I put the gun down. I had almost blinded the poor guy. The light after hours of darkness caused Russ to tell me to do an impossible thing with the unmentionable flashlight. Then, we thanked Sam for being such a good guard. He beamed with pleasure.

They were a bedraggled trio. Sea legs–they swayed as they walked. They had spent seven hours on the way, most of it in rain. They had been cold, and continuously shocked by sparks. In their hoarse voices, they said they were exhausted.

Russ lit the Coleman and I made coffee. The stew was warm, but to warm them a bit before they ate, I served them a healthy glass of Gary's guava wine. It was like brandy. They gulped it down–then jerked and sat up from their slumped positions when it hit bottom. "Wow!" they said, individually and collectively. Then everything was hilarious.

They detailed their experiences, interrupting each other with hoots of laughter. Doc complained in a humorous way that he had enough shocks to stand his hair on end–if it wasn't so full of salt.

"You're lucky the magneto is an old Bosch; it only delivers nine or ten thousand volts."

They ate enormous quantities of food and looked sleepier every minute. Then, Marty did fall asleep. His face dropped into his almost empty soup plate. That woke him, and the boys went to bed.

As I was putting the food away, I asked Russ if they had brought any ice.

"Yes," he said, "and we bailed that out with the rest of the water."

I put the dishes in the dishpan and took them out into the water 'til morning. I brought in a soup plate of the water for my stew pedestal.

Breakfast ready the next morning, Russ went to wake Doc and Marty and called, "Come look." They were gripping the mattress. For them, the boat was still rolling.

A leisurely breakfast over, Russ went out to the pile of boxes and knocked them apart saying, "Charlotte, you and Marty get the nails out, without bending them, and put them in a can." I showed Marty how, while Doc went to the dock with Russ. We had a can full when they came up for lunch.

We were all anxious to see the first complete trap. Russ and Doc had made the framework for several but needed other material. Dishes done, we went to the dock. We needed the drooping roots of the red mangrove trees to complete the traps. When young, the roots are spongy and quite flexible. Using them instead of laths we saved money and didn't have to travel for them. Another feature was that they required no pre-soaking. Only a minimum of ballast was needed, just a rock or two in each trap. As Russ explained this, I was thinking, good, even I with my rubber-band muscles could haul more than a few a day.

Close to the dock, Russ cut two pieces of red mangrove root, side and end, of the proper size. He handed them to Doc and we went to get some more. Not as easy as it sounds. The tree is dense and the roots are always dropped into salt water. They trap debris, and they are not easy to walk on, or through. We fell into the mud many times when we slipped off the roots. We were a mess when we got the first batch out of the miniature jungle.

Marty had stretched out on the dock and was asleep. It didn't take long to complete the trap. Then, getting a conch, we started to fish for trap bait. Doc woke Marty up so he could join in the fun. He got his first saltwater fish. A piece of wire from the radio cabinet made a nice tie for the bait, rocks for the ballast, heavy fish line tied to it–and it was ready. With the skiff, they dropped it in midstream, and returning, tied the other end to a piling.

Doc said, "Look." A big whip ray had drifted in on the ocean end. Turning around now, facing the tide, it rippled its wings and held position. After this graceful performance, we saw a little saucer-sized whip ray drifting out from under it. It moved awkwardly. Just learning how to swim! Another one, and we realized what was happening–altogether mother whip ray had fourteen of these little saucers. We had been provided with a grandstand seat to watch them enter their watery world.

Marty and Doc took the skiff out to look at the trap and gleefully announced that several large crawfish were going towards it, and they were going to watch it until there were enough for supper. Russ marked out more frames and I went to get other things ready to eat. Before long they returned with two tails for each of us. The bait had hardly been touched, so they put the trap back.

While I was cooking, the boys swam out front. They took the muddy clothes with them to rinse, and returning, hung them up.

Hungry? Well, no scraps were left for the ducks that night.

Because of the quick success of the trap, we all worked hard the next morning. Doc and I got muddier than before in an effort to gather roots faster. We quit at noon when I suggested a swim. Baths were out. The boys ran ahead to dress.

My last time in Miami I had bought some fabulous bargains, two two-piece rubber suits. They fastened, top to bottom, with snap fasteners. One dollar each! I gave Russ the bottom half of one and donned the other suit. We took our muddy clothes to the dock and rinsed them. The bushes made a handy clothesline.

We all piled into the powerboat to go around bayside and look for a nice sand bottom at least nine feet deep. In tropical waters it isn't safe to walk on the bottom. All sort of hazards, such as sea urchins and whip rays, hide under the mud. At the base of the tail, a whip ray has a barb that makes a stab-type wound. On that is a substance that affects the nerves.

Russ told us about a friend who had stepped on one. In spite of the fact that he was a powerful swimmer, he found it hard to swim–or breathe. He would have drowned if his friends hadn't pulled him out. Breathing was all he could manage, he said.

We had dropped the anchor now and the boys were in the water. I stayed aboard for the first watch again for sea critters. Then I saw a gray fluttering thing near Russ. It sort of drifted and had no definite shape. Looking at Russ, then, I saw that he and his rubber shorts had gone separate ways. It was hilarious–to us! He grabbed them and coming over to the boat tried to struggle into them. Above the laughter of Doc and Marty, we heard a small boat approaching. Russ was mumbling, "You and your fabulous bargains. Don't do me any more favors! Hell!" By then Russ had the tight fitting pants as far as his knees. He took them off and threw them into the boat. Now I had two suits of my own!

Marty was too nervous to enjoy himself and wanted out. Remembering Russ' experience, I eased over the side.

As we walked towards the house later carrying the now dry clothes, Doc said, "I'd sure like to get that varmint!"

Russ grinned, "Well, you can try. I've got a five-pronged fish spear with a 20-foot line on it. A ray has tremendous power, so it will be hard to hold."

Dressed, and down there again, we saw it cruising with just lazy wing flutters. Doc stood poised to throw. As I looked from it to him, I saw that he had wrapped the other end of the line around his wrist. I called, "Doc, if you happen to snag that thing, you'll be in trouble. Take that line off your wrist. I finished talking just as the spear entered the saddle of the creature's back, and it took off.

What happened then should have been taken with a high-speed movie camera. We had to combine our descriptions of the scene. With a violent reaction, the ray flew its wings, spraying us all, and darted forward, pulling Doc into the water. It was over six feet deep there, but he seemed to bounce right back on the dock with his legs hanging over it. While he pulled his legs onto the dock, I looked for the ray–I was just in time to see it going into the bay. Its speed was so great that the shaft tilted back at an angle and the wake was clean and sharp.

Just then Doc said, "My cigarettes," reaching into his hip pocket. "Son of a gun!" He held them out, only the one on the end was damp. "Thanks for telling me to get the rope off. I don't remember doing it, but thank God I did. What a wicked ride that would have been."

Then he pulled in the crawfish trap and there were plenty for supper. During supper we made plans for the next day. They felt sure they could complete twelve traps. I was to fish for duck food and supper, as well as for bait for the boys so they would have fish to take home.

Bedtime was early.

I caught two unusual fish that morning, a chub with its human-like teeth and a parrotfish with a bird beak, both inedible. They nibble on poisonous coral. The flesh will make you sick, sometimes even paralyze you. Barracuda eat parrotfish sometimes. The old-islanders had a method of telling whether barracuda was edible or not. They cut a slit near the backbone and inserted a silver coin in it. If the coin became discolored after a few minutes, they threw the fish out.

Now we had thirty traps complete. Two trips were necessary. When the boys stacked half of the traps in the powerboat, there was just enough room to squeeze themselves in. They went into the ocean to set the traps and I fished for supper. It was ready when they had finished.

The following days continued to be lovely and we accomplished a lot and still had time to fish and swim. Now we had forty traps and each caught at least eight legal-sized crawfish a day. Our car was filled as well as a number of apple boxes with burlap bags nailed on the top. These were tied to pilings. Now only the largest fish were put in the fish car. It was so packed, there was just a little wasted space between them.

The boys built a new crawfish car the day before they were to leave. The slats were closer together. The legs and feelers of those in the old car had been eaten off by chubs and parrotfish. While hauling traps that day, they saw a white, shining spot on the beach. Investigating it, they found the stress-torn cover of a lifeboat. This they folded and put under the bow.

They hauled the traps at daybreak that morning and put the crawfish and fish in burlap bags. Home for breakfast and changing into town clothes, we were ready. Yes, I was going along. Animals fed, I made sandwiches and filled the water bottle. We took a flashlight, in case.

The crawfish in bags, fish also, were well stowed but taking up so much room, there was barely enough room to sit on the seat. No leg room, foot room only. Russ and I on the stern helped trim ship—we were counterweight to two hundred fifty pounds of crawfish and one hundred of fish. We were very low in the water as we left the barking dog on the dock and headed for Miami.

"It will take us an extra hour, but there's no hurry," Russ said.

Seeing a squall building, about an hour on our way, Russ said, "Rainwater will kill the crawfish and make them inedible. We have to cover them. Charlotte, you weigh the least. See if you can crawl forward and get the canvas out from under the bow."

All he wanted was a tightrope act! Stepping on the things would kill a lot, but the gunwale wasn't wide. As I came up, after falling into the water a few minutes later, I said, "Well, you can't say I didn't try!"

The boat was stopped now and I went to the bow and managed to climb up and snatch the cover out. Holding one end I sort of threw it to the boys. We spread it and weighted it down with bags of fish. Back into the water again, I swam to the stern and clambered aboard.

All this time the squall was coming closer. I had never seen anything quite like it. We were in the sun and in front we had a dark, gray-green curtain hanging from the sky. "Get out the bailing cans! There's a hell of a lot of water in that! Looks like a cloudburst."

The boys reached for the cans and said, "Well, here we go again!"

Russ glanced around and said, "We are about half way—Soldier Key is back there. The wind is directly from Miami. That's a break. I'll just keep the wind in my face and we'll get there!"

I was afraid of that blackish curtain. The boys didn't say anything, but they didn't look happy. Then we went out of the sunshine. From calm to choppy seas and the rain was so thick it was hard to breathe. Now, "Better bail fast. Keep the water level below the crawfish."

144

I noticed it getting ahead of them, so I dumped out the drinking water and lowered the jug into the water. It required dumping quite often. I had to time it so as not to bump heads with Doc.

It seemed like hours before the rain slackened off and we could see the marker buoy of Government Cut just ahead of us. Then the motor started to sputter. Russ pulled the sculling oar out from under the canvas and sculled to it. We tied up. Wet and tired now, it seemed peaceful there, and we waited for a passing boat.

Much later, Roddy Burdine, in a powerful speedboat, stopped and asked if we needed help.

"Can you sell us some gas?"

"No, I don't carry spare gas, but I'll be glad to tow you in. Where do you dock?"

"Atlantic Marine. I sure would appreciate it."

Doc threw the bow line to Mr. Burdine. He tied it to his stern cleat. Then he was off and running. We all fell backwards and yelled like panthers when we saw that the speed he was making was towing the bow under. Just as Russ handed Doc his sheath knife and told him to cut the line, he heard us and slowed down. I think he had planned that surprise. He grinned and then moved slowly ahead. The rest of the trip was peaceful. Arriving there, he eased into the dock, threw his line to be caught by a man on the dock and said, "Fill it up."

Russ went over and offered to pay for the tow. Mr. Burdine refused payment of any kind, even crawfish. Then he left for his dock up-river. We gassed and then sold the crawfish at the market for a very fair price and paid Doc and Marty.

At Everett's again the boys unloaded their fish and clothing and put them on the truck bed of the car Doc called *Mehitibel*.

The following is from a tape recording I made with Doc Stocker recently [approximately forty years after the fact–ed.] when I asked him for corrections or additions to his part in our adventures:

"At the request of Charlotte, I'll made a slight correction here. The name of the automobile was *Esmerelda* and it was kind of an unusual vehicle. It was mostly Model T Ford. I found the frame and the wheels in a field. That was fairly common back in those days. The rest of the car I assembled from various odds and ends of junk through the courtesy of the people who were shipping the scrap to Japan and stockpiling it out in the open at Port Everglades. Also, there was a guy named Rooney who lived in back of me–he had a paper route. He was a junk man and he started to bring that stuff home. He started a pile in his backyard and very often this saved me a lot of travel to the Port.

"Rooney had a 1916 Franklin and two or three other jalopies. He used to deliver the papers in the Franklin. One day when he got to complaining about the amount of gas the thing used, we got to talking. The theory behind it was that if six cylinders used that much gas, three cylinders would only use half that much. We took out three cylinders and it still ran like a top. Less gas, too.

"I didn't bother about fenders, but I recall the tires were 30-inch solid tires off a concrete mixer. They originally had holes in them from side to side, but the tire was worn off so bad that each wheel looked like a gear with rubber teeth in it. When we went down the road at forty miles an hour, which was full bore for that thing, it used to pick up rocks and clamshells from the poor roads we had then and throw them straight up in the air. If you weren't going fast enough, you ran through your own barrage and got clobbered. The rear wheels had regular pneumatic tires and they were mammoth, 400 by 21, something like that. Different from the front wheels anyhow."

I said, "Doc, they used to throw tread?"

"Yeah, they did use to throw the rubber off. You got used to dodging it though. I remember one time on your brother Dode's paper route, his motorcycle was down and we decided to deliver his papers on Esmerelda. Well, one back tire wasn't so hot and over the course of serving the paper route, we had four or five blowouts. In those days, you fixed it yourself and blew it back up. We didn't have any patches, so we used the Fort Lauderdale *Daily News*. We got four and a half to five miles out of a copy. The paper wasn't so great on mileage.

"I don't know how old it was when I found the carcass in the field, but it had a surprisingly long life after that. Two or three years, wouldn't you say, Charlotte?"

"Easily that, Doc," I answered. "I remember one trip when we were going to Miami from Fort Lauderdale on the old Dixie Highway. We all had to go, that is, we girls did, and you just said, 'The next filling station.' They were few and far between in those days. The car kept running. We didn't have tire trouble, so you just wouldn't stop."

"I'm still inclined to do that. I think my wife Ginnie has got the largest kidneys in Broward County as a result of this. I hate to stop while something's going good. I hate to shut it down. Well, anyway, the car's name was Esmerelda and it was quite a vehicle."

"The back end—you didn't have a body. It was a truck body."

"Well, partially. What would normally be the afterdeck if this was a roadster. It was the engine cover off a one-ton concrete mixer, laid sideways, that's what it was. Incidentally, Dode has a picture I gave him the last time he was up to see me. He's sitting on it, out in front of the house on Ninth Avenue. It's a hazy picture, but the only one I know of.

"That pretty well covers the story of Esmerelda. It had its good points, I guess. There was at least half a ton of junk in it that the Japs didn't get to throw back at us. So I guess the whole operation was worthwhile.

"Here's a little addendum to this thing: the guy who was with me, Marty (his last name was Fehn, and he was from Philadelphia). It was my understanding that he went with Walt Disney out in Hollywood. This boy had a tremendous affinity for sketching and cartooning and he was very, very clever. I don't know whether World War II got him or not. I don't have the faintest idea, but I'll make some effort to look him up. I think I can find some of his relatives in Philly who might know where he is."

Now to continue. No one stole Esmerelda. Everett said they wouldn't. We said good-bye to Doc and Marty. We took time to buy meat and ice and were on our way home. It was an uneventful trip and the last quarter of the moon helped us find our way.

Fiddler was on the dock waiting for us, and when we went up, he ate his neglected meal. He just wouldn't eat when we left him alone.

For a change we knew it was Sunday and got up early to pull traps before the Sunday fishermen did. We returned in time to see and hear a fisherman shoot a moray. He told us, "I don't mind losing leader wire or hooks! I'm not about to have one of those dirty things in my boat. I always carry a gun for them! Say, if you want these things for bait, you can have all I catch."

"Thanks a lot, we'll try them. So far we have only used fish."

He shot two more in the next few minutes. We thanked him. Well, we would live and learn…

On our way to the house, Sam came out of the jungle with his left hand full of greenery. When asked what he had he told us that his frying grease had caught fire and he didn't want to burn down the cookhouse so he grabbed the pan and threw it on the lawn, burning his hand. The greenery, he said, was "salve bush." We later learned to call it *aloe vera*.

"Mr. Russ, please take this thing, cut off the roots and the thorny edges, and mash it up with some lard to hold it together. I need to put it on my hand."

At the house, Russ put waxed paper on the plug and used the lead beater to prepare the stuff. He put the completed mix in a wide-mouthed jar, then applied it to Sam's hand thickly, according to instructions. His hand was twice the original size now. "No bandage, Mr. Russ. It works better left in the open. This stuff–without the lard–is good for stomach trouble, too."

Thinking of his burnt breakfast, I made enough for all of us. While we ate, Sam said that if Mr. Fossey or anyone else came from Miami that day, he would "take it kindly" if we would arrange transportation for him. "Can't work with a bad hand. Besides it's close to school time. Got to buy my young'uns school supplies."

Considering his age, this came as a surprise to us. In answer to "How many?" he said, "Mr. Russ, I don't rightly know. I know now, though, I'm supportin' seven. Two by my wife, she's younger'n me, two by another woman, and three by another woman."

Wow!

I went outside then and Russ helped Sam dress and pack. He paid him so he would be ready if someone came. Mr. Fossey came that day and Sam went back to visit with his families. In addition to the "young'uns," he told Russ he had several grownups.

Their tough skin made it difficult to cut the morays the next morning. Fortunately, for some reason, Russ didn't put them in with our fish bait.

At the traps, now, we baited first with the fish, finished with the moray, and threw the extra pieces away.

The next day we pulled and baited as usual until we got the moray-baited traps. All we found in them were ugly, hairy, red worms about four inches long. They were on the entire inside of the traps. Using one of our burlap bags, Russ squashed them and re-baited the traps, after a thorough rinsing, with fresh fish.

We wondered whether it was the worms, or the bait, that kept the crawfish away, and we found out the next day. The same thing happened in spite of having baited with fish. This time Russ had brought a scrub brush, and he used it on the traps.

Back to the dock to build more traps to replace those if we didn't get crawfish in them the next day. We built six and took them along the next morning.

Starting this time at the moray end of the trap line, we found the same condition. Russ cut the line a few feet above the traps and abandoned them. I wanted to untie, but he didn't want any part of the line that might have touched the trap.

Pulling the other traps, we added them to the pile on the boat and moved them to another location further down-island. On the way home, he said, "We haven't been very efficient—you have just been a passenger in the boat. After you pull the trap, I have to leave the motor and do the rest of it. You either have to handle the motor—or the traps.

"I'll handle the boat. Sounds like fun!"

I looked forward to it. I knew the waves in the ocean were higher than those in the bay, but I wasn't worried. I had tried to memorize the north and south markers that we used to locate the third point of the triangle where our traps were, three miles off shore. It looked easy. Russ had called my attention to them often enough and our new location wasn't far from the old.

With more traps in the boat the next morning, I went confidently out the cut into the ocean. The wind was increasing. We were only a little wet when I got to what Russ said was a quarter-mile south of the end of the line. By this time it was only possible to see my shore landmarks when the boat crested a wave.

I made a slight turn to correct course and the boat fell into a wave trough. This set us down on a coral rock the size of a house! I was thrown off the stern seat towards the engine. I grabbed the side of the boat; then getting my balance, I looked at Russ. I was scared! I had expected him to grab the swinging tiller and make things right. The boat was still under power, but rolling and pitching in the waves caused us to ship water.

He sat on the passenger's seat as complacently as if nothing had happened. He said casually, "Take the tiller and keep looking for the traps." Then he started to bail out some of the water we were shipping.

Then I asked him to steer, he refused! "You'll learn."

I said, "The boat will sink."

"Well, I'd hate to lose the boat, but we can swim to shore. It's only three miles, and we might have to if you don't get the boat under control. This water is getting ahead of me."

After I spent several minutes telling him how mean he was, I realized I'd have to do it, and taking the tiller, I eased us into a wave.

Soon I saw one of the pieces of wood we used for a trap-float. I managed to pull alongside it, but when he pulled it, a sudden wave snatched us up and broke the line. The second one was soon visible and suffered the same fate. When that happened, he said, "Well, I guess it is a little to lumpy to pull traps today. Take us in."

I pleaded with him and he said, "I'm just a passenger today."

I managed to turn the boat towards shore without swamping us and looked for my landmarks. On the crest of a wave, I spotted them and corrected course. It was easier going in, but the following waves looked bigger each time I stole a glance at them.

I was exhausted when I docked the boat—from emotion, I guess. Knowing Russ as well as I do now, I realize he had counted on my stubbornness to make me follow through.

That afternoon he made a sculling lock for the skiff and called me. He sculled the skiff with one of the small oars around into the calm bay. I was just riding along looking at things on the bottom when he said, "I think it's a good time for you to learn how to scull. This oar will be easier to handle than the big one." Then he went to the bow and sat down.

Well, I'd asked for it, so I tried it. It's about like learning how to ride a bike. After many scrapes and bruises, it seems impossible, then suddenly you can do it! I amused my husband by my antics for over an hour. Sometimes he laughed aloud. The rest of the time, he just snorted.

How did I manage to get a black and blue chin? Oh, it's easy. Just stand too close to the end of an oar.

"Russ, where's the other oar? I want to row us ashore."

"I thought you didn't notice me put it on the dock. Scull back to the dock."

In silence, then, I managed that because the tide was flowing out. I was grateful for the assist it gave me. After I tied the skiff, he said, "Now, I feel much better knowing you can scull. If you have motor trouble in the future, you'll still able to make it home."

Somehow that hadn't entered my mind.

CHAPTER SIXTEEN

Bob Craig's Story of a Nice Bonus.
He Protects Me While I Hire Help.

We had been talking about getting help to work in the big grove, and heard three whistle toots. George was on his sandbar again.

We took our boat and pulled him off. He had Bob Craig with him and six raccoon dogs. George took his passengers to shore and then came to visit us. He brought with him some fresh fruit and magazines. It's odd how you get the answers to questions. One of the magazines was *Esquire*. In it was an article about the rare sea worms. The author asked for specimens–we never saw another one.

We could hear Bob on Sands, "Damn you dogs! I'll cut off your damn ears if you knock my tent down again."

After George left, I told Russ it would be worth a jar of jam just to hear Bob talk again. He agreed and went over to invite him to supper.

When Russ went back later to get him, he was waiting. They brought prepared crawfish to the house.

Although he is a Georgia cracker, he called himself an "Everglades tramp" because, he said, he could "live off the land."

"But sometimes, like just now in Miami, I have to work to get money for bullets and tobacco, and a few drops of shine," he said, while spooning down the last of the jar of jam I had given him. "Only worked a couple of days and got a nice bonus from the boss. I hired out as shotgun guard at a secondhand car place. He was losin' lots of wheels, tires, and stuff from his fenced lot.

153

It had a high fence and one gate, but it didn't hinder the thieves. Boss told me if I catch one and find out about the gang, he fix me up real good. He did, too.

"Next day, I talked some with the boss and worked that night. I wandered around and while I was on one side of the lot, they got some hubcap bait I put on other side. It purely burned me up!

"Next day the boss let me use real good bait. We put a car with real good tires three cars back from the edge. We nudged it out a little so those pretty little tires showed up, and I went home to sleep.

"Took my own gun that night, loaded with bird shot so I wouldn't hurt no one permanent-like. I walked around on the outside for a bit, then a big truck went by, and I snuck in the lot unseen. I pussyfooted over to the car next to my bait, slid under it, and got comfortable as I could. Figured it wouldn't hurt none to take a nap.

"Guess the guy's flashlight woke me up. Anyhow, some colored guys was lookin' at those tires. I just lay there and studied about it. Pretty soon I heard a thunk as something heavy hit the ground near the fence. A guy comes back with a jack. He puts it under the car and starts hikin' it up. He was workin' on the tire right by me. I waited 'til he dropped the axle on the ground, but I been easin' and inchin' out. I got up then and bellowed, 'Stop, you thief!' Boy howdy! He took off like a jack rabbit running towards the fence.

"He was part way when I let him have it in the rear end. He yipped and yelled, still runnin' with his knees most hittin' his chin. Next time I yelled, he stopped.

"I made him hobble over by the phone and I called the boss and told him to call the cops. Didn't have no trouble with him while I waited for the boss. He whimpered a lot, but I didn't let that bother me.

"Cops came around about the same time the boss did. He brought a new guard with him. I handed over my gun to him while I went with the cops to take that boy to the hospital. Had to testify, and I wanted to go.

"I got in back the police car with him. He couldn't sit down, just sort of squatted 'tween the seat. He just wouldn't open his mouth, Real stubborn!

"In the emergency ward, the doc takes one look at that guy's pants and says, 'That seat won't cover you again,' and he cuts the guy's pants open so he can look. He makes him lay on the table they got there; takes out some fluffy cotton, pours alcohol on it, and wipes off the blood so he can see how bad he's hurt. Boy, that guy yipped when the doc did that.

"I tell doc, it ain't nothin' but little old bird shot. Doc takes out a pretty little knife, he tells me it's a scalpel, and he gets real busy picking out them bird shot. Cops keep askin' questions. All the guy does is yip and yell. Pretty soon I got it figured. If that guy don't talk pretty soon, I won't get my bonus.

"I eased over by the doc and winked at him. Then I took out my old fish knife. It was pretty rusty, some nicked and dirty. That guy was layin' with his face toward me and I waved my knife around some as I talked to the doc. I told him that my knife wasn't clean as his, but it wasn't fair he should have all that fun. I wanted in on it. Got me a little closer and the doc cooperates. He makes believe I'm pushin' him away.

"Then, I touch the guy in a *certain place.* He starts to yell, 'Please, please, don't let him work on me. I'll tell, I'll tell.' Boy, did he! Tire man so and so. Wheel man name so and so. Hubcap man name. Cops had to tell him to slow down; they couldn't write that fast. Wasn't long before they had the names of the whole thievin' gang and the guys who bought from 'em.

"The cops told me then to make my report in the morning, and they go out to make a round-up.

"I do that, come mornin',' and I get real happy when the cops tell me that they got all the thieves but still lookin' for a couple of the buyers. I go back to the lot and tell my boss. He calls the cops to hear about it and he's real happy. He gave me a fine bonus. I got my gun and go home. I can afford a long vacation now!"

This had been better than going to a movie! I was still laughing as I handed Bob an after-dinner jar of jam in appreciation.

"It's gettin' kind of late," he said, after finishing the jam.

"How about spending the night here?"

During a pancake and syrup breakfast, Russ told me to go to

Princeton to hire help. Bob spoke up then and said, "I'll go along and protect Charley. Be glad to take care of Charley." He had called me that since we met. "I thought you was Russ' brother on account of that haircut and pants. Your voice is sure low for a female!"

Russ gave me money for our groceries and some for the men I would hire, and we left with the water bottles.

"I always pick calm weather when I go in a boat, course it's always calm in the Everglades. I can pole a boat as well as any injun there is. Let me steer the boat. I know how!"

When I asked how he knew, he said, "Sure, I steered some for Mr. Deen!"

The waves got bigger as we got about halfway and Bob was scared to death. He kept mumbling about being in a boat with just a female to steer it. He didn't know a thing about cloud navigating and thought I was lost. We had a following sea. It was his first time in a small boat and he thought every wave would come aboard.

All big-eyed he said, "If Russ had knowed how rough it is out here he wouldn't a let you get started, turn back!" I tried to calm this big brave man who was going along to protect me. Finally he gave up. After saying, "Durn stubborn female," he kept quiet and quivered visibly.

Some time later I was glad to call his attention to the smudge on the horizon that was the mainland. Then he relaxed a bit.

When we arrived at the canal and traveled up it, Bob was his usual brave, casual self again. During the mile-long walk to the settlement, Bob said, "Now Charley, you know Russ sent me along to protect you. I'll do all the talking to the colored men when we get there. I'll hire them."

"Okay, Bob. Just make sure their shoes are good enough for work in the lime grove."

Indignantly he said, "I know just what to do!"

When we arrived at a store where some men were standing, Bob didn't say anything. I waited another awkward minute.

"Charley, give me fifty cents."

I was furious but handed him the money and started to interview the men. My first question was "Who wants to work?" And they stepped forward. My next, "Who wants to work on

Elliott Key?" Four stepped backward. Only three in line now. Only one of those had good shoes.

He said, "You just call me Preacher, suh, I am one."

I told him we paid the going rate, $1.50 a day and living quarters. He would share a small house and boat with another man. Then I told him to get his work clothes and meet us on the main road to Cash's grocery. We walked towards what looked like a barber shop about a hundred yards away. A board in front was painted red and white with alternate slanting stripes. I nudged Bob forward.

As we got there, Bob said, over my shoulder, "Charley, give me fifty cents!" He smelled like a brewery.

All the men had heard and I couldn't refuse. Dammit! I gave it to him and watched as he handed it to a boy who came forward. In a few minutes the boy returned and extended the bottle towards Bob.

I grabbed it and said, "This one's mine. I paid for it!" Bob looked disillusioned and sad.

I proceeded to stare him down. Then, questioning these men, I found only one qualified. His name was Tom. When I told him the salary and where he was to meet us, he ran off to get his work clothes.

Bob trailed along in a wobbly way. I was just furious and called him to hurry up. Soon he demanded the bottle. I refused him and he seemed startled. The men came trotting up then. At the grocery, I told the men I would give them part of their wages to buy supplies with. They spent about four dollars each and I had them sign the grocery slips so Russ could deduct it from their wages. They then filled the water jugs, and I told Bob to show them the way to the boat while I finished my shopping. They carried all the jugs there.

Mumbling "Durn stingy," he also shouldered a water jug.

Mr. Cash had raised eyebrows when he saw the bottle in my pocket, but he didn't say anything. I phoned Mr. Weeks from the store. He was glad to hear that he would soon have lime trees as he had recently received several more orders. He told me to stop at his dock for burlap bags.

Before I got into the boat I had to tell the men to put their clothing and groceries in the bow. I didn't think it necessary to explain about possible spray. I put my groceries behind them on the floor by our feet. Bob was sitting on the back by me.

As I started down the canal and Bob raised his empty bottle to show me; then said in an abused tone, "I would thank you for the spare bottle!"

I stopped for the bags and then, saying, "Wait a minute," I tongued the bottle and tipped it up. While I was pretending to take a drink, some of the nasty tasting stuff slipped past my tongue. I shuddered. Bob took the bottle from my hand and took a thirsty drink. Then said, "Thanks Young Charley!"

The men were watching from the middle seat and didn't notice that we were in open water until they turned forward again. Then I saw their backs straighten up when they saw the waves and turned back to look at the receding shore. By now there was some spray. Both men were gripping the edge of the seat firmly. Everything was under control, and I was steering for my cloud, due east.

Apparently the men didn't know Elliott Key was off shore. It had been bad enough to know Bob was afraid. Now I knew that I had three frightened men aboard. I found out neither of the new men had crossed a river in a rowboat. I told them that we still had about eleven miles to go and they got real quiet and looked longingly backwards. There I was with two frightened men and a frightened drunk. I wondered if it could get worse. It did.

I saw a drink gurgling down Bob's throat and grabbed the bottle. He said, "Charley, let's go back and get more of this."

Taking the cork from him, I re-corked the bottle and put it in my pocket, saying, "No, be quiet. I'm busy!" Right then I was heading into one of those larger waves. The spray shorted the magneto, and we stopped.

The colored men were all excited. I told them to sit quiet–I'd fix it. I gave Bob the tiller and told him to point the pointy end of the boat towards my cloud. I showed him the cloud I meant. All through my instructions Bob kept saying, "I know how, Young Charley. I know how."

I climbed forward between the two men, dried off the mag and finally got the motor started. Back in the stern again, I looked up and saw that Bob was steering for Miami and we were just rolling around in the wave trough. When I tried to take the tiller from him, he was insulted, "I know how. I KNOW HOW, Young Charley." I yanked and pulled until we were heading towards my cloud and then fought it out with him. Yanking and cussing, I finally got the tiller. The men were more frightened now than before.

The battle over, I had a marvelous idea. Taking off my large straw hat, I handed it to Preacher and said, "You hold this over that thing you saw me wiping off."

You guessed it. Preacher's hand shook so much that he shook the water off the hat onto the mag. Out again!

I had no choice, so again I called Bob's attention to the shape of the cloud I was now watching and repeated instructions. I thought how much easier it would have been if I had left him on the island. I went forward accompanied by his mumbling, "Dammit, Charley, I keep telling you I know how. I do, I do."

I took the drinking water forward and poured it over the magneto, then wiped it, cranked a half dozen times and we were on our way again. This time, towards Caesar Creek.

I fully expected the motor to drown out while I yanked on the tiller to get us in the proper direction. We were really rolling. Bob was much more belligerent this time and we fought for the right to steer the boat. He kept insisting he should steer because he was the oldest. I was damn tired of cranking that motor and I was the only one aboard who knew how to adjust it. Struggling now, he was much stronger than I, I finally called him a damn drunk. That did it!

He released the tiller snarling, "Do it yourself, if you're so damn smart!" Then, he got onto the floor and sort of curled up under the seat the men were on.

I eased the boat slowly into the waves and was on my way. I knew that with that weight moved more forward I would have to slow down. Preacher was shaking so much now that my hat was useless so I took it and put it on my head again. I felt a bit better knowing that Bob had passed out. The waves got smaller as we got in the lee of the island. I thought my luck had turned.

Not so. Both men stood up and did what most people do when they are cold and frightened, they voided. (It was a good thing Bob had called me Charley.) I had an idea, then, that they

159

needed some false courage.

I pushed Bob with my foot, he just grunted, so I handed the bottle to Preacher, after first pretending to take a drink. "Don't take more than your half, now, and give the rest to Tom." He was fair about it. When Tom finished his drink, he tossed the empty bottle over the side. For a few minutes, they looked almost happy.

The motor stopped again. It was easier to start this time, no trouble with Bob. Elliott Key was visible and I called the men's attention to it. They seemed to relax when I told them we were more than halfway. At least, they started to talk to each other. They hadn't done that before. Soon they were doing too much talking for me–all about a big dance they had been to and certain events regarding their girl friends. Under the circumstances I was forced to appear casual and uninterested.

Closer to the island now, I had no more problems and went towards the small cove that was the entrance to the big grove. We were much closer now, and I saw the men looking down into the clear water. Then, at the same time, they said, "We wade in from here!"

They made the mistake most newcomers make. They thought it was shallow because they could see the bottom. I said, "Oh no! I don't think you'd like it. Tom, you take that big oar and see if you can touch bottom. The oar is sixteen feet long."

He took it, as though to humor me, and pushed it into the water. He almost fell out of the boat when the oar went in almost full length. He managed to fall back in the boat, wet to the elbow. He had a weird expression on his face as he carefully replaced the oar. They weren't about to doubt "Young Charley" anymore and sat quietly for the rest of the trip.

When I stopped at the shore, it was necessary for me to tell them to get out. I was glad to see Russ and hand him my problems. The motion of the boat as the boys moved to get their clothes and groceries awakened Bob. Just as Russ was asking where he was, Bob crawled out from under the seat and unfolded in a very wavy fashion.

He glared at the colored men and said, "Which one of you bastards stole my bottle." Then he started cussing them both.

Before Russ could say anything, I yelled, "Shut your mouth!

I paid for it and I disposed of it."

Bob's condition was apparent to Russ and he said, "Sit down, Bob, and wait. I'll be right back." Bob did, but not before glaring at me. He sat on the middle seat.

I could hear Russ as he called the men's attention to the little house, to the cooking water and told them to stow their groceries in the boxes nailed high on the walls. He showed them where they were to cook outside. They returned to the shoreline and Russ told me to throw ashore the two fishing lines we kept in the boat. He showed them how to remove the chitons from the rock and remove the small piece of pink flesh for bait.

I had been having another bicker with Bob. He wanted to search for the bottle in my grocery bags. He was very bitter when I wouldn't let him. I stood guard over my groceries. I had enough of him for one day. I faced the necessity of having him as a supper guest, but I wasn't going to let him spend the night.

During supper Bob kept moaning around and asking for a drink to help his headache pains. Russ finally convinced him we didn't have any. He took him home while I did dishes.

On his return, he told me that he had given him two dollars for his trouble.

I hit the ceiling! I said, "The trouble was all mine," and proceeded to tell him what had happened. He had difficulty keeping his face straight and I became more indignant.

As I finished, he almost laughed, then he snorted.

I said, "In the future, I'll go for help alone!"

"Like hell you will," he said. "I'll go myself."

CHAPTER SEVENTEEN

Captain W.R. Russell Rescues Our Hired Help.
Dinner on His Sponge Boat. I Learn about Sponges.
War with Japan is Predicted. Sawyer's Treasure.
Would-be Thieves. Superstitions.

Russ left with the skiff in tow the next morning. Then I remembered I hadn't told him the men didn't know about boats. Boy! What an oversight that was.

He worked with them until about two in the afternoon, told them to set the alarm for five in the morning and showed them where he had tied the skiff. Preacher said, "Mr. Russ, show us again how to get the meat out of those little things. They curl up and we can't get at em."

He did and said, "Do it quick. If you wait a few seconds they make like an armadillo.

I was fishing when he returned and he said, "They work all right, but I'm not sure I should have left the boat there." Then I told him.

We had a leisurely breakfast the next morning. Russ had decided to see if the boys were dependable enough to work in his absence before making rigid rules. Captain William Reno Russell came to the house as we finished. We asked if he wanted some water.

He said, "No, thank you", then he chuckled and said, "I was down-bay sponging yesterday with Reno. Came late evening I thought I saw your skiff with two colored men in it. I sculled over and questioned the men. They were just sitting there drifting and they had quite a few fish in the boat. They didn't even seem to realize they were so far from shore when I called their attention to it." One of them spoke up and said, "We work for Mr. Russ and Young Charley in a lime grove some place around here."

"I thought it very unseemly that they should call Mrs. Russ that. Didn't want to discuss it with them though. It took me the most part of the night to sail them back to the grove. The wind was against me. They slept most of the way back, just acted sort of wilted like, glad to hand someone their problems.

"Do you know," he said in an unbelieving voice, "I had to show those boys how to row the boat over to the sailboat? Then, I told them that the next time they were out a little ways they should drop their hook and they wouldn't drift. Mr. Russ, you will find this hard to believe, but they asked me what a hook was. I had to point to it in the bow of the skiff. The anchor string was still neatly coiled. You better tell those men to be careful 'til they learn about boats.

"Never did I see two grown men so stupid and they were scared too. Any six-year-old Conch boy can use a skiff! When he gets to be eight years old, we give him one of his own."

Captain just sat there and shook his head. Anyone who didn't understand boats was in a different world from his! *Hook* and *string* are Conch terms for anchor and line.

Russ explained that the men had meant no offense when they called me Young Charley. They had heard Bob Craig use that name when he spoke to me. After hearing most of the story, he said, indignantly, "I can do very well without meeting such an unseemly man."

Captain Russell simmered down a bit and then asked if he could build a sponge kraal near the big grove. "It will be on your water path to the grove and I'm sure no one will bother it when I'm down-bay fishing sponges."

"We'll be glad to keep an eye on it for you."

I didn't know what Russ had offered to protect and I said, "What is a sponge kraal?"

He thought I was joking. Russ felt obligated to tell him that I was just a city gal learning the Conch ways.

He explained then that a kraal was made by driving stakes into the soft bay bottom. Along the top of the stakes ropes were woven to make the kraal semi-rigid. The stakes were long enough so they stuck above the water six inches or more at high tide. He further explained that each fisherman had his own round-bottom skiff. A small deck on the bow is where they stood while poling the boat with a 20-foot pole on the end of which was a three-prong sponge hook. The teeth were about five inches long and formed an arc.

It took knowledgeable maneuvering not to tangle the hook in unusable items as they poled along, looking for marketable sponges, such as sheepswool or glove. A quart-sized milk bottle, almost filled with oil, was lashed to the clamp strip on the starboard side. In the bottle was a stick with a small piece of rag tied to the end. When the water was too ripply, they threw a few drops of oil on it by shaking the stick. This oil covered a considerable area. Twenty drops was enough to make a hundred-foot area mirror-like.

Now I was glad that Russ had said I was a city gal. I asked him what kind of oil they used. He told me that Key West had a shark industry. One kind of fishermen caught sharks. The hide could be used for boots and shoes. The shark liver gave up many quarts of this fine oil. Any other oil left a colored film on the water. The marketable sponges were thrown into the boat all day, and the heat of the sun killed the little sponge animal. At the end of the day, these were thrown into the sponge kraal to keep them safe. The tides helped clear some of the substance from the sponges. When the weather was too rough, or the sponge kraal was full, they cured them. A kraal was also useful as a pen for the large green turtles that formed most of the spongers' diet. Any extras were taken to market in Key West.

"I left Reno on the other side gathering stakes. I should judge he has plenty of them now. I must be on my way."

We thanked him for taking care of the colored men and he said, "It was a welcome diversion. Sponging sometimes gets monotonous."

Russ towed him to where Reno was, passed the time of day and continued to the grove.

The men had tied the boat properly, and were sleeping. He thought it more important to teach them to row than to work that day. He woke them and made them get into the boat. He taught each man separately, and, he told me, they almost knocked each other out of the boat when they crabbed an oar. He told them about the danger of an anchor line on the bottom of the boat. They might fall over it and go overboard.

Back on shore he gave them a lecture. "No trees, no money!" That really woke them up. They really worked the next few days. Got more trees out than Russ had expected.

Because of possible embarrassment, I didn't go to the grove during the time Preacher and Tom were working there except for one occasion. That time, Preacher asked, "You Mr. Russ' nephew?" I said, "Yeah." A little later Tom asked, "You Mr. Russ' brother?" and I answered the same way. Then I looked around for Russ and told him I was walking home.

They wanted a spree, so Russ took them along when he delivered the trees and arranged to meet them in three days. When he returned he told me that the men hadn't acted nervous. "They just might lose their fear of water."

The following evening we received our first dinner invitation. It was from Captain William Reno Russell, and to be "this evening." Any time after two was *evening*. None of the spongers carried a watch. When we asked for a more definite time, he answered, "Should have enough daylight to eat by. We only have an anchoring lantern to hang in the rigging when we are in the Key West Harbor."

He was too polite to say anything about Fiddler, so Russ said, "Fiddler will stay home, to watch the house."

He left then, saying, "See you later."

We did our washing that morning and got ready to leave for dinner out. Time to spare while Russ dressed, I turned to reading. Then he called attention to my clothes and said that this invitation called for my sailor whites, he had some on.

He fixed Fiddler's supper while I changed and it was time to go. Fiddler barked a bit as we left, but after we reached the sponge kraal, we didn't hear him. There we saw Reno, Captain Russell's son, working rib deep in the sponge kraal. He had a paddle in his right hand and was beating a sponge in the other. Half-inch diameter holes had been drilled in the paddle. Whenever he hit the sponge, a phosphorous smelling liquid oozed out. Rinsing the sponge, he then repeated the process. The clean sponges he threw into the skiff tied alongside the kraal.

I saw a large turtle come to the surface and swim towards him. I called out and told him, knowing that I wouldn't want to be bitten by anything that size. By the time I finished telling, he had swiveled around and brought his knee up sharply under the turtle's head, shoving it against the upper shell. It seemed to me I could almost hear it scream. It didn't move for a few minutes, then sank slowly as it drew its head back into its shell.

Boy! That must have hurt!

Reno kept on cleaning the sponge until it was finished. He hadn't lost his rhythm while dealing with the turtle. He picked up another. I saw it still had the black outer skin on it. This sloughed away as he worked. Finished now, he said, "You go on to the sailboat now. Papa's waiting. I'll be along in a little bit."

We tied our boat to a stern line that Captain threw us and went aboard the 24-foot sailboat on which they lived while out sponging. I found that on a sponge boat the coffee is always simmering on the little Shipmate stove fastened to the deck. The stove was 12 inches by 18 inches and had a little 2-inch railing around the top to keep things from sliding off when the boat rocked. If the level in the coffeepot got low before it was used, they just added more water. Needless to say, it was almost thick. They burned buttonwood, pencil-box sized pieces. It provided an intense heat and very few ashes.

Captain said that many smaller stoves were used, and they had to be mounted on a metal covered cabinet to bring them to a reasonable height for cooking. In the winter, these were used to warm the cabins.

I sat on the deck with my legs crossed. Russ and the Captain squatted, Conch-style. While drinking coffee, I saw Reno moving farther out into the bay and asked his father why he had to go so far out to rinse the sponges.

He said, "Part of this milky sediment you saw him beating out is seed. It is important that the sponges get their final rinse in deeper water so the seed won't be thrown ashore by waves." That was their method of planting sponges for the future.

I sat facing the mast and noticed some pieces of meat, about the size of an individual steak, dangling from fish line in the rigging. I asked about these and Captain said, "That's the main part of our dinner. Reno got a couple of nice big turtles yesterday evening. Parts of the flippers are hanging there. That's a real choice part of the turtle. Got to string them though and let them drip most of the day to get the wild taste out. They make real fine eating!"

When Russ asked about the price of sponges, he said, "The price sponges bring in Key West right now is fantastic. More than anyone in Key West has ever gotten before. We keep raising our minimum prices and those little yellow foreigners just keep buying them anyway. I never saw them before this year; believe I heard tell they are Japanese. They surely must be planning a war before too long. That's always when we get our best prices, when a war is being planned. Especially sheepswool and glove sponge. They use a lot of those in hospitals.

"When the auctioneer in the warehouse starts chanting, those little people start bidding. They outbid all the white folks. There are so many of those foreigners in Key West. I never saw but one in my whole life before. Gotta be a war coming."

I knew nothing of the use of sponges and asked about it. He was a true gentleman. An ordinary sponge fisherman would have hooted at me for my ignorance.

He carefully explained. "In a hospital they are used only for cleaning wounds, no lint to shed! Could be made much more sanitary and they are more absorbent than any other material. On the battlefield they were used for sponging and cleaning weapons. Nothing can stand that rough treatment as well as sponges."

As far as I ever found out, no one but the sponge fishermen ever noticed this particular phase for the preparation of war, and they always minded their own business.

"Where are the best sponge beds?"

"Hard to say exactly. Things got all changed around after Flagler put in his railroad. When he put in his fill beds on mud flats, he disturbed the natural flow of water. It started new beds and ruined a lot of good sponges in the old beds. No good can come out of man changing the natural flow of water like that. If we ever get a big blow like we got in 1906, it will just ruin the sponges. Stagnant water trapped where it never was before–when that gets mixed with the rest, something bad is sure to happen."

It wasn't too long after the Labor Day Hurricane of 1935 that we first heard of the Red Tide. This disease almost decimated the sponges as well as killing uncountable tons of fish. The sponge fishermen had slim picking in the Keys for many years.

During our conversation, Reno had finished his seeding process and returned. Tying his boat alongside, he reached to the bow of the sailboat and got a thin bundle of twine pieces, the narrow inside rim of a coffee can, and a large needle. After threading the needle, he picked up a sponge and put it on the metal rim. Seeing my interest, he explained that if the sponge fell through the ring, it would be illegal to sell it. Those they kept for their own use. Others were strung on the twine, all of the same size on one string.

It really took training to judge the size of sponges in water twenty feet deep. The twine Reno used was 4 feet, 8 inches long, the standard size. A few inches were left for tying. Tied in a loop, it was called a *bunch* or a *string*.

Now Captain Russell turned to the stove. He was squatting between it and the cabin. He lifted the lid of a two-quart kettle there with a fork and lifted out something on the surface. He raised it up and prodded the contents. When I asked him what it was, he seemed surprised but politely said, "Plum duff." I had never seen any before and didn't know anything about it except from my reading. I knew it to be a favorite English dessert, but any account seemed to think everyone knew how it was made, what it consisted of, and how it was served.

"It's a favorite Key West dessert. The duff is well cooked now and ready." It was in a sugar bag.

Suddenly I remembered the pint of sugar, strawberry jam and ripe sapodillas we had brought for them. I was closer to the stern, so I went into our boat to get them. Things had been so interesting that we had forgotten. Reno considered the jam most important, but Captain Russell exclaimed over the fresh fruit.

Then I noticed that Reno had thrown the sponges onto the sailboat and was bailing his skiff. I was fascinated by the bailer. It was the front half of a large horseshoe crab. It made a perfect bailer. Captain Russell asked me if I was aware that the only things that had come through the centuries without any evolutionary changes were the cockroach, the shark and the horseshoe crab. I hadn't known it before. Funny, one land and two sea creatures.

Reno washed his hands a final time in the ocean and climbed aboard dripping wet. Going to the bow, he hung his sponges in the rigging to dry and squatted on the deck near Russ. This canted the boat a bit and the dripping water ran off the deck.

Captain Russell handed his son a cup of coffee and Reno said, "Thank you, Papa, I surely hope you aren't going to make me change into dry clothes."

His Father smiled his sweet smile and said, "No, Son, I reckon our company's been around too much to mind."

While I had been listening, I was also watching. He had taken some bacon grease from a jar and put it in the frying pan. He stood up then and untied the steaks from the rigging. Then he put them on to fry. While they were cooking, he leaned over, reached in the small cabin and brought out the plates, knives, and forks. At his invitation, we each helped ourselves to a knife and fork.

Soon the steaks were well cooked and he spread the plates on the deck and served them. Then he opened a tiny oven I hadn't noticed before and took out the cutest loaf of bread. He had baked it in a coffee can. The oven was just a little higher, wider, and deeper than the coffee can. When I said, "Oooh! Fresh bread," he said, "I make some everyday, sometimes twice." He cut it into four pieces and put it on the plates.

I had never before considered a table as a luxury. I was sitting with my legs crossed and it was a little difficult to cut my meat. I couldn't stretch my legs out–there simply wasn't room. Finally I put my plate on the deck in front of me and decided to cut my meat, all of it. The golden brown crust of the bread looked lovely and it smelled heavenly. It had been many years since I had had any oven-fresh homemade bread.

As Reno had started to eat, I did too. I can't remember anything tasting quite as good as that dinner. The bread wasn't buttered, but I saw Reno dipping his into the juice of the turtle steak, and I did too, and experienced another taste treat. I have had many turtle steaks since, but none that equaled the flavor of that one. It was delicious and the combination was wonderful.

When we had all finished our food, Reno said, "Kindly hold your knives and forks. I'll do the dishes." Leaning over the side, he washed them in the clean ocean water, poured a little fresh water over them and shaking them almost dry, he put them in front of his father.

While he was doing this, his father was preparing to serve the duff. He poured the water off it into the ocean, then putting the kettle on a slightly scorched piece of wood just in front of the little stove, he removed the lid and untied the string again. I had never seen food cooked in this manner and was very interested. He rolled the cloth bag down, then with a quick twist of his wrist deposited the whole thing upside down on his plate. With a fork, he raised the cloth on the top and pulled the sugar bag off. It was slightly larger than the loaf of bread had been. This he also divided into four portions and we started on our desserts. It was very thick and chewy, like soft caramels. It was very tasty and I said, "Mmmm good." Captain Russell just beamed at me.

No one had talked during the meal. I opened the conversation by saying how good the food had tasted and asked for the recipe of the duff. Nothing pleases a good cook more than to share a recipe. He was no exception.

Smiling now, he reached into the cabin and got a pencil and paper so that I could write it down:

"Cream together three-eighths of a pound of butter and one cup of sugar. Add three well-beaten eggs. Mix well. Then add a twelve or fourteen ounce jar of your favorite jam or jelly. Mix two teaspoonfuls of baking powder into three cups of flour. When this is well mixed, add the mixture of butter, sugar, eggs and jam. This will become firm. I have tried many ways of cooking it. The best way is to put it in a sugar sack. In tying it, one should leave room for expansion. (Some people prefer to put it in a greased pan with a tight-fitting lid.) The put it in a kettle and add a bit more water than it takes to cover it. Then set it over a slow fire for three hours. When we are home in Key West, where everything is available, we cut it in thin slices and a butter-sugar sauce is poured over it."

I thanked him and returned the pencil.

Then I asked him, "Reno, how did you capture the turtle in

the sponge kraal?"

"Well now, I'll tell you how I get them. It just depends on how many barnacles they got on their backs. Those are wicked things to scratch yourself on. Takes a long time to heal those scratches. See that burlap bag on the middle seat? It's a real tight weave. Mostly I spread it and safety pin it in front of me on my pants. Then, I scull or push-pole up to 'em soft like, real close. Then I just jump on his back and ride!

"I land on the back half of him and grab his shell far enough back so he can't get a bite. That beak is really wicked! You tilt his head up when you land backside and he can't go under water with you. If he does that, you might just as well give up. No man can hold his breath as long as a turtle. Thing to do when that happens, sometimes it does, you let go real quick when he sounds for bottom and get in your boat real quick so that mad turtle can't bite a chunk out of you. That hasn't happened to me in a long, long time.

"Once you're riding him you can steer by leaning to whatever side you want to go. He just doesn't have a choice. He can't steer when he's tilted back. He gets kind of hysterical and swims like mad. I usually ride him around in circles for a while to wear some of the fight out of him. Then I usually steer him over to Papa's skiff so Papa can grab hold of the shell and help me put him in the boat on his topside. Just stay away from his mouth, then, and he can't bite you or get away.

"If I see some without barnacles and they aren't too big, I just go in like I'm dressed now. You know, you can't put more than one of those in a skiff? Have to take him to a kraal before I can get another one. You ought to try it, it's fun getting a free ride like that."

I wondered how he jumped out of a round-bottom skiff without turning it over, but I hesitated to ask.

Meanwhile, the conversation got around to the disappearance of a sponge fisherman named Sawyer. He and his family had abandoned his house in Key West. All of the furniture and most of the other contents of the house were still there. Reno told the story:

"Most sponge fishermen stayed away only two weeks, but it

seems that after Sawyer was gone three weeks, then Mrs. Sawyer started to pack up some things. One morning without saying anything beforehand, she and the kids just took off on the bus. Without hardly more than good-bye to those few early rising people who saw them leaving. No place to go from Key West but north. Those that saw them said that they had a lot of suitcases and cardboard boxes with them. No one goes to visit kinfolks with cardboard boxes.

"Funny, she left before Sawyer got home. Sawyer was a very seemly, sober, hard-working man. He was always ready to help someone out. He had a lot of relatives who kinda used him because he was so big-hearted. He and his family got along real well together.

"Some of the boys said they saw him in Miami. He acted real strange, just kept sculling his skiff all around and through the boats anchored in the Miami harbor. He acted just like he was lookin' for someone. He hung around an 80-foot schooner for a while, then a rope ladder dropped over the side, and up he went. Seemed he stayed on board most of the day. Then he went back on his sailboat and just sailed off, somewhere, didn't say nothin' to no one.

"When he come back, he anchored his boat and sculled over to the same schooner. All day long he stayed there. Then come evening he and the guy from the schooner went away, some place on shore. Seems as though they stayed in a hotel overnight. In the morning, some of the boys saw Sawyer sculling the guy back to the schooner. Pretty soon, down comes a loaded lifeboat from the schooner and the guy sculls to Sawyer's sailboat. Sawyer follows him and he ties up there; then he gets in the lifeboat with the guy and a lot of gear. He sculls over near a cabstand and talks a while. Then up comes a cab and they put the stuff in it and the guy shakes Sawyer's hand and goes off.

"Then the darndest thing happens, Sawyer hadn't said a word to any one of his friends. Now he goes all around and tells everybody that will listen that he will sell his boat to the highest offer by six o'clock that night, cash money. Boy, did he get took. He didn't get only about half of what he should have and he didn't gripe either.

"No one saw him that night after he sold his boat, but next

173

morning, all kind of bags and boxes got loaded on the schooner, went on all day long, it seems. The first mate seemed to be bossing things there.

"The next morning, here comes Sawyer and his wife and his kids in a cab! All loaded down with boxes, suitcases and stuff, they get aboard the lifeboat and Sawyer sculls over to the schooner. Everybody goes aboard and the mate helps carry up their gear.

"He puts the lifeboat on a longer line and the mate goes up the ladder. Then the sails start raising, the anchor gets pulled, and in a little handkerchief breeze, that schooner gets underway. Rope ladder still hanging over the side!

"People on other boats call, 'Where away, man?' and Sawyer calls back nothin' but 'South, man, South!'"

After Reno finished telling the story, Captain Russell added thoughtfully, "They do say that the ring-bolt where black Caesar used to tie up to is not there anymore, just a fair-sized hole. Could be that Sawyer found some of that pirates' treasure. If so, could be he figured he had helped support his relatives long enough, and it wouldn't last all of them very long."

Some years later while we were constructing a honey-processing plant in Fort Lauderdale, we heard what we believe to be the end of this story. A Mr. Chochiese was the low bidder on our plastering contract and we had several conversations with him during the process of the work. I asked him where he was from, as he had a slight accent. He said, "Sao Paulo." Russ asked then, "Did you know a family by the same of Sawyer down there?"

"That is an unusual name in Brazil. I didn't know the man personally. A family by that name came to the coastal town where I lived some years ago. They had an 80-foot schooner. Mr. Sawyer is engaged in coastal hauling. The original schooner is only one of several he owns now. All are busy."

Russ said, "Yes, he found the treasure," and then he told the story to Mr. Chochiese.

Suddenly we all heard a splashing sound and looking towards the kraal we saw the turtle trying to climb out. Reno quickly got into his skiff and sculled ashore and looked around, searching for something. Soon he got a rock and went back to his skiff. He tied one of the pieces of twine to the rock, which had a hole through it. Quickly he was on his way to the kraal again. There he waited a minute and when the turtle raised his flipper, Reno put a loop over it, slip knot, of course. The turtle got sort of lop-sided then, and soon he went back under water. We all had been watching this silently.

When he came back to the boat, Captain Russell smiled and nodded his head saying, "Just so, Son. That will do it." Reno was visibly pleased.

A minute later, he said, "Mr. Russ, maybe you can use some sponges around the house. There are some torn and wrong-size ones further down the key, near where we had our old sponge kraal that got *borrowed* from too often. That's why we wanted to build this one near you folks. You're welcome to all of those you want. We already got what we wanted of them."

"Sure do appreciate that, Reno. We have felt the need for some. We really won't let them go to waste. We will look in the morning. Why don't you two come to the house for a coconut pancake breakfast?"

Captain said, "Thank you, but–"

Reno completed the sentence by saying, "Papa and I are going to Key West come daybreak. When we come back we sure would like some of those kind of pancakes."

Captain said, "Yes, we better go. Those foreigners might stop buying as suddenly as they started. I'm not going to hold for a bigger price like some are doing. I'll get it while it's there."

We had our thick after-dinner coffee now, and we had to leave before dark. We said our thanks and good-byes and left.

Turning to look just before we entered the cut, we saw the sailboat against the last pink of the sky. As we got into the cut, we heard Fiddler barking madly and growling. Russ got his sheath knife from under the back seat where he left it while we were on the sailboat. When we were nearer the dock, he cut the motor and when it had drifted in, he said, "Tie it."

Jumping ashore, he ran up the path. Nearing the house, he saw three men trying to hit Fiddler. Two had sticks and the third had a board. Russ yelled, "Hold it" and let them see his sheath knife.

One of the men said, "That damn dog attacked us."

Now, Russ saw evidence that they had tried to pry the door open. He pointed to it accusingly. "You were trying to break in."

One of the men took a step towards him and Fiddler bit him on the ankle. A quick nip that Russ had taught him. It temporarily paralyzes the leg. The man screamed, "I been bit!" and fell down.

Then Fiddler went over and stood by Russ, snarling, his hair on end. Looking at him then, Russ saw the mark of a dirty footprint on his rear leg. He thrust out his sheath knife and the other men stood still. Then he pointed at one of the men, "You, go take off his shoe and look. The skin isn't broken. You are just a bunch of thieving cry-babies."

When the sock was off, we all looked. There wasn't any blood or a sign of anything. They were incredulous.

"Now you damn dog beaters, get the hell out of here. The next time, I'll shoot!"

The nerve pinch Fiddler had given the man was now easing off and he got to his knees. One of the others gave him a hand and they all went silently down to the beach where they had left their skiff.

We watched them scull away down-island.

"Good, good Fiddler! You protected our house for us! Come on inside. I'll make you some pancakes for supper." At the word pancakes, Fiddler's ears twitched, his tail wagged, and he looked up at Russ with a silly smile, his tongue hanging sideways out of his mouth.

Before too long, he was happily eating pancakes with syrup, mostly with his eyes closed. It was a trick he had when he ate his favorite food. He finally stopped eating. There were two pancakes left!

The next morning we went to look for the sponges. The sailboat wasn't in sight. Before long, we saw the large pile on shore and looked with wide eyes.

Ashore, Russ started quoting prices for comparable sponges. We looked at first one and then another, and we took them all. One sponge was a real beauty. It was doughnut-shaped, eighteen inches across. The hole in the center meant nothing to me.

Home once more, I went through the sponges until I found just the right one to fill the hole and make the sponge complete. Then I had the pleasure of sitting on the first padded surface I had had on the Keys in eighteen months! A luxury! This sheepswool sponge was used as a chair cushion for years, on the Keys and in town. When it became compressed after a time, I renewed it by a freshwater dip and it again expanded, and became fluffy and comfortable.

Russ remarked that he thought it strange that Captain William Reno Russell hadn't really given an opinion of our neighbors, except to say that he didn't approve of how some native Key Westers were *borrowing* all the time, giving all the Conchs a bad name.

"Charlotte, did you know that when he was younger, he was the master of an ocean-going vessel. With that background, he had a right to consider himself superior to some of the Conchs who just barely learned to read and write. A good many of them, according to him, were just too lazy to do honest work. He told me that he respected the sea as all good sailmasters do and didn't have time for superstition and nonsense practiced by these other people in the course of their everyday lives. They have many weird beliefs that seem most strange. For instance, they won't go walking in the moonlight because they think the moon will make them lunatics. Before making a difficult trip, and always at night in their boats, they sing a chant to the god of the sea. They believe in various symbols and signs, almost relating to voodoo. For instance, a knife placed under the steps of your enemy's home will bring misfortune, perhaps disaster, to him or her.

"Captain Russell also said that they had more practical ways of disabling an enemy's boat with water or sugar in the gasoline. Another method, a bit slower, was to put a small quantity of sand in the engine oil. He told me that most of the Conchs get their crawfish by bullying or grabbing. They are very successful with these methods.

"Listen to this now! We should have known it before. They have a unique method of getting rid of competitors who trap crawfish in their locations. They haul the man's traps and re-bait them with moray eels. The odor permeates the traps, and, as we know, they will never again catch another crawfish!

"A good many of these people work harder and spend more time trying to outwit other people than it would take to earn a good living. I wonder how many hours those fellows wasted just watching the house to see when we were both gone at the same time so they could try to steal from us?

"Captain Russell told me that one of them bragged to him that he had *borrowed* seven hundred pounds of his nephew's crawfish, took the whole live car. Next time he saw him, he complained that his nephew had *borrowed* a thousand pounds from him!

"If some of their superstitious beliefs backfired on them, they never attributed it to their own mistakes or carelessness. They believed then that their intended victim might have had better spells than they had.

"Captain Russell told me about Old Billy Brooks, whose relatives were albinos and so susceptible to sunshine that they had to be completely covered while working. The average Conch usually worked without a shirt and had his pants' legs rolled to the knee. They wear large straw hats and most of them develop eye trouble at middle age, from the sun's glare on the water.

"Captain Russell said Old Billy not only fosters these superstitions but magnifies them. He says he could very well picture him speaking at a gathering, that he does seem religious in an odd sort of way. He believes that God gave the Devil control of all the waters of the land as his personal territory. Old Billy Brooks could quote some passages from the Bible to prove his point. Sorry, I don't remember just exactly what they were and it would be a shame to improvise. So, I'll put it this way. He proved his point as well as I do mine when I say, 'Time is money. Money is the root of all evil. Therefore, to rid this world of evil, one must kill time.'

"Some of the nonsense the captain mentioned was clarified when Old Billy continued with his religious explanation. 'While traveling on the territory of the Devil, the waters of the land, it is very seemly to soothe the Devil with special chants.' When in an interested way, the captain asked Billy to teach him those chants, Billy refused saying, 'You are an unbeliever and I can't teach you. It would be wrong, very wrong!' The subject was closed. The captain said, 'I had apparently trespassed on forbidden ground. Old Billy would never discuss anything further regarding the Devil's territory.'"

Sponge Market in Key West
- Photo Courtesy of Monroe County Public Library

CHAPTER EIGHTEEN

Warn Thieves and Shoot. Hex! Hex Backfires.
Fiddler Recovers. Raccoon Hunting. Blood-Curdling Noises.
Fiddler Goes Fishing. Ball and Chain Speakeasy.
Borrowers Rob Us. First Run from New Still. Yarb Medicine.

Some people from Key West were visiting the neighbors and they dropped in to say "howdy." We had the usual coffee and cookies. The conversation swung around to the drought and the scarcity of limes, no rain for three months now. Very casually then Russ said, "I'm getting damn tired of people stealing our limes and I intend to shoot anyone picking in the grove." This statement was made as though he was speaking of third parties, not present.

There were many side-glances and raised eyebrows, but he hadn't accused them personally and they weren't in a position to say anything.

The following morning as he silently sculled the surf boat to the big grove, he wasn't thinking only of saving gasoline, he had brought along his .22. With the boat tied, he proceeded to shoot high into the trees in different directions. We heard the crushing noises of people in a hurry, breaking branches that lay under and around the trees as they left the grove. Russ grinned and said, "Maybe now they'll believe me!" We heard them run towards the oceanside.

Apparently they considered they had been challenged to a game of wits. When Russ fired each time we arrived at the grove, we heard them running away. Each time he fired a bit lower. Soon he was firing into the treetops. The next time he aimed real low. The bullets couldn't travel more than fifty feet without hitting the ground. There was an unusual amount of branch breaking and I was very, very sure that it was close to where we were.

We were on the path following them almost immediately. We hurried, but they were in a skiff pulling towards a powerboat a bit off shore when we got there. They were four of our recent visitors.

One man was perched on the skiff with his bottom over the side. He had his hand on his left buttocks and was cursing furiously. Obviously he had been *winged.*

We returned to the grove and soon located the spot where they had been putting the limes they picked. The burlap bags were almost full. Further searching turned up some partially filled bags. Russ carried the full ones to the boat while I dumped the others together. Altogether they had picked three and a half bags. In order to do that, they had started at daybreak.

Whenever we found it necessary to rest in the grove, we sat on a sawhorse in the shade of a large buttonwood tree near the bayside. This was made necessary because the entire surface of the ground was composed of rough coral rock, some loose pieces on top of solid. The soil lay in pockets in between. This was partially covered with small branches, all of them thorny.

The second morning after Russ had winged one of the *borrowers,* I went towards the sawhorse intending to sit down and wait for him. Instead I just stood and stared! When he arrived, all I could say was, "Look!"

The ends of the sawhorse were slightly wider than the long top piece, as that had been set into the legs. At the front end was a large claw from a land crab opposite a large claw from a sea crab; between them was the skull of a raccoon. In the center of the other end was the raggedy cut sphincter muscle of a raccoon, in back of it, the tail. On each side of the middle were small claws, one of a land crab, one of a sea crab. He silently looked at this odd sight for part of a minute, then reaching out with his work gloves, he brushed the things onto the ground and said, while sitting down on the sawhorse, "Come on, let's get our boots laced and get started so we can quit at noon."

I gulped! I was shook! He looked at me and laughed, "I didn't think you were superstitious!"

"I'm not, but skulls and bloody things nauseate me. What did that stuff mean?"

"It looks as though the Conchs really believe in hexes all right. They are trying to put one on us. Evidently they have been spying on us, must have been for some time now. Anyway, they noticed that we sat here every time we are in the grove. They put that stuff on it so we would make contact with their hex items. They aren't very fussy about whether we die on land or in the sea. Both of them are represented here. Land crab, sea crab, and the other things. The tail is just window dressing. Don't let that stuff disturb you. It can't cause anything to happen."

His explanation hadn't sounded very bright and cheery to me. "I think anyone would be a little shaken by that odd sight and the vicious thoughts that motivated it."

"Well, yes."

We began to pick limes from some of the hard-to-get-to trees that the Conchs hadn't gotten yet. It didn't seem as though we had been there very long when we heard voices and the sounds of more than one person approaching. In a low voice, while leaning close to me, Russ said, "Be quiet. Try to let me do most of the talking."

Before long a man called out, "Hello, Mr. Russ." Russ answered and soon two men came into sight from the direction of the ocean. We knew them only by their Key West nicknames of Hambone and Hoglice. They had been two of those in the skiff on the winging occasion. (We found out later that the bullet had passed clean through the buttocks of one of their companions.)

They squatted down on reaching us and Hambone opened the conversation by saying, "It's too rough to go after crawfish today so we figured we'd visit with you folks a while. Figured you'd be in the grove. How are ya?" He said the last with a sort of sideways smile.

Russ smiled, "We are just fine." Then he hunkered down and copied their position, so I did, too, although it was a most uncomfortable one for me. Then he said, "Oh, Yeah! I almost forgot. Some stupid ass tried to put a hex on me, or us! Poor dope doesn't know that where I come from in Pennsylvania, we know all about hexes, so it's sure to backfire on whoever conjured it up." I had been watching them carefully and the only change was that their eyes squinted up a little more.

Hoglice said, "Oh no! I wonder who would do a thing like that to nice people like you. What kind of hex was it Mr. Russ? A trouble hex or a death hex?"

Russ chuckled and said in an amused tone of voice, "Do you know what the screwballs did?" Then he told them of the things we had found on the sawhorse, and, their positions. They tried to look shocked, but I found it an unconvincing performance.

This was the first time they had ever come to visit with us in the grove and if they had come to see two frightened people, they were disappointed. I was convinced that most of their shocked expressions had been caused by Russ' statement that the hex would backfire.

I was ready when Hambone turned now to me and said, "How are you Mrs. Russ?"

"Fine as usual." Then I asked if they had heard about Gary's new live well. (I had prepared to use diversionary tactics to make them think I didn't consider the hex signs important.)

Both of them said they hadn't so I chuckled and told them the story:

Late evening the night before we heard a boat at the dock and then heard Gary call, "Hello, the house." Russ told them to come on up and I got the coffeepot on. Then Gary said, "We got a real nice bait of fish and we are on our way to the Miami Fish Market."

"Gosh, you don't have a live well; they'll be a long time dead before you get there!"

"Come on down to the boat. I'll show you why they won't be dead. We built us a fine large live well! Then we went right out fishing in the channel in spite of the rough weather. We ran into a school of fish. Boy, howdy! We were busy baitin' our hooks an' catchin' fish. We ran out of bait. Then that didn't stop us! The fish was just so hungry they bit our bare hooks. We fished until our arms got tired, then in a little bit, the live well was full. It was some rugged while we drifted around there fishing and we was glad to quit. We figured to stop for some coffee here then get going."

By this time we were at the dock. He got aboard the boat saying, "I'll show you a fine bait of fish!" Removing the cover, he shone his flashlight in the live well. The surface of the well was so covered with fish scales that all you could see of the fish was a few top fins. A few seconds after seeing this, we all stood around and laughed. Shad was a silent man and he now spoke for the first time, "Guess the fish house will be right glad to get some already scaled ones."

We laughed more at that and Gary scooped up handful of the scales and threw them overboard. We were still laughing about it when they cast off and left for Miami.

Hoglice and Hambone straightened up as they laughed. We stood up also. Apparently, Hoglice didn't want us to forget the hex. He said, "I just can't figure out who would do a thing like that to you folks."

"Don't you worry your heads about us. I really meant it when I said I felt sorry for whoever did it. Like I said before, it will backfire on them. Good-bye for now!"

Saying "Good-bye," the men left on the well-worn path to the oceanside. I wanted to discuss this visit with Russ but didn't because it was more than possible the men would be listening.

"Get busy. We've got things to do."

He whistled a lot of the time and now started to whistle again, something classical. We worked until it got too hot.

On our way home in the boat I told him I thought only nasty people would have thoughts such as were represented in the hex. He laughed and said that it was funny how some people put faith in such things. "Now stop being ridiculous." Then he softened that by saying how pleased he was that I had managed to change the subject and act nonchalant.

"I am sure that it disturbed those men to find that we didn't act as though the hex was important. Did you happen to see Hambone wince when I said that I felt sorry for whoever had done it?

"Say, the moon will be up early tonight and it will make those ripe limes shine out like light bulbs. That tree of mangos will be ripe in a day or two. They'll probably rob us blind tonight."

When we got to the dock, he said, "Help me carry these bags of limes to the house. They'll be safer up there."

By now I had built enough muscles to help and he had shown me the best way to use them. In a half-kneeling position using my thigh and stomach muscles, I jerked a bag up and onto my head as I rose. Holding it was easy and I walked up the path.

After dinner that evening as we sat quietly reading, we heard the most amazing music. We went outside looking for a boat with a radio playing, but none were in the area. It was like the sound of a stringed orchestra. The themes were lovely and almost identifiable as certain pieces of classical music. Occasionally, one of us was caught in the middle of a sentence as we said, "Oh, I thought it was–" We stayed outside until the sounds faded away. Apparently, it was the sound of the wind in the trees, but we didn't think so at the time. I have since heard and read about it. One author described it most fittingly as "the music of the spheres." A lovely evening concert.

Almost ready to go to the grove in the morning, we heard motors approaching from the south. Looking toward the ocean, we saw a Conch boat towing another boat. A third boat behind suddenly started to circle and a voice yelled, "Help! Come back! Come back! Help me! I'm hurt!"

The leading boat, swinging wide because of its tow, went towards it, the skipper yelling, "Turn off your motor, you damn fool! You'll run us down! Hurry!"

We watched a man lurch towards the controls. Soon the boat stopped, and the leading boat pulled alongside. The passenger held the boats together while the skipper helped the third man into his boat. There was some movement there, we couldn't see what, and then the skipper went toward the other craft and busied himself getting and tying the line to the stern of the second boat, which had drifted near.

Once again under way with two boats in tow, he was on his way. Apparently his passengers were down on the deck as they weren't visible.

Later Gary explained what had happened. From statements they had made in Miami, the story was that these three men (their *winged* companion being unable to help) had worked like mad all night gathering the limes and mangos. Then, dividing them, had started for Miami in their boats. Like most other Conchs of their type, they had left the space around the shaft open. "Why put a cover on it? We need to do our bailing there!" The first man to start his motor had stepped to the stern to see if the boat needed bailing. Worn out and groggy, he had stepped through the hole against the setscrew on the shaft and it gnawed a hole in his leg before he could get it out. He yelled and his nearest buddy went over, wrapped the man's shirt around the leg, helped him onto his boat, and put the other in tow. He got under way and the third man followed. In front of our house, the same thing happened to him.

Gary said, "They really got chawed! Right up to the bone. You know, they gave the funniest damn explanation for it! They said, 'a hex backfired.' Isn't that screwy?"

We didn't lose many limes after that. However, we did see one more hex sign. Russ is a precisionist and he noticed that the thick board of our step, was slightly out of line. Lifting it, he saw a rusty knife and a chicken legbone. Kicking them aside, he said, "Looks as though they don't want to give up. They aim to get even with us. Could only be the fourth man, he was uninjured." Heaving the knife and the chicken leg into the ocean, he continued, "Now they are trying to make us get a broken leg, or a cut one."

About that time Fiddler regained the use of his fourth leg. It took him a while to become accustomed to using it, but the leg and foot were normal now. He welcomed the extra mobility it gave him, and he stopped looking from the leg to Russ as though asking for an explanation.

One day, looking out to see why he was barking, we saw he had decided to race an airplane down the beach. His speed was startling. He was well!

Our storage space near the dock inside an old skiff had enticed a family of rats. Knowing how Fiddler tried to play with all wildlife, Russ had to study out a way to teach him to kill these. Fiddler seemed puzzled by this change, but soon learned how to kill them with a quick jerk, breaking their necks.

We were surprised one morning to see George Deen come in and tie to his regular tree. For a change, he had found the channel. Bob Craig and his six raccoon dogs were put ashore with his gear, then George called and said he had to return to Miami. After he left, Bob called and said he had a package for us, from Gary.

Russ sculled over, and his usual first night's invitation to supper having been gratefully accepted, he brought Bob back with him. Bob handed me Gary's gift and when we got home, I put it away without unwrapping it. I saw his face fall. We all knew that Gary made fine guava wine.

After supper Bob and Russ discussed hunting raccoons.

"Bring Fiddler over and we'll hunt some coons."

"He's a people dog. He doesn't know anything about that."

"Maybe he'll learn. Can't hurt him!"

Soon we were on our way to try something new.

"My dogs are used to meeting strange dogs, will Fiddler behave?"

"It will be his first sight of dogs since he was a pup."

Ashore now, we waited to see how they would act. At first, Bob's dogs circled Fiddler on stiff legs, then one of them must have told a funny story because they put their tongues out the sides of their mouths and got a most silly expression.

As soon as Bob saw our dog was accepted by his, he started them off by saying, "Go hunt." Fiddler stayed at Russ' heel when they ran off. Very soon they started baying and the sound came closer. Before long, a raccoon ran in front of us with the dogs following. Fiddler stood still and looked up at Russ. He was puzzled.

"Get it, Fid," Russ said.

Fiddler just stood still with his ears up and his nose wiggling. The dogs seemed to be making a circle now.

"Get it, Fid!"

Then Fiddler he took off, but not towards the baying sound of the dogs. Soon we heard a different type of baying.

"They got a dead one," Bob said. "Let's look." Before we arrived there, we heard the funniest sound of all, a bird dog trying to imitate a raccoon dog—in falsetto yet! Then we saw all the dogs standing around a dead raccoon. Examining it, the men found it had a broken neck. Fiddler had gotten to it first!

Bob put it in his burlap bag saying, "I be a son-of-a-gun,

how'd he do that?"

"I trained him on rats."

"Go hunt!" started the dogs again. A raccoon climbed a small tree; Bob clubbed it, and put it in the bag. Bob said, "Go hunt!" once more, and we waited. Then Bob said, "They got one treed." There, with the flashlight, we saw four raccoons in one large tree.

"I'd better get my leather work gloves from the boat."

"Yeah, this looks tough! And when you get back," Bob said, "you climb up and shake 'em down. You're younger'n me!"

Russ came back with his gloves and climbed up. "Okay! I'm shaking the first one."

The mother dog was closest to it and she darted forward. In a minute, she yipped, crying with pain. We saw the raccoon had her ear in its mouth. Fid got there, and getting the raccoon's neck in his teeth, he gave it a back-breaking jerk as he tore it from the dog's ear—painfully, we heard!

"I never saw a dog like that before. Didn't know a bird dog could be any good with coons. The boys won't believe it, but I saw it. Can you reach that next one?"

"Wait a minute. Yeah, get ready. Here it comes." One of the younger dogs jumped it. Those raccoons were fighters. This one met the dog halfway and snapped down on its lower jaw. The injured dog now made a weird keening sound, louder than the complaints of the mother dog.

"Get him, Fid."

He did. But before dying the raccoon had firmly clamped its jaws. With his gloved hands, Russ pried them apart and released the dog.

The dogs had backed away from the tree now and even though two of his dogs were injured, Bob asked Russ to get the other raccoons out of the tree.

He shook it vigorously and they fell within seconds of each other. Our bird dog killed them both with quick neck-snapping jerks.

While stuffing these into his bag, Bob started his swapping talk. He began by offering two of his dogs for Fid and ended by offering all his uninjured dogs as a swap. "Gotta have him." He refused to accept "no" for an answer. As we sculled to the dock, he called, "You think it over now. I'll consider giving you all six!"

Fiddler ran up the path and Russ called him. "He's too excited to stay outside tonight. We'll take him in."

Because of the injured dogs, Russ took Bob and the dogs to Miami with him in the morning when he went to sell the limes we had gathered.

About his trip to Miami, Russ said, "Those damn dogs were so afraid of the water that I had to flush out the boat before I left the dock."

We hadn't been asleep long the next night when we were awakened by a bloodcurdling noise, quavering warbling!

Russ laughed, "Sounds like Fiddler did the other night. He thinks he's a raccoon dog now. That's the closest he can come to the sound they make."

He called Fid a half dozen times and he finally came home. He acted hurt and sulky when he was led into the house.

The next day, whenever he wandered a little, Russ would call his name and blow the conch horn. Fid soon got trained to come, and it was very timely because he started to hunt again a few nights later. Waking to that sound during the night made your hair stand on end. Blowing the conch horn always stopped the hunt.

The down-island neighbors came to see us and asked if we had been disturbed by night noises. "Some sort of strange something is wailing at night! It sounds like a lost soul. We would purely appreciate it if you would bring the dog and help us look. We can't sleep! We don't want to look alone, come with us! Did you hear it?"

"It's our dog."

"No dog ever sounded so suffering like the way that sounds."

It was finally necessary to go with them into the jungle back of the house. Fiddler followed happily. "Go hunt," sent Fiddler darting off and we soon heard the noises they had described. It is hard to describe their expressions, frightened, then startled, and then they looked accusingly at both of us. Russ then explained about the raccoon hunt with Bob's dogs that had started Fiddler on his hunting. They finally allowed themselves to be convinced that we hadn't done it with malice. Only after Russ had promised to keep the dog in the house at night did they accept an invitation to coffee.

When we spoiled that fun for him, Fiddler started fishing. We heard a muffled bark at the door one morning, and going to look, saw Fiddler with a large snapper in his mouth. It was still wiggling. He was waving his tail happily and seemed to ask that we cook it for him.

"No people around," Russ said. "No hooks in it. He must have caught it."

Fiddler watched as Russ cooked it, and he waited impatiently for it to cool. He was unusual in that he could sort out the bones and leave them in his dish. From then on, we cooked any fish we found on the doorstep. We knew they were Fiddler's.

No fish on the doorstep one morning and Fiddler wasn't in sight! Russ blew the conch horn and we heard a faint bark from the oceanside. Looking out, we saw Fid about a half-mile away. We went after him in the powerboat. We slowed down and came alongside as, his head under water, he made another snap at a cowfish. It was still fast enough to get away from him.

Russ grabbed handful of his fur and skin and pulled him aboard. The dog was exhausted and lay panting in the bottom of the boat on the way home. Another lesson learned. After that, he didn't go more than a block off shore.

I had been hinting for a long time that I would like to go to Miami and have a night on the town, as we used to do while there. Russ never said anything in answer. One nice, calm day, he surprised me.

"The last time I was up in Miami I arranged for us to spend the night with an old friend, Pret Beaudry. No definite time, but we have to get there before he leaves work and call him. He doesn't have a phone at home. Get ready. We'll come back tomorrow morning!"

Boy! Was I tickled. After months and months, I was going to see the bright lights. It didn't take me long to get into my whites and fold up my dress. I put my dress in a paper bag and said, "I'm ready!" Then I got an awful jolt...

"For Pete's sake, how about cooking up some extra food for the ducks. And Fiddler. We can't take him! We'll put him on the back porch with a sandbox, like we did when he was a little puppy. Can't leave him out, he'll hunt raccoons and get us in bad with the neighbors."

Working on all cylinders again, I took care of those chores, he finished his, and we carried the bottles–and my dress–to the boat.

Sitting in the boat quietly anticipating our night out, I thought how lucky that I remembered my lipstick. I'd put some on tonight for a change!

Russ phoned Pret the minute we got to the dock. I tied the boat and sat down. It was then that I looked at my fingernails. They were long and irregular. When I mentioned this, Russ took out his penknife. I reached for it and he said, "Oh no, you always cut yourself when you handle a sharp knife. I'll do it." He made a neat job of it and had just finished when Pret drove up.

On the way to Pret's apartment, Russ made a stop at a grocery store. Back in the car again, he announced, "I bought steak for supper to celebrate our reunion." *Boing!* There went my hopes for a dinner out!

I was prepared to make myself useful in the kitchen, but Pret said that no one could cook steaks as well as he. I was told to take my shower while they prepared supper. It was ready and they called me. I had showered and put on my dress, fussed a bit with my hair, applied lipstick and reached for my shoes. Until then I had felt well dressed. I stared down bitterly at the high-topped tennis shoes. The stores were closed by now and I couldn't buy any others. It had been so long now since I wore city shoes that I hadn't thought of them.

I felt gloomy as I went in to dinner. For minutes at a time as they talked, I forgot my predicament.

"Charlotte, you do the dishes, but just leave the butter, sugar, bread, and things on the table. I'll put them away. They each have their own place." Wow, a precisionist like Russ! He even looked like him, enough like him to be his brother, in spite of the fact that his ancestry was French.

Finished first, Pret came out and was putting things away when Russ returned. "Russ, the fellows down at work were talking about a place on the Tamiami Trail where you can get a drink. It's called The Ball and Chain. Let's go there."

"Well, it will be a first time for Charlotte. She might enjoy it. This could make it a night out for her."

When he said that, I just stood and stared down at my clumsy shoes in dismay.

"Forget it, you walk very gracefully in them now. Maybe if you don't call attention to your feet, no one will notice."

"I wish you were right!"

In the car, we drove slowly looking for the sign. Pret saw it first. It was smallish and on a house-type building. In addition, the word LUNCH had been painted on the two front windows.

There was plenty of room to park the car in front, so we did and walked up the steps. The door was opened for us by a man who just stood there blocking the entrance.

"Who do you know?"

"Mugs Gillette."

The man stood aside and let us enter.

As we went towards one of the empty booths, I noticed that I was the only woman there, and, for a while could forget my shoes. Several men were standing at the long counter opposite the booths, and they were all staring at us. Some had their elbows propped up behind them on the counter. I thought them rude!

One of them came over after we were in the booth and asked what we wanted.

"A round of bourbon."

He studied each of us and then left. All the men at the counter continued to stare.

Soon the man who had taken our order returned with our drinks on a tray. He stood for a minute on the side of the booth near Pret, and said, "Mind moving over?"

Pret looked surprised, shrugged his shoulders, and moved over.

Putting the tray on the table, the man slid in alongside Pret. He said, "Cheers", and raised his glass. We did the same and drank when he did. I thought it pretty odd for the waiter to sit down and drink with us, but knowing nothing about speakeasies, I just sat silently.

"Where are you from? Been here long? How did you happen to find this place?"

Russ answered, then, because Pret didn't want to talk. "My friend heard about it at work. As for us, this is our first time in Miami for months. We live on the north end of Elliott Key. We are sort of stuck there. This is the first time I've ever taken my wife to a speakeasy, and I appreciate your hospitality."

"Who do you know besides Mugs?"

"Flip is a good friend of ours and Mugs often stops to eat with us. We know Big Erskine, too."

Then the man just beamed. "Oh, you're *those* people!" Turning to the men at the bar, he made a signal of some kind, and said, "Waiter, come here!" Then turning back to us, he said, "I own this joint!"

The sound of shuffling feet caused me to look toward the counter. The men had stopped staring and were turning around. You could literally feel the tension ease. Then the waiter arrived.

"Bring us another round–on the house." Then, he stood up, reached over and patted Russ on the shoulder, saying, "You're all right."

When the waiter returned with the drinks, the man returned to drink with us again and told the waiter, "Everything is on the house! Find out if they want anything else. Do you? Sandwich, potato chips, hard boiled eggs, sausage?"

We all said, "Sausage." When the waiter brought it, the man said, "Their money isn't any good here. Give them anything they want." With that, he smiled, waved his hand at us and went into another room.

The atmosphere was now as cozy as a tearoom. We ate our sausages and asked the waiter to give the owner our thanks.

As we stood up to leave, the owner returned to see us off. While going towards the door, he said, "If your wife wants to come in here anytime when you can't come along, don't you worry about her. I'll see she is taken care of and treated like a lady. Send her home in a cab if necessary."

Russ murmured, "Thank you," and clearing his throat, repeated it a bit more loudly. Then we left.

No one said anything until we had driven at least a block. Then from Pret, "Never look a gift horse in the mouth. Say! Those must have been some pretty important people you named to him! Boy, I wonder if the boys at work will believe me when I tell them about this?"

After spending the night at Pret's apartment, we left early for home. Arriving at the dock, we had trouble tying because of a boat there. It was loaded with very familiar things, and on top the pile was our .22.

Jumping out of the boat, Russ got the gun and ran up to the house while I tied the boat. He was just in time to stop the people from removing the last of our possessions. Fiddler, on the back porch, was just hysterical and had almost succeeded in breaking through the screen door.

They tried to explain that they were only *borrowing*.

Russ merely pointed the .22 and said, "Now, we'll go down and get the other things. You will put them where you found them." Quite some time later they had completed this under protest, not too loudly though, as Russ stayed a few steps from them with the pointed gun. The men were all a head taller than he, and were the three out of four on which the hex *backfired*.

When all the things were back where they belonged, Russ told the men that he was going to put a long-time hex on them. "If you ever try another bit of thieving, that hex will really fix you. Now get out of here and don't come back!"

The way they galloped down the path was something to behold.

"As superstitious as those men are, I think they'll leave us alone for now. They think their hex backfired because I know more about hexes than they do! They were pretty scared when I said *long-time hex*."

Returning to Princeton for the hired help, Russ found Tom at the grocery store, with him was a small elderly man he introduced as Old John. Russ asked about Preacher, and Tom said furiously, "That Preacher ain't no place around. I'd like to get my hands on him. When we got here, I stopped at the store to buy some supper things, and Preacher sort of bumped me when I came out. He kept going then and I stopped to buy some shine from a guy standin' there. When I reached in my pocket to pay him, my foldin' money was gone, and Preacher was out of sight! That damn Preacher. What's the use of taking a few groceries home when my wife wants foldin' money? No use hurrying now. I sort of loafed along and didn't get there 'til dark. I wasn't anxious for an ear-beatin.' I went in, thinking she was sulking. No one there.

I lit the lantern and saw a note on the table. Note said, 'Gone with Preacher.'" Russ said that he sounded more disturbed about the loss of his money!

Russ had by then decided to give Old John, who evidently was the replacement for Preacher, a chance to work if he wanted to. He had been standing silently all this time.

They bought their supplies and Russ paid the bill. This was Tom's second trip over to the island and he tried to impress Old John with his knowledge. It didn't work. He was quietly corrected when he misused nautical terms. Russ was pleased that Old John knew boats, no drifting boats this time! The next day, Russ said, "Old John is a slow, plodding worker, but gets more done than Tom during a day. I was lucky to get him. He must be one of their community leaders. Tom is always polite to him."

Things worked out very smoothly and days flowed along. It would soon be time for Russ to take the two men back to Princeton.

Early one morning, we were awakened by a strange sound. It was rain. Now we could have a lovely shower. Taking sponges and soap, we went out into the rain. Fortunately, it didn't last long and we were inside, and dressed, when Reno appeared with his demijohns.

It was unfortunate that there were only a few gallons of water in the tank, but we offered him that and half the remaining gallon in the house, saying that Russ was going to Princeton in the morning and would bring some back. We had twelve demijohns now!

"Thank you kindly, but my Papa and I drink more than that before early evening and we only have a potful now. It wouldn't be enough. Listen, you bring your bottles along. We'll get some from those people down-key. They got a 10,000-gallon cistern. No one ever refuses to share water! We always used to get it from them when this tank was dry, not unless though. My Papa didn't want to be beholden to them."

We hesitated because it was the relatives of those people we had had trouble with about the limes and the *borrowing*. Over coffee, Russ told Reno about those episodes. He added one that Gary had told us:

On one occasion, they had *borrowed* all of Gary's carpenter tools and personal possessions except his clothes. He said, "I can't imagine why they left my duds. They are all as tall and skinny as I am."

He said he hunted most of the day and finally found their hurricane house, back in the jungle.

"I hurried like mad and *borrowed* everything in it. I hid all their things in different places except one–that I put on my bamboo table in the living room. Next day they came to call on me, I was using my carpenter tools to build a chair. I heard them coming and I sort of watched their faces. When they saw I was using my tools, their faces was something to behold! Their eyes bugged out like bugs on a stick when they saw I had nerve enough to put that pretty red water pitcher on my bamboo table. One of the boys said, 'Say, that's ourn!' I just stood there looking at them then and said, 'Yeah, I know, I only borrowed it. I didn't think you'd mind. I got it the same time I found the things you borrowed from me.'

"They looked awful disturbed then. Guess I broke one of their funny rules by showing off with that pitcher. As the saying goes, 'The silence was pregnant' right then.

"Say you know they must have had a helluva time finding their things! I hid 'em in three different places."

Reno said, "Yes, I know, they don't recognize the word *steal*. My Pappy sure doesn't approve of that! They act just like it's a game, but it isn't right for grown people.

"But about water now. No one ever refuses to divide water. They'll give us some, and it's a lot closer than Princeton."

Did you ever notice how thirsty you get when you are short of water? We all drank two glasses apiece then and allowed ourselves to be talked into going to our neighbors.

We carried the bottles to our boat and, tying Reno's skiff on behind, went to the neighbors for water. Arriving offshore from their home, we dropped the anchor of the powerboat and got into Reno's skiff to go ashore. According to him, local custom required one to ask for water before bringing in your containers. They had only come to our house with containers because no one had lived there for a long time before we moved in.

We were most cordially greeted and were surprised to find all the men at home at that time of day. We were told that the lady of the house was visiting kinfolks in Key West. Besides Captain and his two teenage sons, a male guest was there. (It always struck me as an odd coincidence that these people should be named *Russell,* and *Captain* besides, no relatives of Reno and his father, the real captain.)

At that time, Reno said, "I would thank you for a glass of water."

"Of course," said Captain Russell. Then he went over to the drainboard and tilted a five-gallon jug as he filled three heavy coffee mugs, he handed one to each of us. The jug looked clear and sparkling. At the time, I thought it a little strange, but I couldn't think just why. Later, I remembered that on all other occasions they had used the pitcher pump to get water into the house.

We all got our cups about the same time and took long thirsty swallows. I drank mine, and I didn't notice the flavor until afterwards. Pow! I sat down on the floor and shuddered. I looked at my husband. He looked surprised. Reno? He looked happy! I was the center of attraction.

The men laughed at me until they literally held their sides and rolled on the floor. I felt the heat of the stuff in my stomach now and shuddered more. I was just furious and, on my empty stomach, I was on my way to getting plastered. When Captain Russell could finally talk again he sort of bubbled out, "Boy! That's the most powerful joke we ever did on anyone. Oh, hee hee hee, my sides hurt!"

When he could talk later, without laughing, he told us, "You got some of our first run. We rigged up a pretty little still last week! Borrowed a new Chevrolet truck radiator last week and then, some galvanized pipe. We had the washtub at home, so that was all we needed. Gary brought us a bunch of guavas that was going soft and we threw them in with some coconut milk and juice, had some cornmeal gone buggy, and put that in. When we figured it done fermented enough, we went in yesterday to run it off. We found some fool raccoon done committed suicide in it, didn't hurt the mash none, so we just flung him out and got the juice runnin.'"

I could feel my stomach trying to climb out my throat.

"Come on Charlotte, let's get the jugs."

I went with him, Reno followed, and after they had unloaded the bottles from the skiff, they went to the powerboat for our jugs. I stayed there. Russ didn't say anything, just sort of grinned. By now I was in a sort of whirling circle and the beat of my heart jarred my head.

I sort of woke up some time later and I heard Reno talking.

"Mr. Russ, I would purely appreciate it if you would take the skiff and water jugs around to Papa, he is about a mile down-bay. I'm fixin' to stay here and visit a little bit. Later maybe you would please take me around to the sailboat?"

"Sure, Reno."

When we got near our dock, I told him to leave me there. I didn't feel like going along. He stopped the boat and held it as I got off.

"You don't look really bad, just sort of pale green."

I went up the path and managed, by moving slowly, to have supper ready when he returned. We didn't stay up late, and it was fortunate.

In the first light of dawn we heard, "Mr. Russ can I come in?" Russ put on his pants and went down quickly to let Reno in. He started coffee. It smelled so good that I dressed and went down in spite of a hangover. The second cup of the unusually strong coffee seemed to wake me up. I listened while Reno told us what had happened after we left.

"Mr. Russ, you know I just came by here for water! I purely didn't know I'd be running into temptation going down there for water! Those boys and I used to have some pretty good times in a certain Key West bar. They knew I like my fun."

"Reno, you said *bar*, don't you mean *speakeasy*?"

Reno sort of smiled then and said, "Mr. Russ, no one in Key West hardly paid attention to Prohibition. I mean *bar*. Course it wasn't all in the open, but everyone knew it was there."

"Don't you tell my Pappy 'bout that though. Well, they know I surely love that nasty stuff and they gave me another half cup, then they wouldn't give me any more. They made a dicker with me for sponges. 'Bout the middle of the night they kicked me out saying they are going to sleep. Before they close the door on me, they tell me that I have dickered away $75 worth of sponges and I better deliver them early this morning or something bad will happen. You know, Mr. Russ, no man can drink that much money's worth of sponges. What am I going to tell my Papa?" His last sentence was spoken so softly I got the impression that the previous sounds had jarred his head.

He looked terrible. His eyes were red and he was continuously pinching out lime stickers that had broken off in him.

"Where did you get all those lime stickers in you?"

"Got cold outside on the sand and I went back over the ridge out of the wind and slept in their grove. Mr. Russ, I'll thank you for another cup of coffee. You know, Mr. Russ, they sure weren't neighborly!" (The understatement of the year).

Pancakes were ready by that time and it was full daylight. Reno started to eat. Sort of gulped one bit down and said, "Mr. Russ, my mouth hurts something awful. Would you please take a look and see what's wrong?" He pulled a lime sticker from his elbow.

Russ took him outside and had him sit on the doorstep. He tilted Reno's head back and just stared into his mouth. There was a most peculiar expression on his face. Then, clearing his throat harshly, he said, "Reno, don't drink any more of that damn rotgut. That's what your trouble is. You don't have any skin on the roof of your mouth and your cheeks are bleeding inside. God knows what the stuff will do to your stomach!" Reno looked very frightened. He had more coffee, but no food. After breakfast we delivered Reno to his father on the sailboat.

All the way there, Reno talked to himself. "I been a real bad boy. What will I say to Papa? Oh, I can't tell him I owe so many sponges. What will Papa say? Oh, poor Reno!"

We pulled alongside the sailboat and Reno raised his head, looking at his father he said, "Papa, I've been a real bad boy again. Will you forgive me?"

His Father smiled sweetly and softly said, "Just so you come back and admit it, Son. I kept the coffee hot all night."

We said, "Good-bye," and left.

Russ said, "I don't think he'll do that again for a while. It must have been terrible back of the ridge in the lime grove. Mosquitoes and stickers!"

*   *   *

Back in the grove again, Russ asked the men if they would come back and work for him. Tom said he would be glad to. "Having your money in a lump is a fine thing. i'll be able to get some clothes and catch a new wife to work for me."

Old John said, "Mr. Russ, I like to work for you. You don't needle a man to hurry all the time. Maybe later I will work for you again, but not for a while now. This time I get back, I'm going to get married again. I done outlived three wives and I'm only 81. That is, Mr. Russ, if you let me get a croaker sack full of yarbs."

A *croaker sack* is a burlap bag, but unfamiliar with the term *yarbs,* Russ asked what he meant.

Old John then looked at Tom. "Don't mind my business. Just get on with your work." He said this in an abrupt tone of voice. Tom sort of ducked his head and plodded off.

"Mr. Russ, you come with me and I'll show you." Going into the jungle some distance from the lime grove, he stopped, finger on his lips, for silence, and they listened. Sure now that Tom hadn't followed, he continued softly. "I'll get it off real neat so it won't hurt the trees none. I'll show you."

Taking out a penknife, he made a cut about a foot long, slanting the knife at an angle; moving the knife over about an inch, he cut again in the opposite direction, towards the first one. He made end cuts in the same manner. He removed the piece by prying up, saying, "Mr. Russ, I'm yarb doctor for my people and I need this!"

"Old John, go ahead, get all you want. The tree won't suffer if you get it that way."

Beaming all over, he cleared his throat and said in a very dignified manner, "I surely thank you. With this money I can make now I can afford a new wife. You have been awful good to me, so I'm going to tell you all about these yarbs!" He looked around again, as though for Tom and lowered his voice.

"I'm going to cut these careful, in different places so Tom can't see what I got. I'm careful about letting my people know my business. My Pappy was, too. He taught me. His grandfather was a yarb doctor in Africy.

"I make two different kind of juices from this. I boil some in water; that kind I sell to my people in doses. It don't keep long in an icebox, gets moldy, so I make up a batch when I get orders. The other kind I make the expensive way, with grain gin. I sell that to some white doctors in Miami and white liquor bars, too. Especially one in Seybold Arcade. They told me what they charge for a dose! Boy, wish I could get that. I get $5 a pint. They calls it *bitters* but that ain't what they sell it for!"

"What's this medicine used for, John?"

"Well, Mr. Russ, if you is sick, it makes you well. It cures most anything that can go wrong with your insides." Smiling, he added, "But if you is well, it makes you *wanta!*" Then he went on to give detailed instructions for the preparation of the *yarbs* and the required dosage.

Both men wanted to leave the next day. Early the following morning when Russ got back there, Old John was standing guard over a large burlap bag, which he was holding shut with a piece of vine. The bag had originally contained a hundred pounds of duck mash, and it was full. The skiffs were loaded and ready. Tom tied these to the stern of the powerboat while Old John with his *croaker sack* got aboard, and set it down in front of the engine. Russ moved it back of the seat. "It won't get salt spray on it here!" Old John smiled his appreciation while nodding his head.

Tom put the men's gear aboard and they were ready. When they reached Weeks' dock, Russ tied the skiffs there, and in deference to Old John's age, he took the boat up the remaining distance, a bit over two miles. When they got there, a group of colored men came forward. Apparently they had been waiting for their *yarb doctor.* He refused their offer to help carry his bag, but told them to carry his clothing and other things. They asked many questions, but he appeared not to hear them. The respect with which the men treated Old John impressed Russ.

Prohibition had been repealed just a short time before. Russ said that he was curious about this offbeat medicine and would get some gin the next time he went to Miami.

CHAPTER NINETEEN

Mosquito Nursery. Russ Makes Poisonwood Cane.

Any little rain meant we would soon have mosquitoes. They were so bad now that we hated to go outside unless we had a twenty-to-thirty-mile wind. They could fly upwind against anything less than twenty. If we opened our mouths to talk, we got mosquitoes in them–they tasted peppery.

We needed to find their breeding place and get rid of them in a lump, if possible. Dressed for action one morning, a loose shirt on top of one that was tucked in, socks over our pants' legs, citronella on exposed areas, we were ready.

We walked into the low bushes along the shoreline where they were the thickest. Clouds of mosquitoes in our faces made conversation impossible. When Russ finally called, "Here," he got several in his mouth. I reached him and looked at the spot he pointed to. It was a topless cistern. (He told me later that he had almost stepped into it because he couldn't see very well through the mosquito cloud.) Russ was coughing now with his hand over his mouth. He had swallowed some.

The water seemed to boil with the dark wiggling mass of mosquito larvae. Judging by the neighbor's cistern, this one was half full. I got a long stick and stirred the water. It looked black as far down as I could see.

Russ motioned me down towards the ocean. With my hand over my nose in an effort to strain out the mosquitoes, I followed him. At the water's edge there was enough wind so we could talk. While gouging an X in the sand, he told me to gather all the easy-to-burn softwood I could get and pile it near the mark. He picked up a pint bottle and went towards the house.

Returning, he brought a length of garden hose from under the house and the bottle that was now full of kerosene. He helped me in adding to the woodpile. The beach was clean around us now and I watched as he took the garden hose into the ocean and filled it. Holding both ends under water, he said I should press the palm of my hand on one open end firmly enough to keep the water in and then follow him up the hill–*after* I had tied the bandana handkerchiefs from his hip pocket over our mouths so we could breathe.

"Now, leave a sag in the hose and follow me."

He put his end of the hose in the cistern and I lay my end on the slope. In a minute we saw the siphon was working; it was draining out a black, soupy mess. Mostly larvae, just enough water to keep the mass moving. We watched for a while and satisfied that it would continue to siphon, we returned to the house.

Some time before, we had made a mosquito brush to hang outside the back door. All the natives had them and we copied them. It was made from a palmetto fan, shredded, using your fingernails, into quarter-inch strips and tied like a broom. With this, it was possible to swish the mosquitoes off your back before you darted inside to the screened porch. When those that came in with you were killed, the house was free of them.

Mosquito season is when the inside work gets done. After measuring my thin mahogany board some time before, Russ had been drawing a plan for a "trinket box." The hinges for it were still attached to the radio cabinet we had found. He was working on dovetailing the ends of the pieces of wood he had sawn and I removed the hinges from the radio cabinet and thoroughly sanded them with pumice stone. I wasn't allowed to touch the boards as it required absolutely perfect work to get the dovetails to fit into each other. Quite some days later, this was finished, and in the meantime, we were fortunate enough to find some small nails we could use to attach the bottom. I was sanding coconut shells to be used for making various necessary and luxury items for our mothers.

Later he carved an inebriated-looking cat on the lid of the box and painted it white with some paint found on the beach. Orange paint served for the moon in the background. The box was a very useful item then and is still in use at this time.

When we checked our drainage project during high wind the next day, we found that the siphon had drawn out all but a few inches.

"Now we are ready to use the wood. Throw it all in the right hand corner so some of it is above the water. I'll start a fire with kerosene and we'll evaporate the water."

I carried it up while he went for more, and small boards. Then starting the fire, he told me to watch so no sparks lit the nearby weeds while he went for longer boards. No trouble, and when he returned with the heavy boards, he cut them slantwise, set the ends inside the cistern, and we went home, leaving a well-contained fire.

Russ had pulled up a little dead tree in the bushes on the way back and peeled off a bit of bark. It was sort of greenish and he couldn't identify it, but intended making a cane from it. He fastened it to the C-clamp some days afterwards and was making good progress with his drawknife in shaping it. Before long, he was ready for the sanding process and had finished that before supper.

We went to bed under the mosquito tent that night. It was fastened to the rafters and tucked under the mattress. Russ was very restless. Turned and scratched all night. When we looked at his skin the next morning, he remembered sanding the wood for the cane, and he said, "So, that's what *young* poisonwood looks like! It loses its green color when it gets older." The sawdust had really fixed him.

Getting out the hypo mix, he applied some several different times that morning. When the wind picked up enough, we got ready to see what our efforts had accomplished. He took a broom along.

We arrived to find the wood almost wholly consumed and the cistern dry. The bottom was covered, inches deep, with the larvae carcasses. Leaning over, Russ carefully moved the broom to clear one corner, then jumped in and fanned the carcasses into a pile.

"Get the bucket!"

I returned to find that he had thrown all the remaining

pieces of charred wood out. I tossed him the bucket.

"We have to clean up after ourselves. If we continue to stay here, I'll roof this thing over so it will catch water for us."

Filling the bucket with mosquito larvae, he handed it up while telling me to dump it in the ocean. I did and watched as many small fish came and ate. They were almost transparent and soon their stomachs were visible as small black blobs. Altogether we got four full buckets of the things.

When the mosquitoes from the previous hatching died, we again enjoyed some nice mosquito-free weather. Russ finished his cane, using the cartridge case of a Colt .45 as a ferrule. Happy and Al had given it to me after some target practice they had one day in our backyard.

A few days later we explored the vicinity of the cistern, and then saw the house that must have been next to it. It lay on the other side of the ridge, apparently blown there by a hurricane. Except for a few bad floorboards, which allowed us to look inside, the house was in excellent condition. Looking at it more closely, we found it had been built with wooden pins. Instead of a door and drop shutters, there was a clever arrangement of sliding door and shutters, all parts made of wood.

"The craftsmanship that has gone into this house shows that it was made by an expert ship's carpenter for those he loved," Russ said.

Going towards home, he picked up a small floating can and found some shellac in it. "Now I have what I need. I don't want to discard that cane after putting in all that work."

Some linseed oil was in the house when we got there. I'll put a French finish on it and coat the surface. Then, if we need it, we'll have a cane."

Getting a rag, he put the oil on it, added some shellac and started rubbing. I noticed that it seemed to get harder to rub and offered to take my turn.

"Not now, I'll finish this; I have to rub faster now to set it up. You can start on another side while I rest my elbow."

When it came my turn, I found out what he meant—your elbow gets hot. I was glad to let him finish it for me.

Now that we had gotten rid of the mosquitoes we still had

the sandflies. No way to eliminate them. To protect ourselves from them in the house, we oiled the screens and burned pyrethrum powder in a burner Russ had made with a pumice base and slotted coconut shell top. When we had to go out, we applied Vicks salve to exposed areas. Eventually we discovered a screen paint that kept most of them outside. Mothballs dissolved in kerosene helped keep these *flying teeth* out.

Fiddler

CHAPTER TWENTY

Freeze. Step on Spike. Huge and Miniature Fish.
Effects of Gasoline. Ants in My Pants.

The morning we had picked to go by boat and pick up our
stacks of dock lumber was quite cool. Russ was dressed as
usual, but at his suggestion I was wearing two pairs of his woolen
pants. Locking the padlock and putting the key into my pocket,
I followed him to the dock.

Towing the high-sided skiff, we went down to the first pile
of dock boards, anchored and went ashore in the skiff. With
these aboard, we went to the boat, loaded them, and motored
down-beach to the next pile. The wind had quite a bite to it now,
but I was quite comfortable.

Going ashore for the next pile of boards was pleasant. The
bushes broke the wind and the sun was quite warm on shore. We
went down-beach a way to explore and found a large ship's ladder and a wide plank. Here was the wide gangplank we needed.
With the wide board on it, the ship's ladder would serve nicely.
At that time, it was possible to find almost any type of lumber on
the beach.

Loading this pile aboard weighed the skiff down and we had
to move it farther out into the water to finish. We got wet
halfway to our knees in doing this, but the water seemed warm.

The powerboat was still afloat when we got there, but by the
time we had put the ship's ladder on top the pile, it was aground.
Now the tide was really going out fast. We returned the ladder to
the skiff, but it made no difference—still aground!

"Tie the skiff to the stern. I'll push the boat off and let the

209

tide take us out to deeper water. We'll have to tow that barge the way it is, in spite of the fact that it will surely make trouble for us when we try to go in the narrow channel. The wind will take it sideways and pull us with it."

He climbed aboard then and I had started the motor a few minutes afterwards. The sun was four o'clock low and no longer warm. He was thoroughly soaked and started shivering. Halfway home now I hadn't succeeded in getting him to take off his wet pants and put on a pair of my dry ones. When his teeth started chattering, I draped the pants around his neck, tying the legs under his chin. The seat of the pants protected his back from the wind and he settled down to shivering instead of shuddering. I got colder just watching him.

The skiff was dog-walking off sideways, and when we finally turned left into the cut, it pulled the stern of the boat towards the shallows. We went aground, lengthwise; the tide was still going out and it would be two hours before it reached its present level on the incoming tide. It didn't enter our minds to anchor the skiff and go ashore. Later we wished we had.

While getting the sculling oar from the pile of lumber on the boat, he went aground again. When the same thing happened the third time, high tide was an hour closer. It was a dark, moonless night and Russ, almost warm from his exertions, decided we had to wait for high tide.

Fiddler was on the dock just crying. He never liked to be left alone and sounded quite bitter as he now added a warble to his barking. Telling him to wait, we'd be there soon, Russell started shuddering again. His teeth began chattering so badly he could hardly cuss the skiff.

Knowing we would be warmer if we lay down next to the partially warm motor, I suggested that. He told me to do that, but I refused, and he finally allowed himself to he pushed down and against it. I got the canvas motor cover to put over us and lay down on him. We held the edges of the canvas against the motor and the deck to keep out the wind and managed to get a bit warmer.

He finally stopped shuddering. We relaxed enough to fall asleep and were awakened by the rocking of the boat. The tide had shifted. We were now in the cut, hanging on the anchor line.

"Charlotte, before we get out into the cold again, we had better decide who does what. I think it best if, the minute we push the canvas aside, you go forward and pull the anchor. I'll start the motor and have us at the dock by the time you get the anchor aboard. You'll be right in position to tie the bow line. I'll tie the stern, and we'll run right up to the house. The skiff will be all right where it is. I didn't know it could get this cold in Florida! Keep moving or you won't be able to! Now!"

It went like clockwork, and we ran up the path with Fiddler. He had greeted us as though we had been gone a week.

Reaching the house, we were again in the full force of the biting wind and I reached into my pocket for the house key–it wasn't there. It had been in the pocket of the pair of pants Russ was wearing for shawl, and I turned to him, searching for it in those upside down pockets. No key!

Chattering out some choice cusses, he went out back and climbed the water tank, from there to the roof, and breaking out a screen, he entered the house. Second thoughts, he told me later, caused him to go back out and lower all the shutters before going back inside.

These exertions had helped him warm up a bit, but I had been stupid enough to sit on the doorstep. When he called me from the back door, I couldn't move. He helped me up and into the house. I took one step inside and fell the rest of the way, too damn cold to move or care what happened next. He helped me again and in the living room draped one of the rag rugs over my shoulders and started the fire.

Hot cocoa was soon ready, and we only burned our mouths on the first cup. It cooled quickly. Fiddler lapped up his share gratefully. We all had three cups each.

"Shake out all the rugs, all but one will go on our bed, that's Fiddler's! Take them up and get our extra clothes to put on the bed. All but the whites. I'm going down to get the motor cover, we need it more than the motor does!" Then he ran out in his wet clothes!

I finished in time to go out and help him button the downstairs shutters down. This would keep out the wind, at least, and make it a bit warmer inside. We shared another pot of cocoa, and draping the rug over Fiddler, we went up the ladder.

211

We nearly froze as we changed into dry clothes, then put the motor cover on the bed and our wet clothes on top. We managed to crawl in under all those substitute blankets and were soon warm enough to go to sleep. The temperatures dropped to the low thirties that night.

We awakened to a most astonishing sight. The windows were frosted over and we could see our breath. Russ got up and rubbed a clear spot in the window. "Get up and look!"

When I reluctantly did, I saw many fish lying along the shoreline, and the shallows off shore from them were thick with more! All sizes, including sharks up to five feet in length.

"Did the cold kill them?"

"Not actually, they are cold-blooded. When the temperature goes down, it makes them sluggish and they lose their sense of balance, then they are at the mercy of the wind and tide."

We lost no time in putting on several more layers of clothing that we fished out from under the motor cover. Breakfast came next. We were empty. The pancakes cooled before we could eat them.

"There are a lot of saleable fish out there. We'll gather them in burlap bags and tie them in the water at the dock. They will stay alive."

Getting bags from the back porch, we went out into the bright sunlight and found that it wasn't warm. The wind had a saw edge. "Come see what I found in the seaweed. This trumpet fish is only three inches long, and look at this tiny barracuda."

We filled our bags with many large snappers of both varieties and taking some empty bags along, went to the dock. There he showed me some rare sea snakes. Throwing those into the bushes so they would die, he explained that they were poisonous.

We both found more miniature fish, including a real treasure, a three-inch sailfish, its sail spread.

"We'll sun dry these little things," Russ said. He then put them about four feet off the ground on the slanting trunk of a large tree, and again started to gather fish.

I moved ahead of him so as to have different territory to work in. After filling my third bag, I wandered farther, just looking. I wasn't too warm, my feet were getting numb. Seeing a huge red snapper drifting towards shore, I grabbed it by the tail and pulled it in. It was at least as long as I was. Lifting its head and putting part of the bag under it then tugging and tugging, I managed to get it almost completely into the bag. The large tail was still out when the head reached the bottom of the sack. I started in the direction of the dock. The large flapping tail made me hold my head sideways. The loose mesh of the bag caught on everything and I spent a lot of time getting it untangled. A bit tired, I went some ten feet without snagging anything. Then, I stepped on a long spike that protruded from a 2 by 4–my foot wasn't too cold to feel that!

When the first wave of pain had passed, I opened my eyes, and looking down, saw that about two inches of spike was sticking out the topside of my shoe. Only then did I drop the fish and call Russ, knowing he was over a hundred feet from me. When he said, "What do you want?" instead of "I'm coming," my feelings were hurt and I yelled, "Nothing. Dammit."

I hadn't moved until then, but now I grabbed at some of the bushes near me for balance and lifted my foot. I mean, tried to lift it. Nothing moved but my flesh. Another wave of pain, then I sat down, put my good foot on the board and tugged the other off the spike. Russ was anxiously calling me now and I hurt too much to open my mouth and answer him.

Finally I was able to breathe more naturally and called, "Here." Then by grabbing the bushes, I managed to stand up and went towards the path. By now I was wet with perspiration and getting colder. I almost bumped into him when I reached the path.

"Why in hell didn't you answer me. When you called me you didn't sound disturbed and I was looking at a baby swordfish I had just found. Why did you call?"

In answer, I pointed at my foot. By now a puddle of blood was seeping out from under it and the top was bloody, too.

"Wow! It must have been a big spike to do that. I'll carry you to the house."

My feelings still hurt and I said, "No thanks!"

"I guess you're right at that. Walk and make it bleed. The blood might carry out some of the rust you got in it." With his arm around me to improve my balance, he helped me limp to the house. Many magnified minutes later, we got there. Helping me to the first bedroom, he told me to lie down on my face and left to get some things to dress my wounds.

Chatting during this period, he explained that he needed a probe and was going to get my largest darning needle, sterilize it, and look for rust flakes in the entry point on the sole of my foot before he disinfected and bandaged it.

Supplies on a chair by the bed, he told me to lift my foot so he could take the shoelace out. He did this so gently it did not add to the pain.

"Now," he said, "grab hold of the mattress. If I snatch off your shoe and sock, it will hurt less."

I felt that pain clear up to my ear tips. Then he lowered my foot to the mattress.

"Hang on now, I'm going to probe."

The blood seemed to be surging in my ears now, but I heard him triumphantly announce sometime later, "I got several flakes of rust, but I would like to explore a bit more if you think you can stand it. I don't think I'll have to probe in the top of your foot. How about it?"

In short bursts, I managed to say, "If-you-have-to-yes."

Many star-spangled minutes–could have been seconds–later, he said, "I'm satisfied there are no more rust flakes in there, and it is bleeding freely. "I'll just blot it up and–"

When he gripped my foot so firmly, and it hurt more, I should have expected something. It was when he poured the alcohol into the wound, I learned the meaning of a description I had only read, *exquisite* pain. I didn't quite hit the ceiling, but I do believe I came close to it. I yowled and I only managed to stop when he applied pads of gauze with Oil of Sol on them, wrapped the foot loosely and put a new white cotton sock on.

"Now sit up and put your shoe on. I'll get the cane. You must walk on it today or you won't be able to tomorrow. Don't lace it tightly! Look here!" He picked up a few more rust flakes from the bloody towel and put them with others on a clean handkerchief. "Sit still a few minutes, I'll be back." He took the handkerchief with him.

I waited and thought–that sort of thing is more exhausting than working was.

214

Russ returned and said, "I examined the flakes on the board and the spike. I'm more content now because I am sure they are all accounted for."

I was just one big ache when he helped me outside while insisting that I move and *try* to put some weight on the foot. Down at the tide line, I began looking for tiny fish there. Stirring the weed with my cane, I found some. Using my cane then to balance, I picked them up and put them into my jacket pocket.

Russ came back dragging a large dead fish, then cut it up to cook for duck food. Moving even as slowly as I now did, I was warmer than I had been in the house.

"We'll have to move the wood stove inside the back porch for tonight. I'll start that as soon as it cools off when the duck food is done. Take it easy now, I'm going down-beach to get some boards to slide it on."

He returned with four boards and found the fish cooked, so he put it in the duck trough and cleaned out the fire box of the stove. While that cooled, he measured the size and height of the stovepipe where it bent at the joint. At the back of the porch he cut a round hole in the shutter and the screen.

Now, he helped me inside, and brought out a chair. When I sat down, he handed me a pile of burlap bags and told me to rip the seams and open them, he was going to *paper* the walls to keep some of the heat in.

He split up some thin boxes to use as slats for nailing. Now the stove was cold, and using the boards as slides, he pushed it towards the door. I helped lift it up and into the porch and he did the rest. Once the pipe was installed, he lit the fire again. My cane came in handy now for holding up the bags so he could put the slats over and nail them.

Top pieces fastened, be sent me in to start supper. Corned beef hash would be the easiest. I couldn't balance well enough to prepare this in the kitchen, so I brought the things to the table and worked there. I put everything in the Dutch oven and left the peelings for Russ to take care of. My foot was giving me fits now.

"I'll put the dinner on to cook," Russ said. "Now, you go out and walk at least a block. You must keep the foot flexible. I'll finish the papering job."

It was colder than hate in the dining room and I did get slightly warmer *walking* around outside. I was pleasantly surprised on my return to the porch to find it several degrees warmer. Russ had put on the coffeepot, and when I sat down in the chair near the stove, he draped one of our army blankets on it and wrapped it around me, and started out.

"I'll get enough firewood on this trip so I won't have to get any more before breakfast!"

By leaning over the stove I got a bit warmer, from the top down towards my waist.

When he returned with the wood, he lit the lantern after first fastening a four-foot wire on the handle. "Mustn't scorch the roof!" Hanging it on a handy nail on the rafters, he brought out our other chair and with the blanket was soon cozy. The room looked warmer now, but when I put my fingers on the Dutch oven to warm them, they weren't uncomfortable. Every few minutes Russ would heckle me into flexing my sore foot. It seemed to hurt more each time, but I noticed a surprising thing–the pain seemed to make me feel warmer!

When the food was ready, Russ got the silverware and plates. The plates felt icy and the food cooled immediately, so we put it back into the kettle and ate from there. Our cups on the stove kept the coffee warm.

We let the fire burn down so we wouldn't have to worry about it and the food on the stove, just put the lid on. Too cold tonight for the bugs.

"I'll put the plates in the sink. When I return, you be ready to stand up, go into the house, and up the ladder."

With my cane, I had managed to stand when he returned. Snatching our blankets off the chair, he was at the door in time to help me up that step and into the house. At the ladder, he boosted me up and put my good foot two steps up. He held me as I grabbed a higher rung and pulled myself up onto the bedroom floor. I took off my shoes while he spread the blankets, and I crawled under everything.

When he returned after feeding Fiddler and settling him for the night, he brought up some of our hoarded newspapers. The light from the lantern on the dining table shone up through the open trap door and I saw he had also brought up some clean ban-

216

dages and other things. In spite of my protests, he used a flashlight and checked my wounds. I managed to keep quiet while he did what was necessary, then I exhaled and it was a very visible breath.

"Now, would you get up and help me put these newspapers under the mattress?"

"Why?"

"They will shut out more cold than an extra couple of blankets on top, and we don't have those."

I managed to hold the folded-back mattress while he spread the papers. Finished with that, we remade the bed. I was going to climb in, he insisted we undress and put on clean long underwear. "We'll rest better than we did last night."

The next morning, a degree or two warmer, he told me to stay in bed until he had breakfast started at which time he would come up and get the blankets for our chairs. Then I should get dressed and hurry down.

When it came time, I managed by sliding over the edge of the bed, and using my arms, I got down to find he had put my cane near the ladder. My foot was very stiff now, but I managed, and hopped down the step into the porch, over to my chair.

We ate our grits and scrambled eggs out of the pans on the stovetop and kept our cups warm on the stove. I wanted to sit there after breakfast, but I was in for another wound dressing. Moving the Coleman lantern near my foot, Russ unwrapped the dressing and without warning fiercely pinched both top and bottom wounds at the same time. When I asked why he had hurt me so much, he said, "I had to squeeze them to see if there was any matter in them. There isn't any. It will heal all right, so don't worry." Strange, I hadn't even thought of the possibility of infection.

More alcohol. When it dried, more Oil of Sol, and I could breathe again.

"Now I'll take care of the dishes. You put your shoe and sock back on and be ready to go out with me when I return."

"I'd rather sit here and read."

"No! You *must* exercise that foot. Even if the spike most fortunately went between your bones, it damaged some muscles and you have to exercise."

217

He helped me move until I could do so without losing my balance, then I went again to the shoreline and looked for small fish. He went down and unloaded the skiff and powerboat. Stacking the lumber on the dock, he replaced the gangplank with the ship's ladder on which he placed the board.

When he returned, he took the fish I had and put them on a leaning tree near the house and went to get the potato rakes he had brought to the island some time before. I never could figure out what use they would be. Today they more than paid for themselves.

"Should I use these as crutches?"

"Well, you can try them if you want, but I have another use for them. Follow me and see."

I tried to use them by swinging on them, putting my good foot forward. They were too long to use as crutches. My arms soon became too tired, and some warmer now, I asked for my cane, which he had been carrying. We swapped and I arrived to find he had put the skiff bow on shore so I could sit on it and swing into it.

Aboard now, I looked at the water. It was a startling sight! Fish of all kinds and sizes were being swept by the tide through the cut. They were lying on one side with the fin of the other waving in the air.

He sculled out and dropped anchor. I watched him for a minute, then copied his actions as he raked fish near the boat and got them. This was a lazy fisherman's heaven! Before long, I was as efficient as he was and we had so many fish on the bottom of the boat, he was afraid they would die. He took them to the dock where he prepared many apple boxes with pieces of burlap partially nailed over the tops and short lines nailed to them. These he filled and tied to the dock stringers. With the crawfish car and the fish trap also solidly packed, we had *quite a bait of fish*.

Four burlap bags were soon filled. Even sitting down, my foot had gotten a good deal of exercise and was more flexible now. Russ helped me ashore and I wobbled sedately to the house under my own power. Seems as though it took some time. When I arrived there, he had the fire going and the rest of the hash from the night before was almost warm.

Wrapped in our blankets again, we were soon eating. When

we finished, Russ again needled me into walking and we arrived about the same time at the slanting tree trunk in front of the house—just in time to see Fiddler perched there, securely as any cat. He was just reaching for the last little dried fish. He chewed on it with his eyes closed, a most pleased expression on his face. He looked puzzled and hurt when we fussed at him. Why all that excitement when there were so many larger fish on the beach?

We got a few more fish and put them on a cross-piece of the water tank, hoping they would be safe.

The next morning almost the same as yesterday, more fish gathered, large and miniature. The second batch of tiny fish were gone. Fiddler again. He must have decided that we were putting them there for him. How in hell had he learned to climb like a cat?

Wound redressed I went out again. It was a bit warmer today.

"Tomorrow I'll take the fish in to sell at the market," Russ said. "The ones we have might die if I wait any longer. I'll have enough room in the boat for a few more burlap bags full. Let's rake them in."

We gathered more fish, and again supper was ready when I got to the house.

After a daylight breakfast, Russ went to load the fish. Returning, he put on dry clothes, got more wood for the fire and told me I could sit and read until he got back. I was happy to do that. When he returned around the middle of the afternoon, he brought back, among other things, a copy of the *Miami Herald*. There were many colored pictures in it. These showed the results of THE BIG FREEZE, as it was called. Those taken in The Exotic Gardens were the most amazing. They had turned on their mist-sprinklers in an effort to save the many subtropical trees and plants. The result was not what they had hoped, but a spectacular frozen waterfall through which one could see the brilliant flowers and the many plants and trees. One item in the paper told of a ten-foot reef shark near the Bahia Honda Bridge. [A record low temperature of 30° was set December 12, 1934, in Miami at midnight—ed.]

"My first thought," Russ said," was to get more long underwear. Using Everett's phone I called all the major stores. No luck.

I went to get groceries, and the men all looked funny. I looked again and I saw why. It was a bit unusual seeing pajama pants showing below the pants of otherwise well-dressed men. Their pajama pants differed only in color and length. Everyone was wearing them."

"One man was wearing a Yankee topcoat, and I heard him refuse many fantastic offers for it."

During supper that night we were almost comfortable enough to remove our blankets. It was quite a bit warmer the next morning. During breakfast Russ said, "I want to go to the flats on the west end of the cut today to look at a large drum I saw there yesterday."

On our way we saw it was still there, but in a position so we couldn't reach it with the powerboat. The wind was too strong to go by skiff, so if Russ wanted to get it he had to wade over. Taking one end of a line, which he had fastened to the stern, he waded towards the drum with a large wrench in his hand. It was deep in the water, and the vent was under water. With the vent on top, he rolled it towards the boat and used the wrench to open it. Tilting the drum a bit caused a cold liquid to flow out. He put his hand in it and said, "It's too cold to tell by the odor what it is." Then he tasted it quickly and plunged his hand into the water. "Wow! My hand is freezing–it's white gasoline!" He replaced and tightened the screw top, put the rope around the drum and secured it, and waded to the boat, soaking wet again! I started the motor, but he took the tiller, "It requires special knowledge to tow a full drum. If you go too fast, it will sound and pull the stern under."

I watched and learned. He found the exact speed needed, and we slowly gained against the tide. "You tie it; I'm freezing."

Soon he came back with dry clothes on, still shivering–but not shuddering–with cold. He gave me one of his rare compliments for the way I had tied the drum so that it had drifted ashore near the east end of the dock where it was very shallow.

Then he said, "Untie the rope and throw it when I get near the drum."

I did. I went slowly down the gangplank to help. Our combined weight didn't equal that of the drum, but we managed to get it into shallower water, and using boards to pry with, got it up on dry land. By that time, my foot ached up to my eyebrows. I sat down and rested for a time, almost freezing my bottom.

"I'd like to see how it works in the stove," Russ said. "I'll siphon some out." He did, and put it into a two-gallon can that had held oil. Then I was shocked to see him slosh it around and pour it out over his toolbox. Being so conscious of carrying everything we needed for such a long distance, I was startled, but he said it would keep his tools from getting rusty. Starting the siphon again, he filled the can, boosted me to my feet, and we went up to the house. There I was amazed to see an almost invisible blue flame on the burner. It also burned better in my cigarette lighter than the lighter fluid.

Now to try it in our trash barrel, a metal drum with an open top and holes chiseled near the bottom for ventilation. It was full of tin cans, boxes and other things. Why tin cans? They rust and disintegrate more quickly if heated first. He got out the cracked cup we used for measuring, filled it to the usual level, poured it over the contents of the drum, and tossed in a lighted kitchen match. It didn't burn—it went whoosh! Some two hours later we had managed to gather up all the trash that had been in the drum. Almost all—Russ was on the main house roof nudging things off onto the ground. Perversely, every tin can that had been in the drum had landed upright on the higher bedroom roof. Strangely, all this happened silently. We had been very startled, and then, very busy.

Russ dropped down off the roof, grinned and said, "Wonderful gasoline! Complete vapor explosion. Let's try it in the boat!" The trip from Miami had left the tank almost empty so Russ filled it. We were getting ready to start when we saw an extremely large fish drifting into the cut. He ran to the house to get his lily-iron rig. I managed to keep an eye on the fish. It rolled over a little, almost got its balance, and headed towards the ocean.

"Now, you handle the motor, and for gosh sakes, don't make any quick stops or starts. I've been wet and freezing once today." He went forward and stood on the bow deck, poised to throw the lily-iron. As we got near the fish, he identified it as edible, a blackfish. It was as long as the boat. It managed to dodge when he threw the weapon. Each time, I slowly approached and

221

maneuvered the boat near it, it darted away. It was an interesting game, and the fish did seem to be tiring. The sun was warming up the air today for a change and it was pleasant.

After wobbling a bit when I changed speed, Russ had grabbed the bow line as a balancing aid. He was poised at all times, ready to throw at his target. I was again slowly closing the distance between us. "This time I'll get him, slowly now, only ten feet more—"

You guessed it—we ran out of gas. A full tank lasted for five hours. Where had that time gone? We looked towards shore for the first time since leaving the dock, Russ said, "We are about five miles out now and it is almost six o'clock, judging by the sun. No moon tonight. And I left the damn sculling oar ashore, just a skiff oar aboard now. Oh well, it's a good thing we have the sound of Fiddler's barking to guide us ashore later. Otherwise, we would have to try and drop anchor and spend a very cool night out here. I'm afraid we don't have enough line to reach bottom here. Thank God we put the motor cover back on board before we left this morning."

Russ held the oar between his knees and with line from the lily-iron rig bunched a piece of canvas and fastened it to the end of the oar, stretching the canvas, then he did the same thing further down. Clamping the oar blade between his legs he sat on the stern steering. We took turns in holding the canvas extended into the little breeze.

Sailing slowly home with our little spit of a sail, we discussed various methods of handling the large fish had we managed to capture it. None of them would have been possible. "Do you know that fish weighed between fifteen hundred and two thousand pounds. We couldn't possibly have used it all for bait or duck food."

In the small hours of the morning, we finally reached the dock. Fiddler was in ecstasy. We thanked him and let him kiss us. Without him, we would have gone ashore somewhere, but not to the dock!

The white coral of the path looked fairly bright as we followed it to the house. Fid kept telling us how abused he had been and kept bumping into me. Russ had to help me balance.

From our emergency supplies we made an easy supper.

"It is utterly stupid to take the sculling oar out of the boat. The first time we needed it, we didn't have it. From now on it stays in at all times."

It was very pleasant to awaken to summer weather again the next day. A bit windy but not too cool. Now I could take our clothing off the bed and put it back on the shelves. I was getting the washing together when Russ came in and said that we would have a squall around noon and it would be more logical to work on the dock. I cut the boards to the proper lengths while he placed the pilings and stringers. We started to nail them, and I hurt my hand.

Throwing the saw ashore for safety now, Russ said, "We'll only have time to put one nail in a board and anchor them against the wind. Lay down on the loose boards and hang on when it gets here. There is a lot of wind and rain in it."

In trying to hurry now, my hand suffered more. I could hardly hold the nails to get them started. The wind picked up considerably, and we didn't want to lose those boards now that we were at last using them. The hammer got heavier, I got clumsier. Then the squall hit and I put the hammer down and spread my weight on the loose boards near me. It started to rain. Now that my hand wasn't being beaten, my foot hurt worse. I noticed it for the first time in quite a while.

"Hang on to the stringers!"

I did, and turned my head from the beating rain. It was a wicked squall for the short time it lasted. When it slacked off a little, it was much colder.

"I'll finish nailing these boards. You go to the house before the next squall hits."

I hurried along but when the next squall hit, I looked back to see him lying on the dock still nailing boards.

The next day we put in all the necessary nails. My oversized hand made it difficult to hold them but I was so careful that I didn't hurt it. Everything went smoothly.

As our addition to the dock was larger and stronger than the original, people preferred to tie to it. It was on the west end of the original. A bushy tree there kept one from seeing the boat at the dock when you looked from the house. It annoyed me!

The days seemed to blend with each other, and we were arguing as to whether it was Saturday or Sunday when we heard the motor of our usual nice weekend visitors. For some days now, I had been asking Russ to cut the tree down. We needed to see who it was at the dock! I didn't bother looking that morning. I knew I couldn't see through that damn tree anyway.

I hurried into better clothes, my whites, and went down to say hello. There were eight in the party this time and Mr. Fossey said that four of them would spend the night at the house. We had planned on conch stew so increased the amount of ingredients so we could share with them. Supper that night was a community affair–we ate their steaks and they ate our stew. They played bridge for a while and then went to bed.

With supplies from the yacht, we had bacon and eggs for breakfast. After a short visit, they went down to fish, saying that they planned to leave around noon.

We gathered some limes for our guests and around noon went down with them. The dock was crowded as they were doing some last minute fishing there. We stood on shore, me with my cane in hand, feeling quite jaunty. Suddenly I felt a fierce bite on my thigh. A red ant! I looked at my white pants–nothing. But my shoes had a wide stream of ants that disappeared from my sight as they climbed my high-top shoes. As anyone who knows about fire ants will tell you, they are very well organized when they make a sneak attack. As many as a hundred of the little stinkers will get into position, then the leader gives a signal and they all bite at once. That happened then.

I hop-darted towards the bushy tree, now grateful that it was there. I took off my pants and started to brush off the ants. When I unbuttoned the top of Russ' boxer shorts, which I was again wearing, I heard a roar of laughter. Now I realized that there had been a few minutes of silence before this. They weren't laughing at me–the tree was bushy enough. I couldn't see them–how could they see me? Just in case though, I re-buttoned my pants and clawed at the ants under them. Scratching bites, killing ants, fluttering my shorts to dislodge others, stomping my feet all the time, including the sore one. I might have looked funny enough–if they could see me. But they continued to laugh.

When I heard Russell's delighted laughter coming closer, I

turned toward him. He was laughing so hard, he couldn't talk. Finally he said, "Look!" and pointed towards the bottom of the tree.

I did. I saw that I was protected from the view of anyone on the dock—from my waist up! I turned my back on the spectators and continued to search for ants. I was hurting. And, really furious!

He managed to stop laughing long enough to tell them that I had been after him for some time to cut the tree down, and he had finally trimmed it early that morning as a surprise for me. It really was!

CHAPTER TWENTY-ONE

Introducing "Wilbur." Russ Makes Bearing and
Yarb Medicine. Russ Cures Don's Poisonwood.
Don's Prohibition Days Stories. Zigzag Path.
I Bring Mumps to Russ. Make Bamboo Beastie.

We were near the dock the next day when we heard a powerful motor on the ocean side. It seemed to be coming
towards the cut. I hurried down to the dock. The shallow, narrow entrance to the cut from that end wasn't used by sizeable
boats except at high tide. It was about medium now. Some
stranger was arriving. As I passed beyond the bushes, I saw a pretty Hacker-craft sedan, 26 feet long, towing an 18-foot skiff. He
veered from where I knew the channel to be, towards the dock
on a straight line, at full speed.

A man handling a new and unfamiliar toy would do that! I
waved him out, but he accepted my directional wave as a saluta-
tion. He kept on in the same direction at the same speed. This
would take him directly over top of a sunken motor near the
shallows; he might hit it and rip his bottom out!

He kept heading in at full speed and had to make a turnout
to avoid the dock. This took him a few feet from it, fortunately
for our boat. He cut his motor then, didn't throw a line, and
drifted beyond the dock before he stopped coasting. The man in
the skiff almost fell out as he threw himself forward through the
clutter of things there, in an effort to push against the stern of the
Hacker-craft to keep the heavy bow of the skiff from ramming a
hole in that pretty little boat. He fell forward at the bow and
managed to push the skiff sideways, toward our boat. It went for-

227

ward now and bumped the side of the Hacker-craft, audibly.

"That man is an utter damn fool. He is probably looking for the brake pedals now." Russ had arrived.

The man in the boat started his motor again and drove the man in the skiff slightly batty as he tried to hold the skiff from contact with the Hacker-craft as it reversed, then went forward again towards the dock in back of our boat.

Russ reached over, took the bow line from its place and tied it. An older man came out of the cabin towards the stern and threw a rope to Russ. He watched as Russ fastened it. Then he said, "Will that hold it?"

"If the rope is strong enough, that same method will hold a battleship." Apparently he was not familiar with the loop-over-loop method of tying.

Boy, what a caravan that was. Everything was new. In the skiff were three 20-gallon garbage cans, various paper cartons and bags of food. On the floor, visible to the eye, were shovels, axes, machetes, and a thing I found out later was a post-hole digger. For a coral rock area! Another strange-looking thing was a wire-stretcher. What was *not* visible and figured greatly in their future plans was a transit. The price tags were still on most of these items.

Later we found out that the garbage cans were full of an assortment of canned goods and bottled spring water. The contents of both boats included everything that any greenhorn considered necessary for camping.

The skipper of the Hacker-craft introduced himself–I will call him "Wilbur," because, to the best of our knowledge, he is still alive. He was a very nice-looking man, a blue-eyed blond with impeccable manners. He appeared to be in his thirties. His build was medium, he was a bit over six feet tall, and his muscular development was about that of the average librarian.

With Wilbur in his boat was a small white-haired man who was introduced as "Pop." We never heard any other name for him. He was the cook for this group. The man who so deftly managed the skiff in this fiasco was introduced also. Knowing he is now dead, I will give his right name, Donald Bowen. He was about five feet, nine inches tall; he was heavy-built, but not a blimp. He appeared to be a friendly soul with many laugh wrinkles around his blue eyes. Those and his nose were about all you could see of his face because of a black bushy beard. His voice was low and resonant, very pleasant.

Wilbur got out of the boat then, and said, "I bought a piece of land down the island a ways. It is near something called "Billy's Point." There is a survey marker just on one end of my land; if you know where it is, will you show it to me?"

"Yes, I know where it is," Russ said. " You just follow me, but slowly. The channel is tricky so you turn exactly where I do. Not when, but where!"

We took Fiddler with us, and it was a treat for him. Mostly we left him home to guard the house.

Wilbur followed closely and did the right things. I told Russ, then, we had better give the man a few instructions about water travel.

"I was thinking of that guy trying to get through that twisty channel by himself. I'd better show him how to tell shallow water from deep. He acted as though the boat should be able to go any place he saw water, without thinking about how deep it is. I'll bet this is his first time in a boat."

The point we were looking for was about four miles down. Russ signaled Wilbur to cut his motor, and going ashore, he grounded our bow there and verified the marker number on Wilbur's deed. "Throw out your anchor. This is the place."

Pop got into the skiff with Don and they rowed ashore. Unloading the skiff, they returned to take more equipment from the Hacker-craft. During this time Russ had put our boat along-side Wilbur's and was telling him how to tell water depth by the color. Further conversation was airy. In fact, in all the time we knew him, he never told us anything that had a bearing on his occupation or anything else personal except that he was from Boston. He was a master of small talk. As they talked, I watched the men unload some firewood (of all the ridiculous things to bring to that area). The skiff was again loaded, with tents, gasoline stove and other things. As they left to go ashore, Wilbur said, "I'm not used to roughing it, do you have a spare bed? I brought some food."

"Of course, just follow us home."

Wilbur called to the men, "See you later."

When he got to the dock, Russ and I tied both boats. Wilbur stayed aboard for a few minutes and then slid a large metal box out from under the seat. "Russ please come aboard and give me a hand. This is a bit too much for me to handle."

Russ did, and emerged from the cabin carrying the box. Wilbur explained they were his personal supplies. "Wait a minute, I'll get my linen." Apparently he had planned to stay with us! We didn't know at that time that he had his own grapevine.

Opening that box at the house, he brought out six small steaks and other luxuries which we cooked for supper. We had some of his cold drinks while this was cooking. Everything in the box was in threes or could be divided that way.

He was a pleasant person and welcome company. During the evening, he told us his favorite joke, something about four Harvard graduates who had planned a reunion ten years after their graduation. He also mentioned that he hated to wear socks and whenever possible, as now, he wore his shirttails out. I guess it was in retaliation for having to be such a well-dressed young man during his youth.

During breakfast with more of his supplies, he told us that he would be back in a few days with more supplies and would like it if he could leave *his* bed made up. "The men have orders to clear some land and build me a fishing cottage."

After Wilbur left, Russ asked me if I had heard some of the odd sounds the motor had made the day before.

"No."

"It sounded to me as though it needs a new bearing—sort of ragged! You run the boat alone a good bit of the time now, and it would be a good idea for you to learn what makes it tick. You tear the motor down, I'll only help when it's necessary."

"Good, I have always wanted to mess with machinery and no one would ever let me. I'll put on my oldest clothes. Hey, second thoughts! What good will it do to tear down a motor to replace a bearing that we don't have?"

"Never mind—wait and see!"

He freed up the bolts so I could manage and supervised my work for a bit and went off. He returned with a can of kerosene. "Drop all the little things in here. We have to wash them before reassembling the motor." Helping me remove the motor head, he pointed at the items I was to remove from the motor, and let me struggle. When the parts were removed and washed with some kerosene on the dock, we saw that he was right. The bearing was bad.

"You go beachcombing; I need a piece of Spanish cedar at least four inches square. After you find it, bring it along to the dock and scrape the carbon off these motor parts."

It had been days since I had gathered Spanish cedar for my outside cooking stove, the remains of the kerosene stove, so I found quite a bit and finally got a piece the size he wanted. Putting the rest on the porch, I returned to the dock. I had heard an occasional dull thumping sound while I was searching and wondered what it was. Now I saw what caused it.

Russ was in the water, chest deep and was raising a large hammer-like thing for another blow. With a grunt, he brought it down on the sunken motor Wilbur had come so close to wrecking his boat on. He was in the process of breaking it apart.

As he stood there for a few minutes waiting for the murky water to clear, he threw the hammer thing ashore, and reaching down into the water, he came up with his hands full. "This should be enough."

I looked at the junk in his hands, "Enough for what?"

"For the bearing I'm going to make."

"Where did that hammer thing come from?"

"It's a railroad spike maul. More usually though it's called a *John Henry*." I found it under the dock.

"How come a maul is to have a people name?"

"The name came from a legendary figure who, according to the story, could out-work any ten-man track crew in laying track, moving railroad ties, or setting spikes."

When he handed me the scraper then, I passed over the piece of cedar. Looking at that black greasy mess, I decided to wash it off *me*, rather than my clothes. It was pleasant working in the late afternoon sun–then the sandflies hit. I was miserable for a few minutes while I washed enough of the stuff off my hands so I could use the kerosene to get them clean enough to carry my clothes to the house. I made real good time on my way there.

While I made supper, Russ worked on the cedar on the back

porch. He had sawed it in half and was doing a bit of rough carving on the inside of the pieces.

At the dock the next morning, I got the other piston out while he did some carbon scraping for me. I watched and was amazed at how effortlessly he did this. Finally, handing the piston to him, I returned to the scraping, and while I tried to do as he had done, I didn't have much success so I just kept chipping until it was done.

He sat on the dock and did some more carving on the cedar pieces, occasionally fitting the cleaned piston into one or the other of the pieces. No micrometer available, just eye measurements.

"I'm finished now. I'm going to wash."

"Wait a minute, I'll look! Well, it's better than I expected. Go ahead and wash. I'll finish it later." This was the sort of backwards compliment he often gave me.

I was making sandwiches when he came up and lit the stove. "Get the big cast-iron skillet on and set it on this flame, I'll get the metal." He returned with an empty coffee can, poured water off the metal pieces in the bottom, and set them on the door step to drain.

"Why did you put that junk in water?"

"To leach the salt out. That 'junk' is going to be our new bearing. Now, hold the door open and stand aside. This will sizzle for a minute." He put the junk into my very hot frying pan. Boy! "Now, come on out and hold this piece steady for me." I did and he chipped off the remains of the old bearing.

"Go in and watch now. Let me know when that Babbitt is melted." I looked out and saw him sanding the inside of the pieces with pumice. Soon he had them looking like a mold. Now he went to the radio cabinet on the back porch and returned with wire, just as I called to tell him that the junk was now liquid.

Bracing the door open, he came in and with a hot pad, grabbed the handle, and took it outside. There he took a straight piece of wood and tilting the pan a bit, he scraped off the fuzzy top. As it hit the sand it sizzled. Back inside he put it on the fire again and said, "Give me a hand now."

He carefully positioned the part of the piston into the pieces.

I held them while he wired them together.

"Go watch the Babbitt. When it has more fuzz on the top, let me know, the heat is bringing the impurities to the surface. Removing them once more should be enough."

I watched as he went to the ocean edge with a little wooden cheese box. There he partially filled it with wet sand. While I held the cedar, I had noticed several small holes had been drilled in it, and when he returned to the front of the house, I asked why.

"To let the air out when I pour in the metal."

"More fuzz on it now."

"Just a minute, I have to position this thing in the sand. Prop the door open and it'll be ready." Again scraping the fuzz off, he very skillfully poured the hot metal into the small hole in the mold. We had been too busy at the time to pay attention to the boat that we had heard slowly coming into the cut from the bay side. Just as Russ was completing the pour, Wilbur came up.

"Wow, that wood is smoking! Won't it catch fire? What in the world are you doing?"

"The wood won't burn, merely char. That is why I picked Spanish cedar. If you aren't too impatient, just wait and see!"

"Russ, I managed to get in to the dock because it is still high tide, but I sure would appreciate it if you would ride along with me to my place. I brought some wood for tables and benches, an outboard, and a mechanic. I have to take all that down there."

I had been looking at my cast-iron pan in amazement. I hadn't been sure I would be able to use the thing again, but it looked polished.

"Sure, but wait a few minutes until this thing cools a bit," Russ said. "When it does, I have to open the mold so it can cool a bit faster. I guess though that I can do that at the dock."

He picked the mold up with the hot pad, and we went down. There, he removed the wires and pried it apart about a quarter of an inch and put in a pebble to hold it that way. Then we were introduced to Kurt, the mechanic. Beyond acknowledging the introduction with a German accent, he had nothing to say.

For some reason, Russ didn't speak German to him. When I asked him why, later, he said, "You hear more if people don't realize you understand them."

When they returned, Wilbur said, "I told the cook to fix dinner for all of us. We'll go down later on. Now let's see that thing you were working on."

"Wait a minute while I get a file. Then, when we get there, I'll let you see where it fits in the motor."

The metal was quite cool now and Russ trimmed it a bit with the file, then fit the part into its proper place in the motor.

"I thought you required a fully equipped machine shop to make something like that. I'll have to get a picture of you, holding it. Wait a minute."

Going aboard his boat, he returned with a camera. I stood along side of Russ. I suggested that I take a picture of Wilbur and Russ together. Another picture taken at that time was one of Fiddler and me with Sands Key in the background. I then took a picture of Wilbur posing in his boat, and standing by it.

We changed into older clothes then, and while he watched, we got busy with the re-assembly job. Soon again it was a two-man job, and I held the wobbly pistons while Russ lowered the head over them and the other parts. Many skinned knuckles, mumbled obscenities, and it was finished. (Three years later when we sold the boat, the bearing was still good.)

About the snapshots. Wilbur said that he would have the film developed and bring us copies of all the pictures. When he did bring them, some time later, only the two that he had taken were there. By way of explaining this, he said, "The rest of them were strangely fogged. They didn't turn out well enough to print."

I assumed that he was blaming me. I didn't say anything, but I couldn't imagine how I had fluffed such a simple thing. We weren't to know the real reason for quite some time.

It was around four o'clock when we had cleaned up and changed clothes to go *out* to dinner. We went in his boat. As we approached, Don got the skiff out to meet us. Russ threw the anchor. Knowing when the lumber was delivered, we were surprised to see they had already constructed a sturdy table and benches.

Kurt was working on the outboard motor and continued until called for supper. He had very little English and didn't speak much. Pop was cooking on the little gasoline stove on one

234

end of the table, and the steaks were served piping hot on metal plates. Open cans of vegetables with spoons in them were passed around, and it was all very good. Then pieces of canned cake were passed around on paper napkins. It was the first I had ever seen. It was surprisingly tasty!

I couldn't avoid seeing Kurt. He was gobbling. Pop and Wilbur were discussing the amount of lumber needed for a work-bench, when Russ interrupted to tell them that a little beach-combing would provide them with whatever they needed. I tried then to keep my eyes averted, but Kurt almost ruined the meal for me. The men ignored him. He ate great quantities of food, ran into the bushes and audibly lost it; then returned to do it again. Finally he ate more slowly and managed to retain it.

Kurt had told Wilbur he was a Mercedes mechanic. When he went to work on the motor again after the meal, Wilbur asked Russ if he would please look and see why the outboard didn't work. "It's a secondhand motor, but it ran fine just before I bought it!"

Don said, "Please, Russ, we are all tired out from cranking it!" Kurt had been hired to take care of motor trouble and apparently he couldn't fix it.

Russ went over to look at the outboard, and he just stared. It glittered! Kurt had painted the whole thing with quick-drying aluminum. It was an excellent paint job and the paint was well set.

While everyone silently watched, Russ took out his small pocket knife and carefully scraped the paint off the spark plugs, then removed them with a pair of pliers, and saw that the insides had also shared the paint. He scraped this out and checked the terminal wires. After scraping the paint off them, he pulled the cord and the motor roared. "No possibility of the motor running with paint on those parts!" It was so quiet—all we could hear were a few late song birds. Kurt watched this work with a sort of bewildered expression, which changed to surprise when the motor started. When he looked at Wilbur it was plain that he expected some sort of punishment.

Wilbur, in a soft tone of voice said, "Kurt, you never saw an outboard motor before did you?"

Kurt silently shook his head. Wilbur surprised me, then,

when he said, "Kurt, don't ever paint the spark plugs or terminal wires again!"

Kurt simply shuddered. Then he looked worshipful. His loyalty had been won. At that moment it became apparent that he hadn't been so kindly treated before. It was impressive.

The men had picked up a tiny kitten in the shipyard, just before they came down to the Key. Now it cried plaintively for food. One of the men picked it up and threw it into the water. I was startled and indignant. In answer to my remarks, Kurt said, "The damn thing is always crying."

"Maybe it's always hungry. Why don't you feed it?" The little thing swam hesitantly to the shore and Russ called it. It went partways toward him and stopped. Its little ribs were showing through the wet fur. Russ asked Pop for some canned milk, and mixing it with a little water, he put it on the plate and set it in front of the poor skinny little thing. It seemed to inhale rather than lap it up.

We complimented Pop on the meal, and Don rowed us out to Wilbur's boat. The wind had picked up considerably, so when we got to the dock, he asked Wilbur for an extra length of rope for a spring line.

"What's a spring line?"

Russ explained, and using a piece of our rope, fixed Wilbur's boat safely. He looked surprised when he saw how the line held the boat off the dock. He definitely was not a boatman.

That night Wilbur told us about hiring Kurt. "I never saw Kurt in the shipyard the other times when I went to get my boat, but this time he was hanging around. When I bought the outboard, he loaded it on my boat and then in lousy English asked for a job as a mechanic. He said, 'Mechanic. Mercedes.' With that, I hired him. He didn't have any gear at all. Got aboard empty-handed. On the way down I managed to talk to him some, with some of the German I remembered hearing at home. He told me he was an orphan who had grown up in the Kaiser's Germany. He always had to scramble for his food and never remembered having enough to eat. Finally, just recently, he got a job as seaman. When the boat got to Miami, he got shore leave and couldn't believe his eyes. The prosperity here decided him and he jumped ship. He hadn't even seen butter before."

Prosperity? During the *Great Depression?*

The next morning before leaving, Wilbur said, "I'm going to get fishing gear. I'm going to get the big jewfish you showed me in the cut." The fish was approximately six feet long and estimates made of its weight ran over four hundred pounds.

Trying out our motor that morning, we found that it ran very smoothly. Russ made a quick trip to Miami and was back before nightfall with gasoline and other supplies—he did take the time to get some grain gin for the off-beat medicine.

In the morning, Russ went into the jungle to look for the same type tree from which old John had removed his strips of bark. Before long, he had filled the five-pound sugar sack he had brought to put it in. I soon got the necessary bottles at our beach store, washed them, and he was ready.

Thin strips almost filled each bottle and he poured gin on them, allowing some room for expansion. He stood them upright in a smallish kettle of water, and put them on the fire. After the water had been boiling for some time, he turned off the fire and corked the bottles.

Just then we heard a knock on the door, most unusual, we hadn't heard a boat! It was Don. He had a colorful silk handkerchief tied around his neck. It was an odd addition to his sweat-stained work clothes. When I commented on it, he said, "Well, it was clean, and when my swollen ears popped open last night, I put it on to catch the drips and keep them from running down my neck."

I can't imagine how I missed seeing those swollen blobs sticking out of the black jungle of hair before. His blue eyes weren't twinkling, they were almost swollen shut. He looked pathetic. When he sat down at the table, Russ gave him a glass of water, which he drank thirstily.

"I waited for daylight this morning so I could see. I asked Pop about taking the boat. He wouldn't let me so I just lit out on my own with my machete."

On hearing that, I put the coffeepot on and started to fix him some breakfast.

"Them coral rocks was so hard to walk on that I got in the water along the edge. Then it got so muddy, I was plowin' like.

So I went ashore again. Those prickly bushes there didn't want to cut and slapped back at me, so I went into the jungle. More mosquitoes there, but it was easier walking. I made better time. I don't know how long I been on my way when I hear the sound of your voices and I found a little path right to the back of the house. Boy, I was glad to get here. About what time is it?"

"Ten o'clock, Don. A mile an hour in that going is fair time."

"Boy, you know I had a hell of a time. Especially when I got in those trees that kinda flipped their lids and let their roots down from the top branches." (Red mangroves.) "Course all the time there's mosquitoes. I tried to remember not to hit 'em on me, but sometimes I forgot, and then I saw stars."

"Don, mosquitoes don't cause that kind of swelling. Tell me what kind of green stuff you were handling, have you been doing some clearing?"

"Yeah, we've been doing some clearing around the camp." Then, hesitating a minute, he blurted out, "Wilbur wants a path cut and we been working on it. We cut a lot of trees there and got 'em off close to the ground. Hey, maybe that's it! I saw some kind of milky stuff on a machete and when I took it off with my fingers, it made strings like rubber. I showed it to the boys and told 'em I found a rubber tree. You know that damn stuff turns black when it gets on you and sticks to your hairs something fierce. Those mosquitoes in there was rough too, we kept busy slapping 'em."

I saw Russ shaking his head, he said, "Poisonwood!"

I had fed Don and he talked through breakfast. He was finished now so I gathered his dishes and Russ went to make up the hypo mix. I washed Don's dishes in the hot water the *yarb* medicine had been in. The medicine bottles were safely in the closet now, cooling.

Russ gently dabbed the hypo mix on Don's ears. "Your whole face seems to be swollen. We'd better just pour this stuff on." Getting a wash basin then, he put it in Don's swollen hands and told him to tilt forward a bit, then he poured the stuff over his forehead and sort of massaged it into the beard. Then, back into the jar and again over his entire face area. When it had sort of stopped dripping, Don put his hands in it, they weren't quite round. He sat sort of slumped and apparently felt better because he seemed so relaxed.

I showed Russ the beautiful Dubonnet color of the *yarb* medicine and said it would make a beautiful dye.

"Yes, but damn expensive. We could try it with boiled water sometime though."

We hadn't made any attempt to talk quietly, but when we looked in at Don, we saw he was asleep. Russ woke him and put more hypo mix on him before we left for the grove and told him to apply some more to himself when he got uncomfortable.

We didn't stay in the grove too long, the mosquitoes and the heat were too bad. Fishing for supper now, we discussed the reason for Wilbur's path. Russ said it had to be for illegal purposes. The key was quite wide there and no one would cut a path merely to go to the ocean side. I left him at the dock fixing the fish and went up to start the potatoes.

On purpose, I made a noisy entrance and Don woke up and put some liquid on himself. When Russ arrived soon after, he completed the job for him by pouring it through the beard again.

"My legs are just plumb wore out. I just couldn't face the mosquitoes at camp. Please, could you put me up for tonight?"

We had expected him to stay and felt rather silly when we had to be asked. I made up the bed and Russ did the dishes. Then at Russ' suggestion, I went up to bed and he helped Don undress. His hands were too swollen for him to do anything like that for himself.

We heard him stirring several times in the night putting on more liquid. We had coconut pancakes for breakfast, and had intended going to the little grove, but we got so interested in some of the stories Don was telling that we didn't get anything done that day. After his naps through the day and most of the night, he was rested. The hypo had reduced the swelling so much that his ears no longer dripped and he said he felt wonderful by comparison.

He started off by telling us that he and Wilbur had met in grade school, and been pals ever since. "He had a funny way of talkin' even then, sort of clipped and proper. His folks was loaded and I had to scramble for my spending money. Guess I got him in trouble, once anyway. I figured out how to rob a candy store and he wanted to go along. He was clumsy and got caught. You know, he acted kind of proud of it later. Tell you somethin'! He didn't squawk! His folks got him out of that. Had it been me, I'da gone to Juvenile Hall.

"You know, when we was kids, he was the original hard luck boy. If we sat down under a tree, it was Wilbur the birds picked to shed their mess on. Even the dogs acted funny with him. Two times, I know of, they used his leg like a lamppost! I could be next to him and never get touched.

"After high school, he went on to college and we got separated. I could always count on him for a loan when I needed it. He didn't heckle, I just paid him back when I could.

"Then comes Prohibition and I had it made! I had some pretty good contacts, but we needed organizing, so I looked up Wilbur. He's got the brains to run anything. Pretty soon we had an operation of our own."

He told many short stories that day, but he didn't refer again to the operation. Dabbing the liquid on himself from time to time as he talked, he said, "This is wonderful stuff."

Towards the middle of the afternoon, he and Russ went to get crawfish for supper. Don was as intrigued and excited as a child, he didn't want to stop, so they gathered many more than we needed and put the extras in the live car when they came up, quite late.

We went to bed early that night. The next morning, Russ went to the little grove and I prepared to scrub the floor in the kitchen. When I scattered dry sand on the floor, Don asked why.

"We can't spare fresh water for this. We scrub the floor with salt water and sand. Then rinse it with more salt water."

"Give me the bucket, I'll get it for you."

Finished, with the doors propped open, we both sat down to read. I was very interested in the story I was reading and I heard him say, "I feel almost well again. I'd like to get the loan of a razor so I can get this hot, tangled beard off my face."

Knowing it was heavy, and full of the salts from the hypo, I said, "Oh, no, you don't. It would take a half-dozen razors to get that thing off. I'll get you a pair of scissors to use first. Here is a mirror to use. You go outside so we don't have the mess in here. Trim that shrubbery before you waste a razor on it,"

He talked to me occasionally from outside and interrupted

my reading. Nothing important or I would have remembered. Coming to a stopping place in my story, I got the razor, a can of fresh water, and the saltwater soap. These I put on a ledge near him, and went back inside. He looked rather weird, all sorts of furry tufts sticking out on his face. He was whittling them down as I looked.

The story I was reading was really good and I was interested in it. The next time he spoke from right in back of me, he sounded real pleased with himself.

"How do I look now, Charlotte?"

I had turned to look at him just as he said "Charlotte." Without that, I would not have recognized him. I can't explain what happened next. I laughed. It was involuntary and no more easily stopped than a cough would have been. When I finally did manage to stop, I tried to explain why I had laughed. I made a poor job of it. I could think of nothing better to say than, "Because you look so different you startled me."

Russ arrived just then and he hesitated in the kitchen before coming in; he could see Don over the top of the partition.

"Hi, Russ. How do I look?" Russ recognized the voice then, and said, "Oh, you shaved! You surely look different."

That he did! Picture him as I had seen him just before he went out the door. A Santa Claus figure with a four-inch Santa Claus beard, his again-twinkling blue eyes surrounded by laugh wrinkles. It had been startling to see a sober-faced, almost chinless man. His face was lean, not round as it had appeared to he. I thought of Andy Gump, a chinless funny-paper character of that time.

"Don, you must feel real naked and cool now that you are out from under that brush; you'll have to be careful not to get sunburned. It looks tender!"

"Boy, it feels tender, too, but it feels cool and nice."

We had some coffee then and he again got talkative.

"Wilbur and I had a swell operation between Canada and the U.S. Wilbur went over to Canada and rented a warehouse on that side of the river, opposite one in the United States. I went all over, bought a length of chain here and one there 'til I got enough to go across that river. More than enough, actually, because we had to have it double and leave a big sag in it so the boats going up and down couldn't snag it and ruin us. We had some special bottle clamps made in a place in Canada. Then we were ready. One dark night we got a boat and dragged that chain over to the warehouse in Canada.

"Wilbur was ready and waiting. He had bought a lot of liquor and had it ready, along with a big-toothed wheel. We hooked the chain on that. They fastened bottles on it with those clamps and when they turned that wheel the chain started to move those bottles. I wasn't back in our U.S. warehouse long when our man turning the wheel there yelled, 'Here's the first one.' Just about that time, that slow heavy motor we ordered came and our mechanic hooked it up to the wheel. From then on we was busy, busy!

"We had some kinda stupid guy working for us, so there was a space between each bunch of bottles, twelve bottles of good liquor, and a bottle of 180-proof alcohol in each bunch. One guy would open those and put it in a container we had there, like a restaurant coffeepot with a spigot. We had some burnt-sugar water in that to dilute it. We figured 30% booze with alcohol and 70% sugar water. Had a real production line. Filled the bottles when it was mixed, then put on some labels we had printed for us in Canada. They looked most like the real thing.

"We made so damn much money then that we sent some of it to Florida. We wanted to retire in the sun when things got too hot. They did, too! Some of the guys we paid off didn't stay bought.

"Wilbur was the brains of the outfit and he didn't show. I had to handle the runners. I paid them so much a case. We had a silent partner in Canada. He hired the help and took care of that. He was a dope, though, was happy with just a good salary. Some of the runners got careless and got caught.

"Sometimes, some of the big shots didn't want hired help to make deliveries, I had to do it then."

He chuckled gleefully during the time he was telling this. "One big politician was throwin' a pre-election party and I had to make a delivery to him. Made it kinda late. It was a swell joint, the butler opened the door and let me in. The guy had my money ready in cash and I took off.

"Was just gettin' into bed when the guy phoned. He sounded frantic, just about screaming! I asked what was wrong and he just kept hollering, 'You come here and see!' I said I would, right quick. I got dressed and was going out the door when he called again. This time he was more excited, his voice went uphill in squeaks. I told him I'm on my way, to keep his shirt on. Now, I was scared!

"I got there in a hurry and, no butler now, the guy himself opens the door and tells me to hurry. I go in. Boy, I never saw such a sight! A lot of people were draped around, on the floor, on the stairs, across coffee tables. Guess I just stared for a couple of minutes. All that time the guy is yelling 'Do something, I'll be ruined!'

"I pull myself together then and think. We don't handle any rotgut. None of our weak stuff could hurt no one, well, when I thought of weak stuff, I remembered that bottle of 180-proof that comes through with the booze.

"Let's see your bar,' I said. On the way there I feel the foreheads and wrists of some of those people. They're warm! I feel better. Getting to the bar, I ask the guy to show me the bottle he made the drinks from. He handed it to me and watched while I drank the little bit there was left. Then I grinned at him, and before I could explain it was 180-proof, he tried to hit me. He was madder'n a hatter then.

"I had to hold him quiet, but he wasn't very strong. Then, I explained to him that he got some of our extra special liquor, six times as strong as the regular. He sort of wilted then from relief. 'Those people are just plastered, they ain't sick or dead.'

"Boy, when I told him that, he was so relieved he even tried to pay me the extra money for the better booze. I said, 'Nah, you're a real good customer. It's on the house. You make a lot of contacts for us.' Boy, I was sure relieved to find out what it was, made them drop like flies in front of a flit gun.

"On the way home I grinned every time I thought of all those people knocked out with one shot. It was real funny! Wish I coulda been there to see them wake up!

"Not too long ago our grapevine told us the law was catchin' up on us and was gonna pull a raid. Lucky none of the boats goin' up and down river knew what we was doing. They coulda dragged their anchors and hoisted our stuff.

"We shut up business and took off when one of our customers got arrested just as he was payin' off our delivery man. Someone squealed! Hey, I like this Florida weather better anyway.

"Russ, I'm about well and I'm overdue at work. Wilbur might show up and I don't want to have to explain to him. Take me there!"

Russ made up another small bottle of hypo and we took him down-bay. Neither Pop nor Kurt were visible. Don said, "It's all right, I know where they are working. Wait a minute." He called, "Pop! Hey, Pop. It's me, Don. I'm bringing Russ and Charlotte in with me."

Signaling us to follow him, he went up a little ways on an almost invisible path and then into the jungle. There the path suddenly became "on purpose." Five feet wide, all stumps cut off at ground level, and the trees trimmed in a straight line. It seemed to end some twenty feet ahead, but as we got almost there we could see it made a sharp jag and went in the opposite direction. On the fifth leg of this path we saw Pop, with a transit, waving instructions to Kurt, where to tie up the long cord they were using to mark the edges of the path.

Pop had known Don without a beard, but Kurt picked up his machete and wasn't sure he would accept this different-looking man. Pop said, "You damn fool. Can't you recognize his voice?" Turning back to Don, "I liked you better with a beard! You sure left us in the lurch and you got to work extra time to make up for it. It's quitting time now. Let's make some coffee."

They left their equipment where it was and we followed them back down the path. Somehow, without saying it, Pop had implied that there was a time limit on this work.

We were having coffee and cookies when the kitten appeared. Fiddler had been behaving beautifully but now went towards it. Kurt picked it up and threw it into the water. I fussed at him. Pop said, "Oh, crimany, it's learned to swim real good now. It's always crying."

I looked and saw that it was swimming swiftly to shore. Its ribs showed as plainly as before. I didn't particularly want the cat, but I didn't like to think of the miserable life it was leading there, so I asked for it. (Wouldn't I ever learn?)

Fid sat quite still and watched as Russ then went over and pried a chiton off the rock. Taking the bit of meat out, he flipped it in front of the kitten. It eased over and started to eat. The third one brought it close enough to Russ so he could pick it up. Then Pop said, "Be glad to be shed of the crying thing."

We thanked them for the snack, and the cat, and headed home. I held it, Fid came over to get acquainted but was rebuffed by the hissing and the sharp claws. At home, I mixed canned milk with water and put it down for the kitten. It took patience to convince the dog it wasn't for him. All the fussing the little thing did made us wonder if the two would ever get along.

A few days later, we looked outside and saw the cat sleeping on Fiddler's back. He lifted his head a little and sort of grinned at us. He loved it. Little Cat became more friendly and as she gained weight, became more playful.

Wilbur returned the day after we had returned Don to camp, and brought the usual goodies. It was then that he brought the two snapshots he had taken of us. "The others didn't turn out."

We enjoyed a cold Coca-Cola with him and Russ told him about Don's bout with poisonwood. He left then saying that he would check on the men and return. We had said nothing about going ashore when we returned Don to the camp.

Perhaps an hour later, he returned loaded down with an unassembled fishing rod, and a wooden box containing all sorts of hooks, plugs, teasers, and everything a fisherman might want. Depositing this on the table, in a manner that we soon found was typical, he said, "I wonder if you would show me how to put this together. I am going to get that big jewfish you showed me in the cut. How much does he weigh?"

He stood aside, and Russ began to assemble the tackle, saying, "Well it is at least six feet long and the most conservative estimate of the weight is four hundred pounds."

When the pole was ready, they took some frozen mullet from the box, and they went to the dock together. Russ cast off the lines and returned to the house soon after.

"Boy, that guy is dumb. Instead of casting towards the fish, he took his boat over, let the sinker hit bottom, and set the line. I got back aways up the path where he couldn't see me and watched. I saw him wrestle a bit, guess the fish took the bait, anyway. He lost the pole, and the fish box was knocked into the water! He just sat and watched them go. Then he cursed something fierce! I heard him start his motor again, but I'm not going to wait on him too much. I hurried up here."

Soon Wilbur appeared at the house. His face looked pinched with anger. He told us about it and we managed to look sympathetic. "That damn fish can have the pole. I hope the hook gives him a hell of a bellyache. I'm through fishing!"

Because of actions like this on Elliott Key, we didn't consider Wilbur as anything but a bored man with money to spare. Thinking of what Don had said about leaving the north, we thought he had retired. Don's statement about retiring in the sun had apparently blinded us to other possibilities.

"I bought a new double-barreled shotgun when I bought the fishing gear. I'd like to try it out. Will you take me in your boat? I figure to get a cormorant in the bay."

"I don't mind. Come on Charlotte, let's go."

Wilbur sat next to Russ and I sat on the seat in front of him. We went as close to the shoreline as the depth of the water allowed. When Wilbur said something, I turned to look while I listened and noticed he was resting the end of the gun on the toes of his right foot on a chine of the boat just above the water line. That position was dangerous!

"Wilbur, you had better move the gun. If we get jarred you might shoot your foot off, your finger is on the trigger."

He got perfectly livid. He had been so soft spoken that I was startled when he suddenly lashed out at me. "I'll do as I damn please. No woman is going to tell *me* what to do! Mind your own damn business!"

"Wilbur, Shut up! Charlotte is perfectly right. It is not only your foot, but my boat, that might suffer. Move it!"

He looked a bit shaken, apparently he hadn't thought of the possibility that he might get hurt. Muttering some then, but slowly moving the gun off his foot, he raised it to the next chine up.

Five minutes or so later, we scared up a cormorant. Wilbur shot and killed it. He was pleased and appeared to regain his normal pleasant disposition. "This cormorant will make a tasty treat for the men at the camp. Let's take it down there." He put the gun in the same position and sat as before with his finger on the trigger.

Russ turned the boat towards where the bird had fallen, just then the other barrel went off! It made a good-sized hole in the boat just above his foot. Wilbur was real shook. His face went white when he looked at the hole. He pulled his foot back and sort of slumped down. We were with a very explosive guy–on two counts.

Wilbur picked up the cormorant and we went silently to the camp. Throwing it ashore to the men there, Wilbur said, "I killed it for you, cook it."

Turning to Russ now, he said, "That's two bad things that have happened to me today, let's get back to the dock before something else happens"

We did, and when we got there, he got aboard his boat saying, "I'm going back before the third thing happens." Then he sat there and let us untie for him, then left.

His men came to get some drinking water a few days later. The outboard still ran well. Apparently they had kept the "Mercedes mechanic" from making any adjustments on it. Then they told us about the cormorant. Don said, "I skinned it, then I cleaned it. It didn't smell bad until it started to cook. Then it smelled like bad fish, so we threw it into the water and ate salmon." They didn't stay long–seemed a bit disturbed about Wilbur returning and finding them there.

The last time we saw Wilbur was when the camp had been in existence about six weeks. Because of the tenseness of the men when they came for water, we did not visit them. He came slowly into the cut one morning, towing the loaded skiff. He docked sedately in back of our boat and his skiff hardly nudged the Hacker-craft when it drifted forward. We reached the dock when he did.

"I came to say good-bye. In town, they are saying this is getting to be hurricane time. I'm only leaving the table and benches."

"I think that's smart. Build your fishing shack after the hurricane season. Then you won't take a chance on losing it this year."

"Russ, is the tide high enough so I can go into the ocean? It's a lot easier that way! No worry then about the mud flats."

"If you go slowly, it is. Just don't get too close to our boat when you pull out. The rub strip is loose on the stern and it's sticking out some. Back up slowly, then turn and put out past our boat–" He stopped talking, Wilbur was showing his teeth and grimacing with anger. (Again he was being told what to do.)

Shouting, "Good-bye," he turned the wheel enough to miss most of the stern of our boat. The rub rail was made of oak and three inches wide. His boat picked it up on the curve and it started into the boat. More of it was torn loose by the force of his boat, motor still roaring. It passed into the boat, went up at an angle past the back of his head and, after bumping through the spring and mattress fastened to the roof of the cabin, stopped. The ropes of our boat now held both boats immobilized. The forward end of the rub rail was still fast to our boat. Perhaps ten seconds passed before he shut off the motor. His skiff had bounced back after hitting the stern of his boat. A shattered place on the transom showed where it had hit.

Wilbur sat frozen at the controls of his boat. He made no move all during the salvage operation, which Russ supervised. Correction: when Don got on the cabin of the Hacker-craft with a hammer to pound on the rub rail, Wilbur lowered his head a little. Now we could see he was bloody (but unbowed). The back of his head was red with blood, and blood had discolored his white shirt. I judged it to be a good thing that his anger had been caused by an inanimate object. At that minute, he looked capable of anything.

The three men silently did everything Russ told them and the end of the rub rail was finally removed from inside Wilbur's boat. The most difficult part was when they were moving around Wilbur. He refused to move. The minute the boat was free he sat up and yelled, "Get aboard!"

This time, he moved very slowly out the cut and didn't increase his speed until he was in the deep water of the ocean. The boat didn't look very new now with a hole in the side roof and a fractured transom.

Some days after that, we were awakened by Little Cat. She bitterly resented having to sleep outside but refused to be house-trained. Now she was on the roof at the east window making the fighting, boxing motions cats make when they scratch on glass.

"Boy, I wonder how long she has been roaming on the roof," Russ said. "She'll ruin our water supply. We'll have to watch her. He unbuttoned the window and let her in. Then he crawled out the window and looked. Unfortunately, nothing was visible.

The first project before Little Cat was allowed out was to remove anything that she could use as a ladder. But when I turned on the faucet a few mornings later, it didn't run!"

Thinking it might be dry, I looked, but the tank was a third full. As I climbed down, I thought of other possibilities. Perhaps a large bug blocked it. I got the ice pick and poked around in it. No such obstruction there. I put a glass under it and continued to poke. When I turned the faucet on then, a mass of wiggly worms dropped into the water. What a sight! We hadn't carried city water for some time now, had plenty of rain. "Russ, come here!"

He looked at it in the sunlight. "I guess we'll have to find another home for Little Cat. I'll load the boat with the water jugs, while you get dressed. Put worm medicine on the list. I'll use the water to do the laundry while you are gone. It'll be sort of pleasant having our clothes all rinsed in rainwater. I'll put Clorox in it first, don't worry.

"There is some water in the teakettle. Strain it and boil it again. We need at least one cup of coffee for breakfast, and it would be best not to take medicine on a full stomach. We'll take the medicine when you get back, and then eat."

It was a beautiful calm day and I had no trouble with the boat. I completed the list with the worm medicine. It was available only in a pint bottle. I filled and carried the demijohns and was glad to rest on the way home.

When I passed Mr. Weeks dock, his young brother-in-law hailed me. I stopped, he asked if he could go home with me and visit for a while.

"Will your sister let you?"

"Yeah, we got a case of mumps at the house and she'll be glad to know I'm safe and busy. I want to fish!"

It didn't sound unreasonable to me. I told him to hurry. He left at a run, but came back more sedately. He had a bundle under his arm and he was carefully carrying a cardboard box, a cake, his sister's contribution to our supper. Bud was really thrilled. "My first visit without kinfolk!"

We were about halfway back when we found a skiff, almost sunk, the bow line had apparently frayed off. We went alongside and took turns bailing. Bud said he would get in and finish bailing as we went towards the island. He had finished and was back aboard the boat before we approached the crooked entrance to the cut.

The wind was quite strong now and the tide flowing out. This combination caused the skiff to close in on me when I made a left turn in the twisty channel. The skiff line got in the prop and tangled it. I drifted onto George Deen's mud flat, out of sight of the dock where Russ was waiting for me.

I was stepping over the side into the water. I had to untangle or cut the rope. Bud, though younger, was much stronger than I and picked me up from the water and set me on the seat. He was horrified that I should have even wet my foot in the water. He looked frightened. Someone must have raised him with some pretty horrifying stories of things in the ocean water. He wouldn't let me go in nor would he do it himself.

Russ was yelling, "What's the matter?"

"This fool kid won't let me go over and clear the line from my prop!"

"Mr. Russell she wants to go in the water. I'm not going to let her get hurt!"

"Forget it, I'll be right there." He sculled to us in the skiff.

"Bud, why wouldn't you let her get the line off?"

"Mr. Russell, you gotta protect women, she was going into the water!"

Russ just gave him a strange look then, grunted, got into the water and freed the rope without cutting it. Both skiff lines tied short now, he pushed us off and I started the motor and steered towards the dock.

Bud helped us carry things to the house and said he wanted to fish. That was fine with us, giving him some conch left from the day before, Russ told him to stay at the dock until one of us called him, and off he went.

I made fresh coffee and divided the medicine into two water

glasses and chased it with a cup of coffee. He took a magazine and supplies when he went down beach. I stayed home.

We made an early supper with a lot of filleted fish Bud had brought to the house. He was so excited he just shouted when he said, "I got about a hundred in the live car. I want to take them home for a fish fry."

I tried to ignore Little Cat as she rubbed on my ankles that evening. I was more than aggravated with her.

Just as we were getting up the next morning, Happy and Al came. They had coffee with us while we ate breakfast and Russ asked them if it was possible that they could find a home for the cat. She was now on Happy's lap being petted. They thought she was cute and took her with them after we had told them why we couldn't keep her.

Later, they said, "Thinking over your story, we had suffered for you and decided to drown the cat." Some distance from the island, Happy slowed the boat and dropped the cat over the side. He wouldn't look back, but Al did. Seeing the swiftly swimming cat, he called Happy's attention to it. "Right then we felt ashamed of ourselves. Happy stopped the boat and when it swam to us, he picked it up, and all wet as it was, he held it in his lap the rest of the way back." From then on, it was their mascot at the Border Patrol headquarters. The Swimming Cat was now an individual, no longer nameless.

After saying good-bye, we gathered all the empty bottles on the beach, washed them and took them to the house. Russ made a funnel by cutting the bottom out of an oil can, tied a folded handkerchief over it, and we strained the cistern water into the bottles, adding Clorox to some. Why? To wash off and sterilize the roof before the next rain. Then Russ climbed into the tank and scrubbed it thoroughly. Then he cleaned the rainspout and set it aside until after the roof had been scrubbed.

Bud spent all his time fishing. There were now so many fish in the car that he removed all the smaller ones and only kept the largest. He had magnificent plans for a huge fish fry for all the neighbors when he returned home.

On the way to the grove that afternoon, we took Bud along. I saw a cluster of almost floating bamboo roots. For some strange reason their appearance appealed to me and I had to have them. Russ didn't object and now I was grateful for Bud's strength. It took the three of us to get the clumsy things into the bow. We were busy then bailing out the water that drained out of them. When we returned to the dock with it, Bud and I figured we had bailed out about thirty gallons of water. It was lighter when we set it on the dock to finish draining. It really looked weird.

Back from the grove again, Bud proudly said, "Mrs. Russell, you go get the potatoes on. I'll bring up more filleted fish." He was a thoughtful and unobtrusive guest.

Russ was always up first in the morning, the next day was an exception. "I have a little headache and don't feel quite right, wonder what's wrong?"

I made breakfast and asked Russ to wake Bud. He came out of Bud's bedroom with a disgusted look on his face. "You, and your marvelous inspirations. I never have had the mumps, so you brought some home for me to catch. Go, look at him!"

I went silently to the bedroom and saw Bud. He was squinting at me out of swollen eyelids. He sort of whined, "I wanta go home! I don't want any breakfast, I just wanta go home!"

"Okay, get your things together, I'll take you," and I went to change into other clothes. There wasn't any further conversation. Russ was filling the gas tank when we got to the boat, and we left without taking the fish out of the car.

I was feeling pretty sick myself now. Not physically, just mentally. I hadn't realized how thoughtless I had been until now.

Bud's family wasn't surprised to see him. Misery loves company. They all had the mumps now! I turned right around and went back.

At the dock, I noticed the bamboo clump was swaying in the wind. I lifted it, only about forty pounds. I managed to wrestle the thing up to the lawn and set it in front of the house. I wasn't really avoiding Russ. I had a good excuse for sitting outside, I was studying the roots. They grow in an interconnected mass. There were main roots, oval shaped blobs covered with broken off rootlets that looked like magnified hair. On the lower parts of these blobs were broken-off small roots that looked like legs. Short broken pieces on top looked like necks for the blob bodies. One larger blob had a two-foot neck on it. Checking the entire cluster, I decided that by using these blob-heads with necks, I could have one large, and four smaller *beasties*. I pictured them as having sea-shell pieces as teeth.

I went into the house now to discuss this with Russ–he hadn't said anything while I sat out there and I would rather be fussed at than ignored. He looked up, shrugged his shoulders and said, "Well, after all we have been through together, what's a little thing like a case of mumps!"

He went out with me and I explained what I had decided to do. He took over then and sawed the thing apart, and reassembled it. It looked quite well after he had drilled holes in some sea shells and fastened them on as eyes. Some yellow lucky-beans made noses for them. By then, I had found the ridged shells for teeth and smaller nails fastened them on. With the buckle end of the wide leather belt that had made a bearing for us on one boat trip, we made a suitable collar. A short piece of chain found in the old dump, fastened to a stake driven on the lawn, completed our "Beastie." Quite a fantastic lawn ornament, it startled almost everyone who saw it.

CHAPTER TWENTY-TWO

Treasure on Sands Key.
Russ Provides Me Some Special Entertainment.

Not long after Russ had recovered from a severe case of mumps, we were awakened about the middle of the night by the sound of a boat. It was strange to hear it now. During Prohibition, we had become accustomed to the sound of boats running through the cut, but this was the first one since. Then the motor stopped.

We both dressed quickly, expecting visitors. Russ got the gun and checked the clip.

"It could be Bill!"

We were downstairs with gun and not yet lighted flashlight, waiting for trouble. No sounds on the path. Then the white path shone up as I looked. In the bright light of a Coleman lantern on the boat, we saw it was tied to the tree on the other side of the cut, ocean end. Another light was moving around in front of the boat, just above the water in the shallows there. Because of the glare of the lights, we were never sure how many men were there. We saw three.

We silently went down the path and didn't shine our light. Arriving near the dock, we saw two men in the water with pick-axes, chopping into the rock near their feet.

"Hello. What are you doing?"

"None of your damn business! If you don't want to get shot, stay where you are!"

When a powerful flashlight was turned towards us, Russ took my hand and quickly pulled me from the path. We walked back up near the path until we were out of the light.

"Quiet now! Let's go look. For God's sake, don't make any noise!"

We went into the bushes slowly and cautiously, towards the cut. Behind some bushes now and near the water's edge, we squatted down to watch. The men were busily chopping at the rock in the shallow water.

Before long, we heard a boat approaching from the ocean. It slowed down and made the turn into the channel, slowing the motor then.

A man's voice said, "What's going on?"

Another responded, "Get the hell out of here!"

Then we heard two shots. The men in the water didn't have guns. There was at least one more on the boat, apparently standing guard. The fine whistles of the bullets didn't seem to be far from us. I sort of shrunk down where I was. The boat immediately backed at high speed, then turned and left down-ocean.

When the intruders had been driven away, Russ eased me to a sitting position and leaned over, "Don't move, not a sound now!"

My heart had been pounding ever since the shots. I was afraid to move.

Soon one of the men started to throw rocks away from the working area. The other one didn't swing his tool, just pecked at the rock, with prying jabs. Now the lantern on the bow of the boat was turned off and we saw three men gathered around a bulky object. From the way they grunted, it must have been very heavy. They slowly moved it to the side of the boat that was close to shore. From our position, it was difficult to see much now, but one of the men stood on the back of another and went aboard the boat. We heard much cursing and grunting, now, and then the other two men were helped aboard after passing the tools up. The boat was soon underway, in reverse. The lantern off now, we were night blind and lost sight of them. We soon noticed the first pale light of the coming day.

Still a bit shaken, we waited till they were out of sight and hearing, and then went to the house for breakfast. I was quite stiff for a while as I had taken Russ' admonition not to move very literally, and I had been quivering from the effort to sit quietly.

After breakfast, we went over to the spot in the skiff. We found it to be a space a little larger than a large washtub. There was a dessert-dish depression in the center of which was a circular hole about two feet deep. Among the rocks in the immediate vicinity, we found some broken pieces of an earthenware or stoneware jug, of approximately ten-gallon size. The rest of it–and its contents–were on the boat. Apparently *some* treasure maps are good!

While sculling back across the cut Russ called my attention to a very large yacht in the bay. It appeared to be at least a 75-footer. Knowing it drew too much water to enter the cut, we ignored it completely.

Not too long after we got to the house, we heard a boat; looking down, we saw the yacht-tender tying up there. We watched a man in sailor whites assist two women in white onto the dock. One of the women led the way up the path.

Russ met her at the door.

"Do you serve meals here?" she asked.

Somehow this infuriated me. I opened my mouth to say "no" when–

"Why certainly," said Russ, "but you will have to wait while we prepare it. Won't you come in?"

I was startled but stood aside as he led the way in to the table and seated the two women at one end and the sailor at the other. It was apparent from the sailor's deference to the woman who had spoken that she was the owner of the yacht. The diamonds on her hands and her wrist were even more magnificent than those of her companion.

"Start the small new potatoes cooking," Russ said. He went then to our storage space and got out three small liquor glasses. After wiping them, he poured a rather large portion of Gary's guava brandy in them, he put them on a plate, put a folded dish towel over his left arm, and went into the dining room.

"Here's just a little something to help you pass the time while we are preparing your meal." I knew he was up to something. When he returned to the kitchen, I opened my mouth, but he shook his head, grinned and put his finger to his mouth. I hushed!

"I'll be right back." He dashed out the door and went towards the dock. He returned soon with the tails of twelve undersized crawfish in the wooden bucket, then put them on to boil.

He set the table for our paying guests, towel again on his arm. On the paper-napkin place mats, our stainless-steel silverware looked quite acceptable.

Returning to the kitchen with the empty glasses, he grinned at me again, and poured out a large portion of guava brandy.

The women had been having an animated conversation between themselves. After that drink, the sailor was included. Then Russ poured a third drink for them.

When the little potatoes had been peeled and put in the sauce of scorched margarine and lime juice, the crawfish were ready. I heated a can of small green peas he handed me. Then (all this silently) he motioned towards the large platter on the shelf. I got that and he put the potatoes in the center of it, put the crawfish in the sauce for a minute, placed them around the potatoes and poured the rest of the sauce on. The peas were put in side dishes.

By now, the women were on very friendly terms with the sailor and asked Russ to set his place near them. He seemed very reluctant to change his seat.

After serving them, he returned to the kitchen, grinning from ear to ear. With his head, he motioned for me to look.

I saw the yacht owner, her arm around the sailor's neck, putting a piece of crawfish in the general direction of his mouth. She giggled and the sailor's face was red. He could hold his liquor better than the women. I had to move a bit to see the other woman's expression. She looked jealous.

"He should be sitting between us! It's not fair!"

They ate all of the food and then asked for the bill. Russ told them it would be $1.50 each. The women fumbled around in their pockets for a couple of minutes. The sailor, almost stuttering, said "Here!"

Russ accepted the five-dollar bill and thanked them all.

On their way down the path, the sailor was very busy helping both women maintain their balance. Without their deck shoes, they never would have made it.

After their motor had started and our silence was no longer important, Russ burst out laughing. "I wonder what's going to happen next, on the yacht. I'd like to be there to see it!"

Boy, what a sense of humor! To do all that work, serve that much food and liquor, at that price, just to see if the dignified women would put on a show for us. Still waters *do* run deep. I was getting to know a bit more about my husband.

Brown Fish Hook

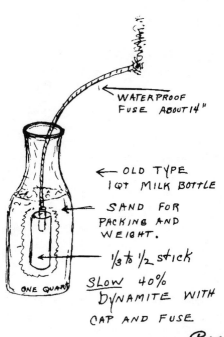

WATERPROOF
FUSE ABOUT 14"

← OLD TYPE
1 QT MILK BOTTLE

SAND FOR
PACKING AND
WEIGHT.

1/3 to 1/2 stick

ONE QUART

SLOW 40%
DYNAMITE WITH
CAP AND FUSE

RM

CHAPTER TWENTY-THREE

Mr. Cole and the Yarb Medicine. Brown Fish Hook.
Sea Caterpillar. Bottle of Tea.
Lime Thieves Are Put to Work. I Sit on a Scorpion.

The *yarb medicine* on the shelf had almost been forgotten when Mr. Fossey arrived with a guest. He left him aboard his boat and came up to tell us about him.

"Mr. Cole is in his seventies and recovering from a long illness. He hasn't been out of the hospital long. He is well enough to do for himself. He won't need any care. All he needs is a lot of sunshine and the peace and quiet you have here. How about putting him up for a week or two. He brought his own linen and groceries."

"Happy to."

"He is an old friend of mine and I know he will really appreciate this. He is a very quiet man, easy to get along with."

They went to the boat to carry up Mr. Cole's supplies. When they had gone back for the second load, Mr. Cole came in slowly, introduced himself, and sat down to rest. He had brought his own icebox to the Keys and it was pretty well filled with packages of fresh meat.

"Sorry, can't stay to visit. Must get back to Miami," and Mr. Fossey was on his way.

"Where is your linen, I'll make up a bed for you."

He said, "Thank you kindly," in a way that let us know he would rather be alone for a while. We went fishing.

"We are running out of duck feed again and I am going to make a dynamite fishhook!"

261

"How?"

"Wait and see! It takes a hell of a long time to catch enough to feed our twenty large ducks. This will be quicker. Go find a milk bottle!"

When I returned I found him waiting with a piece of dynamite. Dynamite in bottle surrounded by dry sand, and a fairly long fuse completed it. Getting the potato rakes from the storage skiff, he was ready.

The tide was going out when Russ sculled to the middle of the cut, lit the fuse, dropped the bottle over the side, then dropped the anchor. As we drifted back on the line, we watched some curious fish going towards the bubbles which arose from the bottle. Then, a sort of bump on the boat bottom.

"Grab your rake and be ready!"

I was soon terribly busy helping him gather in the stunned fish. "I thought they would be in pieces."

"No, that's why I packed the sand around it, that and the slow dynamite just caused concussion."

Altogether, we got a full five-gallon bucket of nice large snappers. We added some salt water and went up to cook the duck feed. While that cooked on the wood stove, we went in the house. Mr. Cole's bedroom curtains were drawn, so we were very quiet as we prepared and ate our supper, then retired early.

When we got down the next morning, we found that he had already eaten and cleaned up his dishes. Apparently he had gone for a walk. We ate and went to the grove. When we returned around five, he was washing his supper dishes. He went to bed while we were eating. The conversation in between times was polite, but meager.

The next two days were the same. The morning of the third day, Russ was to leave for Miami. I thought to check the amount of drinking water in the jug and got aboard the boat to look. While reaching to get it, I looked under the dock and found it hard to believe that I saw what I saw. In the shallow water near the deeper edge was a monstrous caterpillar. Apparently an underwater variety, as it was completely submerged. It appeared to be feeding on something in the sand and mud it was stirring up in front of its face. Including the bristling protrusions on its back, it was more than six inches high.

When Russ got to the dock, I asked him to get the pail, the outside part of a bait-bucket that we had found some time before. "Now, what kind of an idea do you have?" he asked, but he walked to the storage skiff and got it. When I called him to bring a stick of some kind, he said, "For Pete's sake why?"

"Well, it looks like a huge caterpillar."

He just snorted.

"Walk softly on the dock when you come back here. I don't want it scared into deeper water."

Then he looked at me as though I had flipped my lid, but he did walk softly. When he got aboard the boat, I pointed and he looked. "Gosh, I thought you were kidding. I never saw a thing like that before. I never read about one like that either. It's just a great big magnification of one you would see on a bush or a tree, almost the same coloring as the small ones the monarch butterfly has."

He leaned out of the boat, filled the bait bucket, and slid it around the back end of the creature, holding the stick just touching its head. As soon as he had most of it in the bucket, he tilted it, and took it out of the water. The head end also went in then. The caterpillar made one complete circle and most of a second, leaving little room for fresh water.

"It is fully eighteen inches long! What'll we do with it?"

"Why not take it along and sell it to the people who have the marineland and zoo in Miami. They might want to buy it."

This marineland and zoo had been started aboard the Prince Valdimar after the vessel had been blown ashore, almost onto Biscayne Boulevard during the 1926 hurricane. Before the hurricane, it had been one of the largest steam yachts afloat. We were told it had been Kaiser Wilhelm's yacht.

Russ told me later that he had changed the water on the critter many, many times in an effort to supply it with oxygen, but when he entered the river, the busy traffic there caused him to forget it. When he finally docked, he remembered it and looking down, saw nothing but a worm-like mass of innards.

"It was more than possible that it had swallowed its tail and turned itself inside out in its distress when it ran out of oxygen. I dumped it in the river." When I got back from the grocery store, I visited Flip and Bertha. Then when I got back aboard the boat, I remembered the thing and decided to call the marineland and find out what it was. I phoned them from Everett's and asked them about it. They asked for a description and when I gave it, said, 'Yes, that fits! It's very rare! Will you please sell it to us?'

"When I told them I had dumped it in the river because it had swallowed itself, they offered me money for the skin. They were quite bitter when I told them it was long gone now. It had sunk when I dumped it over."

It had just been another strange thing to us, but apparently it would have meant a lot to the aquarium to have it.

"They said it was a *trilobite*, and scientists assumed it has long been extinct. They sounded almost furious!"

While Russ had been gone, I occupied myself gathering more conchs to anchor and then cleaned some. At the house, I began to work on my stew. While I was pounding the conchs to shreds, Mr. Cole came in and asked what I was doing. I explained and he watched in an interested way for a bit and then left for his afternoon walk.

When he returned, I had my cooking well underway and was using all the burners on the stove. I realized it was about the time he usually cooked his supper, but what could I do about it?

Just then, I heard the conch horn. Russ always blew it when he passed Soldier Key on the way home.

"That's our conch horn. It means Russ is only twelve miles from home now. He always signals me that way."

"I never knew sounds carried that far on the water." He turned and sniffed at the cooking food. I told him that it would soon be in one pot and then he could have the burners for his own use.

"It smells delicious! If you can spare a bit, I'll swap a steak for it."

I grinned, "We'll be getting the best of the bargain."

It was at that time that I got a marvelous idea. Getting the *yarb* medicine from where it lived on the shelf, I carefully measured a two-teaspoon dose in a jigger, got another jigger and put some in it, saying, "It's time for my medicine. If it's good for me, it can't hurt you."

Filling two glasses with water, I handed him one, and said,

"Bottoms up!" We chased the stuff with the water. Boy, was that stuff bitter! It had a dry, bitter smell, but I wasn't prepared for the intensity of the taste. It was fierce. I shuddered. He did too!

I had washed all the extra pots before Russ arrived. We stowed the ice and meat and left the other things for later. I always did have a healthy appetite, but I felt as though I could have eaten a horse if it was peeled first. I had to eat! *Now!* I was almost ashamed as I gulped down my first bowl of stew; then I got up to cook the steak. Mr. Cole was helping himself to the second bowl when I returned with the steak.

"My, this is good." He followed it with a third bowl as we finished the steak.

Russ looked at me with raised eyebrows when I refilled my bowl with stew, but was too polite to say anything.

The next morning we were awakened by raps on the bedroom floor. Russ raised the trap door and heard, "Come get it, while it's hot."

We went down to find that Mr. Cole had cooked some of his supplies and the table was set. He smiled at our surprise and I saw then that he had two jiggers in his hand. "Miss Charlotte, I slept like a baby all night. It's the best sleep I've had in years. Would you please share some of your medicine with me this morning?"

Russ gave me a funny look as I ducked my head and went to get it. "Here's some for you, I only have to take it once a day with my evening meal–I'm only about a third your age." Russ' glance now was accusing. I acted as though I hadn't seen it and sat down to eat. I had gotten out of taking that dose easily enough, but what about tonight? I still had to explain to Russ. I had remembered the thin floors the night before and decided to wait for another time to tell him about my marvelous idea to help Mr. Cole get well.

Finished now with the bacon and eggs, I was still hungry and grated some coconut. Russ mixed the other things and pancakes were soon ready. Mr. Cole ate four of them.

"My, I haven't eaten that much breakfast for years. It tasted wonderful too! Seems a long time since I noticed the flavor of food. No, no. Just leave the dishes, I'll do them. I've got all day."

The rest of the conch stew was on its usual pedestal and had been reheated, so we accepted his offer gratefully and left to work in the grove.

As we turned the corner to go down-bay, Russ asked, "Just what monkey business are you getting into now?"

"I had an inspiration. That medicine makes people well, and Mr. Cole needs some. But, boy, is that stuff bitter!"

He just howled with laughter when I said that. "You'll have to take your medicine tonight! No, don't argue with me. You asked for it!"

During the day he chuckled occasionally, and I knew what he was thinking.

When he returned, Russ prepared the medicine and handed it to Mr. Cole and me. Nothing to do but gulp the bitter stuff down and reach for the water. He laughed then, but carefully explained, "Mr. Cole, doesn't she look funny when she makes a face like that and shudders?"

After supper I solved the problem of taking more medicine by presenting Mr. Cole with the remaining contents of the bottle, "Here, Mr. Cole, you take this bottle. We have another. Now, you won't have to wait until I take my medicine." He was very happy to accept and it worked out just as I had hoped. He finished his supper every night before we got home, too hungry to wait! That way he couldn't see if I took my medicine.

We continued to share our breakfast and he was getting more talkative all the time.

Our first gift of manufactured liquor was brought to us by friends who came to visit us soon after Prohibition had been repealed. We joined them in a celebration drink. When Mr. Cole was asked to join us, "Thank you kindly, but, I feel so well now I don't want to do anything that might set me back!"

Russ chuckled when he looked at the bottle. "Listen to this! All the whiskies in this bottle are guaranteed to be at least three months old." It was raw!

We had most of the bottle left when our next visitors arrived. These were the thirsty kind. When Russ saw who was at the dock he quickly put a small amount of water in a pan and put it on to boil; then he added six tea bags and boiled them. "Get an empty quart bottle off the back porch."

I brought it and he filled it with the tea, and added water.

Now it was liquor colored. He put that among our canned goods in the storage space and met our company at the door.

I served coffee as usual and the guests sat around and hinted a bit. We hadn't kept liquor around the house and I didn't think they would expect any, in spite of their hints. "Glad Prohibition is over now, you can drink without being afraid of going blind. Wish we hadn't finished our bottle on the way down."

Someone asked about the Beastie out front. In answer, we went out with most of our guests to tell them about it. When we returned, Russ sort of drifted towards the kitchen closet. He returned with a twinkle in his eye. He tilted his head towards the closet. Before long I got an opportunity and looked. The bottle was almost empty. We knew that anyone wouldn't go back for a second drink of that bitter tea. That meant all of them had taken a quick, large gulp, been fooled, but kept quiet about it. I surely would have loved to see their expressions when they did it.

When I returned, everybody was sitting around the table talking. I just couldn't help grinning at them. Russ grinned too, then got up, stretched a minute and asked, "Anyone care for a drink?" Heads nodded then but no one said anything. He went to the kitchen and, in plain sight of everyone in the living room, he reached up between our syrup bottle and a bottle of vinegar and took down the liquor bottle.

You should have seen their expressions, sheepish and guilty.

Mr. Cole arrived back soon after and joined us in drinking another cup of coffee. They left almost immediately afterwards.

"Mr. Russell, those people were more relaxed when I left than when I got back, what happened?"

Russ told him about the almost empty bottle of tea and then said, "The best place to hide things is in plain sight. Just put it with similar shaped things," and he showed where the liquor bottle was. He laughed heartily and said it should have been spiked with pepper. He was still chuckling about it at bedtime.

The next morning was just two weeks from the time Mr. Cole had arrived and he was apparently in good health now. We heard Mayor Fossey's boat arrive and went down to meet him. He was simply amazed when Mr. Cole met him there. "The improvement in your health is visible. I brought you another two week's supply of groceries. Hope you didn't run out."

Having coffee up at the house, Mayor Fossey told us of an amusing story he had heard in Miami. Mr. Charles Brookfield owned a large lime grove, situated on the bay side several miles south of us. It was kept in better condition than most groves. It was here that someone had finally gotten the best of the *borrowing* Conchs.

For some time before this, Mr. Brookfield had been losing most of his limes to these people and he determined to get the best of them. According to the story, he and his two friends were armed. They anchored some distance out in the bay, apparently fishing. They had binoculars with them. One stayed on watch at all times. They waited patiently through two moonlit nights without relaxing their vigilance. The third night was payoff night! They didn't have any lights on the yacht when two of the local boats went towards the shoreline where the grove was located. After they tied and went into the jungle, Mr. Brookfield slowly moved his large boat closer, dropped anchor, and the three men got into the yacht tender and rowed ashore. Their boat tied just down-bay from the others wasn't visible. He and his friends made themselves comfortable in the bushes near the path and waited. Quite some time afterwards the men returned. This time, each of them had a full bag of limes on his shoulder.

When the fourth man was on the shoreline near the boats, Mr. Brookfield and his friends stood up from the bushes where they had waited and said, "Hands up!" The startled men dropped the bags and put up their hands. This was the first time that an absentee owner of a lime grove had caught them *borrowing*. They didn't make a move; the guns were pointed at them; then Mr. Brookfield told them to pick up the sacks of limes and put them aboard his boat. When they had done this, he again spoke to them. "You wanted to pick limes. Go back into the grove and pick them.

"You have a choice though. If you don't want to strip my grove for me, I'll give you a free ride to Miami and have you thrown in jail for stealing! Make your choice now."

The men looked silently at each other, picked up an empty bag apiece and went back into the grove. Mr. Brookfield and his friends went into the grove to see that the unwilling men worked and didn't disappear into the surrounding trees.

In the early morning, after the exhausted Conchs had loaded the last bag of limes aboard his yacht, Mr. Brookfield told them, "You can go now, but, if I lose any more limes, I will swear out a warrant for your arrest. I know who you are. That means if anyone steals my limes I will blame you for it. You had better pass the word along if you don't want to go to jail. I've got two good witnesses."

These men had picked eighteen crates of limes during the night, in addition to the four original bags they had been caught with. That was hard, fast picking for four men. There are from twelve to eighteen hundred of the small limes to a bag. They were bringing a high price right then and it was the most money Mr. Brookfield had ever gotten from the limes in his grove.

To us it was a really lovely story. Poetic justice.

Mr. Cole told the bottle-of-tea story to Mayor Fossey. He laughed heartily and agreed with Mr. Cole that Russ should have added the pepper.

"This has been fun, but I'll have to be on my way back to Miami," Mr. Cole said. "When I left Miami, I thought I would never go back into business. I turned it over to my son. I've loafed long enough, I'm anxious to get back. Hope the boy managed the business all right." (As Mr. Cole was in his seventies, the *boy* could easily have been in his fifties.)

While he was packing, he said, "I'd like to say thank you by giving you my groceries. I won't need them now!"

We were both happy to say thanks.

He hesitantly said, "If you have a further supply of that good medicine, I would surely appreciate it. My bottle is pretty low." He held his bottle so we could see. Taking it, Russ said, "Of course, I'll trade you Charlotte's for it. That is almost full yet." (He didn't consider it necessary to tell Mr. Cole that I hadn't needed the medicine. Thank God!)

When Russ returned with it, Mr. Cole carefully put it in his pocket to keep it safe.

Mr. Fossey told us later on that Mr. Cole had gained ten pounds during his stay with us, and had again taken an active part in his business. He was disturbed to find that his son now considered him as a partner, rather than full owner.

We had alternately been using our boat, then that of Mug's, to keep the battery charged. He arrived the following morning. We were working on some coconut trinket cases for Christmas presents for our mothers and didn't meet him as usual. We had a pleasant visit. Seems as though there was some technicality and maybe he wouldn't have to serve his time after all. He was out on bail. This time, I thanked him for the use of his boat without any side remarks. He left soon towing his boat home.

Three of our frequent visitors were bachelors who each arrived in his own boat. They came soon afterwards and Russ told them about Mr. Cole and the medicine. They had a good laugh at my expense but were impressed that it had helped Mr. Cole. Then he told what old John said about the other effect.

"What color is it? How does it taste?"

Russ got out the small amount left in Mr. Cole's bottle, and they tasted it. "Same bitter, wonderful stuff. Look, Russ, this is the same stuff they got in the Seybold Arcade liquor store, and they really charge for it!"

"Yes, Old John sells it to them."

"We'll bring the gin and give you ten dollars to make up three pints for us. Okay?"

"Okay!"

The next day it looked as though the drought might break. Soft, puffy-looking clouds were beginning to gather. The very weekend we were expecting three couples as guests! They arrived at the usual time and visited a bit, then took the yacht into the ocean. The bluefish were running, and they had great sport for a time, but they needed high tide to come into the cut and returned before long.

After supper that night we played bridge, in a rather awkward manner. Four people at each end of the long table. It was difficult sitting alongside your opponent without seeing his hand, but we managed it.

During the time he was dummy, the owner of the yacht went out. He returned with liquor and a bottle of mix. Some time later, after the second highball, the bidding also became quite spirited. Six no-trump, and my partner got the contract. I took that opportunity to go the Chic Sales on the porch.

Too modest to signal my intentions, I neglected to take a flashlight to look for scorpions on the seat. Immediately, I wished I had. I managed to stand up after the second sting and before the third. With my lighter, I saw a four-inch scorpion on the spot I had just left. I raised my foot and squashed it.

Rearranging my clothing I decided to go to the bedroom where I could hurt in solitude. I didn't feel very sociable right then and knew I couldn't open my mouth without crying.

I was two steps up the ladder when Russ grabbed my pants, "What's wrong?" I hung onto the ladder and he tried to pull me down. The third time he asked that, I was still holding to the ladder, but I managed to blurt out, "A scorpion bit me."

"Where?" He repeated it several times and I managed to say, "I sat on him!" My pants had started to come off and I backed down the ladder.

Our company now, "Oh, you poor thing. How about a drink, that will be the best remedy for the pain. Guess you don't want to sit and finish the game?"

I accepted the half-full water glass from the man and drank it down. Then going up the ladder, I heard them arrange for the dummy of the other table to take over my hand.

I managed to get up the ladder and fall on the bed. The last sound I heard that night was, "Charlotte, we made our bid!"

Boy did I hurt the next morning. Russ had taken off my shoes only, and it wasn't much of a chore to get dressed. Our guests were most sympathetic about my wounds–and my hangover–with big smiles on their faces. When they left at noon, I relaxed a little.

Hearing the rain on the roof the next morning was pleasant. We hurriedly got out the many bottles of water, added some Clorox to each, and started to scrub the roof. I poured and Russ used the brush. Finished before long, we let that water run off, then poured more through the pipe and fastened it to the tank. By that time, the roof was rinsed and we went down and outside to take a shower. I felt almost new again.

Afterwards, we were prepared to go to the grove when one of our bachelor friends arrived with the gin and a ten-dollar bill. Saying he was in a rush, he left and returned to Miami. Quite a trip for medicine! Russ got the materials and made up the

271

medicine for them. It was hardly cool when another one of the group arrived to collect it.

Each time they returned after that, we were introduced to their *wives*, a different one each time.

We were well into the rainy season now and worked at keeping the old cistern drained so that the mosquitoes couldn't get started there again.

Captain Russell and his son, Reno, came frequently for a coconut pancake breakfast.

CHAPTER TWENTY-FOUR

Hurricane Warning. Hurricane Log.

On Saturday, August 31, Mayor Fossey arrived for his usual weekly visit. He reported that there were no storm warnings displayed so he had come down as usual. The previous Wednesday, Thursday and Friday the weather was very warm and particularly humid. The wind was light, variable, mostly southeast. The mosquitoes were very bad and inclined to fly right into the wind to bite. Our Muscovy ducks appeared nervous as though they were watching for an unseen enemy. They seemed always hungry. They did not go swimming on the incoming tide in their usual manner, but sat facing northeast all the time they were eating.

Russ kept a record during the hurricane that occurred here September 1, 2, and 3, 1935. [Printed here in italics.] We added observations when we could and when we learned more.

Sands Key Cut
Elliott Key, Florida
August 31, 1935

August 31. My wife Charlotte and I are on the north end of Elliott Key. Weather fair, a few mild squalls, wind moderate northeast. The cut between Sands Key and Elliott Key is full of fish.

September 1. Mr. Fossey's party is out fishing. This is the first time no one caught any fish. I have been in the small grove picking limes, and I got half a crate for him to take home. Wind is fresh, northeast. Partly cloudy–sultry.

At 11 A.M. a U.S. Coast Guard plane from the Dinner Key Air Base flew over the cut between Sands Key and Elliott Key. It circled low and on the second pass, as it was heading west over the cut, dropped an orange-colored container.

We waved and signified that we had seen it. The pilot headed around for another pass. We took the skiff and recovered the container. It was canvas-covered cork, painted orange, about eight inches long by four inches wide and two thick. In one end a hole had been drilled and plugged by a cork. Upon removal of the cork, we found a crumpled note from the pilot. It read, "IF YOU WANT TO BE TAKEN OFF – PUT SOME SHEETS ON THE LAWN – WILL SEE NEXT CIRCLE."

Under that we found, wrapped in a piece of oiled silk, an official dispatch, dated September 1, from the U.S. Coast Guard, warning of increasing winds, probably reaching gale force, possibly hurricane force that night or the next day (Monday). We kept the original hurricane warning.

Mayor Fossey and his party immediately began to gather their gear together. We ran to the house so as to be on the lawn, without sheets. The pilot saw us when he returned. He waved and left.

Mr. Fossey wanted us to return to Miami with them. Russ said we would sit it out but would appreciate their taking a few of our treasures with them. It was okay and we managed to carry everything in one trip. Once our things were aboard, the Fosseys left. We were in time to say good-bye to a police captain who had come in his own boat.

George Deen and his party were still gathering their equipment together. George brought his boat to our dock and tried to frighten us into leaving with him. I was content to stay if Russ was.

Not much whiskey was left in various bottles aboard, so George emptied all of them into a quart milk bottle. When a very little mix was added, this was full. We accepted a drink. Never having tried to drink from a bottle before, I spilled most of my drink on the outside of me. Russ took a drink, handed the bottle over and told them they had better get started. And, we had things to do.

12:15 P. M. The cut is deserted.

We pulled the skiffs on shore, preparatory to tying them to trees, and got into the powerboat. In order to start that darn thing, it was necessary to mix profanity with the gas. It finally started and we went to the bay side where the *Gertrude* usually anchored. This and a sister ship were built with 2 by 4's. We had met the men when they came for water.

These middle-aged spongers laughed at us and called us greenhorns for being superstitious enough to believe in hurricane warnings. Sure, they had seen the airplane! "Suppose it did drop the message. What does Mon who sit at desk know about weather? Fishermen knows weather better!" They laughed heartily at the possibility of a *blow*. They believed that because of their knowledge of the weather, they knew everything.

We had noticed that for some days previously we had been unable to get conch in shallow water and had to go much deeper for them–a sign these weathermen who called us greenhorns didn't notice.

The third boat to which we carried the warning was Captain William Reno Russell's sailboat. He said that he had seen signs to indicate bad weather was brewing and was grateful for the warning. "When you see crawfish moving in the daytime heading for deeper water, it is most unusual. They are a nighttime creature.

"Russell, I know of a hurricane creek on the west side of Sands Key and I would appreciate it if you would tow us there on your way home. I'll call and you cast loose my painter when we get near it. Reno and I can tow the boat and the skiffs over the flats to it."

We were soon going back towards Sands Key, near the cut. Captain called and we cast him loose, throwing the line aboard as they drifted forward past us. On our way again, I looked back and saw the two men towing the boat towards the mangroves.

We were tying the eighth spring line to the powerboat when Reno appeared in his skiff.

"Papa says this blow will last for at least three days and we need extra water."

"Go up and help yourself, Reno."

We finished at the dock, tying the skiffs, gas cans, shovels, etc. to trees for safety.

Reno was gone when we returned and removed the drain spout to the tank. The liquid mud in a hurricane would ruin our drinking water if we didn't. The lid nailed securely, we went into the house to plan what to do next.

3:30 P.M. There is a heavy cloudbank in the west.

Until then there was no sign of really bad weather. We remembered that we had a film in the camera and took a picture from time to time.

4:30 P.M. The wind is a strong northeast. Ragged clouds appearing in the east and southeast. Tide is ebbing fast. Many seabirds heading ashore—Mother Carrie's chickens, frigate birds, and others. Charlotte counted several hundred in groups.

About 4:30 we saw many boats in the ocean, headed for Miami. By 5:30 we had moved all things of value to us to the new house up on the ridge. The workmen who erected it had left the day after they were finished, on Friday.

5:30 P.M. Wind northeast about forty miles an hour. Tide is rising fast. We are having short sharp squalls. Dock is cleared. Boats all tied. Couldn't put the powerboat in hurricane creek. No way to return to the old house in this wind.

9 P.M. Wind the same. Squalls sharper. Not much rain.

10:30 P.M. Just had a bad squall, northeast. The wind has not fallen before it. Took a look at the dock and boats. All okay.

Forgot to mention that before returning to dock after warning sponge fishermen, we had gone to Sands Key. Bob Craig had been camping there in a partially built fishing camp, George Deen's. He left two days before and left a Bantam hen and her biddies to make do. We tried to catch them and got one chick in twenty minutes. No more time to spare, need the rest of the daylight for our preparations.

When we reached the house, Charlotte improvised a pen for the chick. She emptied a Bull Durham sack, put cotton in the bottom to spread it. "Little Bug," as she called it, had enough room to turn around in the sack. The drawstring was loose around its neck. She carried it in her shirt pocket while we worked.

We ate a cold snack and had the Coleman burning. Charlotte taught Little Bug house manners, using bits of paper for locations and taps of the bottom for punishment. It soon learned to come when called.

All the wooden shutters in the new house had been nailed down except for one at the back of the house. That had been loosely fastened. We hoped that if the roof went off, we could make it out through that opening and into the jungle.

For such an eventuality, Charlotte had packed the Boston bag with our bathing suits, knowing that the wind would probably blow our clothing off if we had to go out in it. Also packed a jug of water, crackers, baked beans, can opener, small jar of matches and a flashlight. We expected our belts and knives to stay on even if we lost our clothing. Because of the intense humidity, we wrapped our little Seth Thomas clock in a bathing suit, hoping it would keep on running.

Although we had deserted the old house, it was also secured.

12 Midnight. Almost time for high tide. The water shows no sign of slacking. Wind northeast, nearly fifty miles an hour. Little rain, regular high-tide squalls start.

3:15 A.M. September 2. Tide just changed. Had a bad squall just now; it shook the house badly. This is the first time it shook. We are very grateful that it was built on top of the ridge and sand-anchored.

Four foot-deep trenches dug in the ridge outlined the shape of the house. A rectangle formed of 8 by 8 timbers was joined to shorter pieces for the width by long bolts through holes drilled in centers. Ends of bolts were joined to floor beams after the trenches were filled with rock and sand. This allowed the house to "walk". Had it been rigid it would have been blown over the ridge. The house surely did walk. After the hurricane, this tight, well-built little house leaked in every joint.

3:30 A.M. Stars have been showing up to now. Bright and sparkling. Decided lull, with fewer squalls. We are going to lie down and try to get a little sleep, with our clothes on, ready to move quickly if necessary.

We haven't mentioned Fiddler yet. He was with us all this time and getting very fidgety and nervous.

6:30 A.M. Got a little sleep. Wind and conditions are the same as 3:30 A.M. Checked things at the dock. Everything there is okay, and at the house. Expect this hurricane to get worse on high water at about 1:30 P.M.

12 Noon. The squalls are increasing. Wind northeast and more rain now. Tide is rather high. About two feet above normal.

2 P.M. Squalls are very sharp. Wind bursts reach sixty-five to seventy miles per hour, with the northeast wind a steady fifty-five to sixty.

4 P.M. Violent wind squalls lasting from 20 to 25 minutes. Sometimes with bursts to seventy or eighty miles per hour. Very little rain. Wind is still northeast. Charlotte is sitting on the floor in the open doorway. She saw the tide recede fifty feet before each squall, and then return with a rush. Each time a little higher. No waves visible. The wind has blown the tops off. Afraid for our boat at high tide if the wind doesn't shift or the surges continue. The roof of the old house is blowing off in chunks. I can't stop it.

Just realized that we had ignored the ducks after feeding them. Wonder if they will survive?

This new house is really trembling, and in wind bursts, the floor actually jumps. Could not stand upright during my several trips to the dock. It was necessary to lean forward on a forty degree angle and walk against the wind.

6:30 P.M. Fiddler smells into the wind and growls. Strange actions for a dog. I made it to the dock all right once again and the boat is okay. The surges are very bad. Wind is getting variable in bursts. It is trying to swing east to east southeast. I hope it does. Never saw a storm from one direction so long. It should be low tide now, but it is several feet above normal high. If it would only rain hard!

8 P.M. There has been a little lull with wind swing to east and almost southeast in bursts. I judge velocity of wind to be around ninety miles per hour as waves are completely flat now and spray goes by like smoke. It stings like hail. There is much water over the path to the dock. Charlotte refused to let me go to the dock alone this time. She said that if anything happened to me, it should happen to both of us.

Our heavy crawfish car has been carried away. I am glad. It was too heavy to handle and it was dangerous to have it fastened to the dock. The boat is pitching in the waves and surges. It will be okay if the many lines hold, and the tide doesn't get too much higher. It is over the land now and running in surges over the ten-foot ridge the house is sitting on.

If it gets much worse—the house is shaking badly now—we may have to go into the jungle and hope to survive there. The old house is shedding pieces.

Expect the worst part of this hurricane to come at high water, tonight. Wind is a steady ninety or over now. Wind is east southeast and the rain comes in sheets.

10 P.M. Wind almost southeast now, and steady, about same intensity. Very few squalls, almost steady rain. Clouds, when visible, are traveling extremely fast in two distinct layers. The house is swaying now that it has stopped trembling. Water over everything and coming in at speedboat pace. Lots of debris going by. Boat will ride okay if rope and flexible mangroves it is tied to hold. Only big danger is collision with some large object in the water. We almost had to crawl along the ridge to see this. Boat seems to be changing color.

Oh, boy! Just had a squall of twelve minutes' duration. This was the worst one so far. We had to shout to talk to each other. Sure hope this hurricane breaks on the tide. Will try to get a little sleep as there is nothing we can do and we are simply exhausted. Will not undress, as we might have to go into the jungle yet. I hope not. It could be real rugged, trying to hold onto trees, in the racing water—with this wind!

12 Midnight. Had a bad squall for the last eight minutes. The wind is southeast, way over ninety. Just a deafening hiss and roar now. No sky visible. Lots of rain. These dogwood trees near the house are bent double now and crying. The wood makes a high screaming whine that can be heard above the wind sound. I don't see how they can stand it. All other visible trees are broken.

1 A.M. September 3. Another squall, east southeast, about same velocity, only we have more rain now. It is coming in visible sheets. The tide is still rising fast, but it should be full-flood now. House is swaying in the puffs.

3:30 A.M. The worst squall so far. Also the heaviest wind. Lots of rain. Tide just now starting to ebb. Not much chance to look after the boat now. Wind is much too strong.

6:30 A.M. Just getting light. Wind, southeast about sixty, light squalls. Tide ebbing because of southeast winds.

8 A.M. Wind southeast about ninety. Fairly strong and steady. Tide just on the turn from ebb to flood. Down to normal high-tide level now. Many seabirds have come ashore at our dock. Because of the southeast wind, it is somewhat protected. Things are really a mess at the dock.

Our boat is still afloat, but it was so sandblasted that it has an almost perfect camouflage coat. It was necessary to go within twenty feet of it to see it. Skiffs are sunk on shore and everything is covered with coral rock and debris from the ocean, including a life ring marked S.S. Dixie. Some of the dock planking was carried away when the waves and surges broke over it. Sometime during the night, what was left of the roof of the old house started to go—in chunks. It is still shedding like a molting duck. The coconut trees that were not

280

broken are getting to be just bare sticks. With a few exceptions, all the other trees are bare. The leaves that are left look burnt from the salt spray. At times the rain seems as thick as pea-soup fog, and it sure hurts when it hits.

10 A.M. (approximately). Well, salt-laden air has stopped our clock in the Boston bag. Now we are time-less. Wind, southeast about eighty in squalls with steady rain. The tide is rising slowly.

At the next high tide this thing may break, although it covers such a large area, it is hard to tell definitely. The clouds for hours now have had that typical rotary motion that hurricanes give. There are three separate and distinct layers. Each seems to be about eight hundred to a thousand feet apart. The lowest is moving southeast to northwest and just floating by comparison. The top layer is moving at least two hundred and fifty miles an hour from northwest to southeast and apparently right into the face of the storm.

We haven't even tried to eat regular meals. Snacked on crackers and beans as the spirit moved us. The crackers don't quite droop in our hands, neither do they crunch. Pretty tiresome diet—nothing cooked beforehand, and no time to do it.

Charlotte just counted nine frigate birds coming out of the northeast to land in the cut for shelter. These are late. Many others of the same kind came several days ago.

The tide is starting its surging again. Just measured some stakes that I had previously driven in the beach. Find that from fourteen inches to two feet of sand and rock has disappeared along the entire beach. Will have to build a new gangway to the dock as the old one is much too short now. Much land has been lost.

Estimate the center of this storm to have passed about fifty miles from us. Considering the wind velocities it reached, probably less.

After the hurricane, official records showed the center had passed approximately fifty-five miles from our location. A large cypress log, twenty-five feet long and fourteen feet in diameter at the butt, had became stranded in nine feet of water two weeks before—it has been washed ashore like so much seaweed.

These squalls, one of which just occurred, seem to be worse on flood tide and reach peak at intervals approximately an hour and a half.

12 Noon (approximately). Wind, southeast by south southeast sixty-five to seventy miles an hour. Clouds almost south. Tide rising and running parallel with shore, taking out sand and rock fast. Steady light rain with few squalls.

No signs of any boats that went into hurricane creek on Sands Key. That means, I hope, that they are safe. Feel certain that when the wind reaches southwest, the storm will be over. Main part of this storm has lasted over thirty-six hours. It is getting very cool now.

I believe this storm will set a record for wind violence and low barometric pressure.

According to a newspaper report, "A barometric reading of 26.35, the lowest in the history of world weather bureau records has been officially announced by the U.S. Weather Bureau." The barometer, belonging to a charter boat captain, came through the storm unscratched, but had registered such an incredibly low reading that it was sent to Washington for verification. (The second lowest barometer reading, 27.01, was recorded in 1932 by the British steamer *Phenius* in the Western Caribbean Sea.)

4 P.M. (approximately). Wind is south southeast to south, almost fifty miles per hour. We have a light rain. Short squalls with occasional puffs. Clouds still circling. Only two layers visible now. The tide is ebbing. Light spots are appearing in the east.

A few of the frigate birds are flying out to sea. The storm apparently passed about 2 P.M.

Charlotte had seemed to be affected by the change in pressure as one of the violent squalls went by. To get some relief from the headaches caused by the pressure, she sat in the open doorway watching things blow by. As the squalls passed, the sudden drop in pressure would cause the air to rush out of the house, and then return with each squall. The increasing discomfort allowed her to tell me when each squall was approaching.

She explained that this had first happened to her after a twister passed the house she was in during the 1926 hurricane. After the twister roared by, she suddenly realized she couldn't hear her companions. She was deaf for over an hour, and has suffered reactions to low barometric pressure since that time. Here is her story:

It was mid-afternoon and the twister was visible as it plowed up sand, bushes and other movable things in the sparsely settled section of Rio Vista where we were living at the time. Because of the roar of the wind all conversation had stopped. It just wasn't possible to shout over the wind. We saw the thing go by a short distance from us and I followed the others outside to watch. A couple of blocks down the street was a two-story four-unit apartment house which was directly in the path of the twister. More debris was added to the spiral and after it had passed the apartment house, I saw that the whole west wall had been neatly removed.

Plainly visible in the upstairs bathroom, a man was sitting on the toilet. He stood up, looked around at the open space, then instead of going through the door that was visible there, he jumped out the opening and broke a leg when he fell.

6:45 P.M. (approximately). Fowey Rock Light just turned on. Tide is way out and has not changed for hours. Wind south southeast to south. Expect a few squalls on the flood tide tonight.

10 P.M. (approximately). Wind a steady forty now with short sharp puffs of fifty to fifty-five. Definitely south now. Tides slowly flood, something is keeping it out. Clouds still ragged and in streaks. We expect to sleep tonight for a change. The house is like a great big sieve, but what does a little more water matter now? The ocean is a dirty white offshore, and muddy near shore.

September 4. Sleepy but safe. Had breakfast. More beans and crackers.

End of Log

In the morning we decided to see if Captain Russell and his son were safe. Wading and climbing in the mangroves, we managed to unfasten the powerboat. The knots in the ropes had tightened beyond any possibility of untying. We cut them.

We hadn't removed the wicker-covered gallon jug that we

kept in the stern of the boat. We found it in the bow, unbroken. The canvas cover that we had laced around the engine was still in place. We cut those ropes and we poured fresh water over the distributor to remove the visible layer of salt that had penetrated under the cover.

By the time the motor was dry, we had the boat bailed and the assortment of hurricane debris thrown over the side. We couldn't quite understand why there wasn't more water in the boat–apparently, it had blown out. Thank God for that. Strangely enough it didn't act up as usual. Started immediately. We went through the cut towards the flats and saw Reno wading towards us. The water was lower now than when we had towed them towards the hurricane creek.

"Mr. Russell," Reno said, "could you please bring a couple of shovels so Pappy and I can dig ourselves out? Oh, some matches, too."

"Okay, Reno. Boy, it's good to know that you two are safe!"

While Russ cut the shovels loose from the trees to which they had been tied upright, I went to the house for the jar of matches. When we returned to Reno, there was less than twelve inches of water on the flats. He got aboard and we moved to a position closer to the hurricane creek opening.

I held the boat in position with the sculling oar and they started their trench. Soon there was length enough to it, so they tied the two stern lines around their waists and towed the boat after them as they dug. Only a ditch for the keel of the sailboat was necessary. It was more than a quarter of a mile in and took several hours. Mud and sand caved down to fill the hole and doubled their work. Fortunately, we had some drinking water left. They needed it. I wasn't allowed to help. Men's work!

Around noon, we were near the sailboat, which was almost on its side. Here, the fact that the hurricane creek was deeper than the flats leading to it helped a lot. The tide was still going out, and after they had cut through the last of the flats, the outgoing tide helped clear their trench. The sand dug out near the keel of the sailboat raced out with the water.

Finally the sailboat was floating upright and Reno went farther up the creek to get the skiffs. They had been sunk to protect them from damage. Free of water now, they were tied in tandem behind the sailboat and I was told to start the motor and go slowly forward. Reno and Russ pushed and got the sailboat started. They followed along and as I got into the deeper water, they climbed aboard a skiff.

Without our help, they would have had a fantastic amount of work. Without proper tools, it would have been almost impossible.

It was about two in the afternoon when we arrived at the dock and tied. Reno immediately got out the little stove. None of us had done any cooking throughout the time of the hurricane. Our stove was in the old house and Captain's little Shipmate had been stowed below.

Captain Russell moved very slowly and when I looked into the cabin, I saw why. The sails were folded and packed in there, along with bunches of sponges, which had been their beds while they waited out the storm. Only a four-foot space, the length of the cabin, was free and clear, in addition to the space from which the stove had been removed.

After the first cup of coffee, we all felt the need to stretch our legs again and went towards the house. We picked up a couple of coconuts from the debris and opened them to make a pancake breakfast.

Funny. We hadn't missed the kitchen door of the old house until now. Except for debris on the floor, the kitchen was much as we had left it. Of course, it was open to the sky and frayed along the edges, but that lovely stove was there and the fire started immediately.

We set up the table and benches while Russ made breakfast. We still had four plates left and four heavy cups. Reno rinsed them off and we sat down to the first warm food in three days. Never have I tasted anything better.

It was an occasion for real rejoicing. The warm sun that poured in seemed to bless us.

The first batch of pancakes just seemed to disappear, and we finished the second with Fiddler's help.

We had been too busy until then to notice that none of the ducks were around. We looked under the house, at the back of the ridge, and found them all, still huddled together just waiting for whatever might happen next. Covered partially with sand and seaweed, they sure were a miserable looking bunch of birds.

We put food and fresh water out and called them out to eat. They finally started to move sluggishly. Sort of cramped. I guess from trying to stay under the house in the small protection that gave them.

"How did they manage to stay there while the water poured over the ridge?"

"Swam all the time, I guess."

As they thinned out a bit, we saw a large black snake was snuggled in among them. As the snake, disturbed by our proximity, started to move slowly along the length of the house, it was possible to judge its length. It was nine feet long.

"Mr. Russell, we got mighty short of water while we waited out that blow. I got to thinking about it and remembered some of the places we go when we are away from peopled areas. If you ever need water when you are near Lignum Vitae Key, you go in from the ocean side towards the second point of land past the mangroves and on shore there you look for a worn foot-path. It goes up hill a little. You follow it and when you get to where it is level again, you'll see a hole where there is drinkable water. It's sweet water, but very good."

"How did you happen to find it, Captain?"

"I didn't find it. My grandpappy did a favor for the Indians one time and for a thank you, they told him how to find it.

(As I write this, my husband and I have been on Lignum Vitae, now, for twenty-one years. That was the first time I had heard of this key.)

[In 1971 the state of Florida bought Lignum Vitae Key, off the north tip of Lower Matecumbe Key, to make it a state park, naming it Lignumvitae—ed.]

"Mr. Russell, I have been studying just how to say thank you. Without your help, we would have been crab-bait like the rest of those boys. I am going to tell you about a secret I have kept for a long time now.

"There is a shipload of block tin at Longitude—by Latitude—. I know it was insured by Lloyd's of London. For quite some years now, it sat on the edge of the reef in thirty feet of water. This was

286

a mighty big blow, though, and it could be that the undertow of those giant waves out there could have sucked it off the reef into fifty fathoms or more on the Gulf Stream side."

We thanked him sincerely for this information. Later events made it impossible for us to try to locate this wreck. We never seemed to find the time.

"Now we purely appreciate the wonderful breakfast, but we must get to Key West to see how our people there made out."

"You sit still a few minutes, Captain. Reno and I will rig your sails for you, then Charlotte and I will tow you around into the bay so you can catch the wind and get a good start."

He was impatient to leave, though. "Reno and I can rig the sails while you are towing us down-bay. No time lost that way."

We took them quite a way off shore and they were ready to sail when Russ cast off their painter. We called our good-byes and waved back at them.

There was no sign of the *Gertrude* or her sister ship. No wreckage on shore.

It was a shock to look at what had been the lime grove. It was almost gone! There were many signs of twisters having gone through. The trees were splintered and frayed so that they looked like the upright remains of old brooms. Limes were on the ground six inches deep. We were talking of the possibility of salvaging some of the bruised limes when we found a man's body. We went back to the house.

Shortly after we arrived there, a small airplane flew over slowly. ASSOCIATED PRESS was painted on the sides. We gathered our linen and quickly spread it on the lawn, spelling out O-K. Then the plane returned and the passenger waved frantically.

Sometime later we found out that the passenger was my brother, Don Arpin. He wrote an article that appeared in the Fort Lauderdale *Daily News*, saying they had been surprised to find us alive, that we were among the very few survivors of the Labor Day hurricane, how we had spelled O-K with the linen. And the final line stated that Fiddler was scampering around us.

Later that afternoon Happy and Al came. We were very glad to see them and they us. After the first greetings were over, they went to the boat and brought some fresh bread and cookies, a valuable gift at that time.

"That's some paint job you have on your boat now. We didn't see it until we almost hit it. Didn't expect to find you here. Almost everyone else is dead.

"We were sent out this morning to evacuate those keys which were connected by the railroad, particularly Lower Matecumbe. When we got to Upper Matecumbe, we found that the train had been blown off the track there. Only a few people alive there.

"On the north end of Lower Matecumbe where the Bonus Army was camped, it's flat. All the men gone, most likely dead! All places where there were bridges, as far as we went, we saw only open spaces between the keys. The only way you can contact the lower Keys now is by boat or airplane."

We led the way to the house-shell now and they shook their heads in amazement. They drank coffee with us but refused to share the fresh bread and cookies. "We brought it for you!"

The bread tasted as good as cake to me. After the second cup of coffee, Al said, "Gee, it's good to be sitting here talking again. We didn't know what to expect when we got here. Saw so many dead people on those other keys! Sorry to have to go but we have to go back and see if we can help more people–if we find them alive. Thank God you don't need any help!"

On the way to the dock, Russ told them the location of the man's body. Then he offered to go with them.

"You've gone through enough strain without adding to it. We'll find it and take it along to Matecumbe with us."

As we walked back to the house after seeing them off, we decided that being so isolated had lost its attraction. And, there was no possibility of earning our groceries on Elliott Key for a while. We decided it was time to return to the mainland.

Form 2654
TREASURY DEPARTMENT
U. S. Coast Guard
November, 1931

U. S. COAST GUARD
OFFICIAL DISPATCH

UNIT _____ DATE _____

INCOMING HEADING

W A R N I N G   T O   A L L   V E S S E L S

TEXT: *1 September* —

WEATHER FORECAST:

JACKSONVILLE TO FLORIDA STRAITS:

MODERATE NORTHEAST WINDS OVER NORTH AND CENTRAL PORTIONS FRESHENING OFF THE COAST AND INCREASING NORTHEAST WINDS PROBABLY REACHING GALE FORCE OVER EXTREME SOUTH PORTION AND POSSIBLY OF HURRICANE FORCE IN THE FLORIDA STRAITS TONIGHT OR MONDAY WITH HEAVY SQUALLS IN THE FLORIDA STRAITS.

PLEASE PASS THIS INFORMATION TO ALL VESSELS IN YOUR VICINITY

Barometer Reading on Keys Found Lowest in All Annals

A barometric reading of 26.35, the lowest in the history of world weather bureau records, has been officially announced by the U. S. Weather Craig, tiny Key settlement, during the Labor Day hurricane.

The record reading is .66 of an inch lower than the next lowest reading ever recorded, according to Ernest Carson, local weatherman.

Because it was so low that it seemed incredible, United States engineers brought the barometer from the Keys to Miami shortly after the storm and had the instrument checked both by local and Washington weather men.

The barometer belonged to Capt. Ivor Olsen, charter boat owner. It came through the storm unscathed and was pronounced by Washington authorities to be in proper working order.

A preliminary test, made by the local weather bureau, revealed its

(Continued on Page Twenty-one)

BAROMETER

(Continued from Page Two)

accurate reading as 26.38. It was sent to Washington, where corrections were made, with the final result that a reading of 26.35 was confirmed.

The second lowest barometer reading was recorded in 1932 by the British steamer Phenius in the western Caribbean sea. This reading was 27.01.

Miami's lowest official reading in the 1926 reading was 27.61, while on November 4 of this year the lowest pressure recorded was only 28.75 inches.

September 2, 1935

The Aftermath

The Railroad That Died At Sea
- Photo Courtesy of The Historical Museum of Southern Florida

Sending Home the Dead
- Photo Courtesy of The Historical Museum of Southern Florida

The S.S. Dixie
- *Photo Courtesy of The Historical Museum of Southern Florida*

CHAPTER TWENTY-FIVE

We Learn We Are Among the Few Survivors.
Wilbur Shows Me Bullet Wounds.
Souvenir Hunters Try to Buy Our Hurricane Warning.
Load Russ' Father's Car and Prepare to Leave.

Only a few days after their visit, Happy and Al arrived in a new boat.

"How did you rate a new boat?"

"We were going slowly towards Upper Matecumbe when we hit a submerged board. It made a hole in the bottom of the boat and we thought it best to leave it there. Al bailed and it wasn't too bad until we hit something else and it pushed up farther and made a bigger hole. We just did manage to limp to shallow water before we sunk. We just sat there in the boat full of water for hours until some Border Patrol buddies of ours came along. We flagged them down with our shirts. Before then, though, we were talking about those cookies we hadn't eaten. We were hungry! They took us back to Miami and we got into dry uniforms and they gave us this new boat to work with. Knowing you folks were all right, we went back to help those who needed us.

"A lot of Miami people are down in the Keys now helping the survivors. Give us a list of whatever you need and we'll bring it back tomorrow when we come down."

"Can you take Charlotte to Miami with you? We have decided to leave here, and she will make arrangements for my dad to meet me in Princeton with some of our things."

"Sure, and we'll bring her back tomorrow. It isn't usual for civilians to get a ride in a government boat, but you surely do come under the 'Distressed Survivor' clause."

I dressed quickly and Russ made some notes for me to take along. One of the items on the list was a pint of liquor. "Charlotte, we just might need it for medicinal purposes."

The boat ride to Miami was very slow. Al stood up and looked from side to side as we went forward, looking for more bodies. Fortunately, we didn't see any. We did see a fantastic assortment of almost anything that will float, including a wooden headboard from a bed.

At Border Patrol headquarters, I thanked them and left for the Greyhound bus station just a few blocks away. I chose to walk through Sears & Roebuck's store, rather than around it to the back where the bus would be. Because of this, I saw Wilbur again. I noticed him about ten feet ahead of me and called, "Wilbur! Hello!"

Turning, he saw me and stopped. This caused many impatient people to push by him. When I caught up to him, we walked towards the back of the store together. Seeing his noticeable limp, I asked if he had injured his leg. By this time, we were on the outside of the store. He stepped sideways out of the flow of traffic into a clear area back of the open door. Perhaps it was clear because it was partially occupied by a Red Cross worker collecting for the storm victims.

She pulled on my sleeve and almost demanded a contribution. I said, "I'm one myself!" Then she asked for my name, address, and, I said, "According to the instructions on your questionnaire, the maiden name and religion of my grandmothers! Hell no!"

She was furious and temporarily speechless, so I turned to Wilbur; who was grinning at the woman's expression.

"About your injured knee?"

"Oh, no. I didn't injure it." Kneeling down on one knee, darned if he didn't pull up his pants' leg and show me an indented white scar. It was whiter than the surrounding flesh. Sort of puckered, and on the calf of his leg. I tilted forward slightly and saw the other side had the same mark on it.

He seemed to be displaying these scars proudly. "I had polio," he said. "Isn't it remarkable that this is the only result?"

Almost two full years of meeting strange situations head-on

had given me quite a bit of control. "I don't know anyone else who had polio that got off as lucky as you did! How are Pop and Don?"

"They are just fine. Matter of fact, I'm on my way to meet them now."

The departure of my bus was announced then, and saying good-bye, I ran towards it. The trip to Lauderdale seemed short as I thought of this strange conversation. Since when did polio leave the scars of bullet holes. What made him so talkative about a personal thing? It was the first time, and he was friendly. All his conversation on the key had been addressed to Russ. It seemed important that he convince me he had been ill.

At my parent's home, I visited Mother, Dad, Jan and those of my brothers who were home. It was then that I learned about Don having been the passenger of the plane that buzzed us after the hurricane. He choked up when he tried to explain how he felt when he saw we were alive. All reports they had had said everyone on the Upper Keys had died. "When I saw you were both well I–"

Jan just flew into my arms, almost squashing Little Bug in my pocket. I gave it to her then but told her to leave the little bantam in the bag for a while before releasing it. She had to talk to it and get it acquainted with her voice.

They all went along with me to Russell's parents. Not much time to visit, so we visited on the way as well as later on. Russ' parents were delighted to hear we were "coming back to civilization."

I gave his father the map showing the location of the dock on the Princeton Canal and asked if he would meet Russ there to get some of our belongings two mornings later, around eleven. His parents were delighted to do anything to aid us. After a short visit, we left.

At the house again, Little Bug came in for his share of attention. I let it out of its bag, put a square of paper down on the table, and we started lunch. Mom fussed then about "a chicken in the house," so I put it on the floor. Strange how a small piece of bread fell out of Mama's hand a few minutes later. It landed right near the little bantam.

We spent the time that evening reliving the hurricane and

the newspaper reports of the disaster. Very few of the Keys residents had survived. First reports said "None"!

I said that I was sorry but I wasn't used to late hours, then they reminded me of an old family custom. We all knelt down and Mom led us in saying the rosary in thanksgiving for our safety. We usually followed this custom—always in emergencies.

It was just daybreak when Dad took me to the bus station for my return trip. After I arrived in Miami, I asked the bus driver where I could find a liquor store to get the bottle Russ had mentioned. I had a little time left before I was to meet Happy and Al, so I hurried.

This was the first time I ever bought liquor, so I hesitantly entered the combination bar and liquor store. No one paid any attention to me. They were all watching and listening to a crying man at the bar. He was punctuating his statements by slamming his fist on the bar.

"Those damn people told me to come running and get my train ready to evacuate people from the Keys, and that Washington Bonus Army that's camped down there. Look at me, I ran down there in my good suit. [Veterans of W.W.I, owed bonuses, were instead given jobs building bridges for the Overseas Highway—ed.] Look at me! I just now got here. Been gone days.

"Don't do me no good to run down there. Those miserable bastards won't give me a go-ahead sign. I kept phoning them and they say wait, wait. I talked to the rest of the crew and they took a chance on their jobs same as me. We took off without a go-ahead. If they had let me go when I was ready, I could have saved all those people. The bastards didn't want to help the Bonus Army so everyone got lost."

"Look at me." Then he put one fist on top of the other and put them on his stomach. His pants extended beyond them. "Look at all the weight I lost while I waited three days for them to come after me."

Too bad the officials couldn't have seen that angry crying man. Perhaps it would have made them more humane in the future.

Had I wanted to, it would have been impossible to interrupt him. I waited until he went to a booth and slumped down. Then

I made my purchase and hurried out.

At Border Patrol headquarters I found Happy and Al waiting. The waves were high and close together. Now the bay was full of debris from farther south. We had to go slowly and it was a bumpy trip. According to the numbers of coconuts we saw in the water, there wasn't one left on the trees in the Keys.

I was glad to reach Elliott Key again and didn't envy them their all-day patrol. They didn't stay for coffee and left as soon as I was on the dock.

About an hour later, we heard a small fast boat and waited at the house. These were strangers to us. They finally came up and introduced themselves as Smith and Jones.

"The fishing down there isn't very good. Can you suggest where we should go?"

The thought of men coming a minimum of twelve miles, through debris strewn water, merely to fish! No. Ridiculous!

"Fishing won't be good for quite a while! Didn't you know we just had a hurricane?"

"Hey did you get a hurricane warning?"

"Yes, we did."

"Can we see it?"

"Russ held it in his hand and let them read it."

"Say, Jones, that would make a swell souvenir wouldn't it. Mister, I'll give you fifty dollars for it."

That was ten weeks groceries in those days, and I had spent most of our ready cash going to Lauderdale and back, the day before. I saw the strange look on Russell's face then.

"There's something screwy about your offering so much money for this thing!"

Without saying another word, the men left the house. Getting into their boat, they left the area. About two hours later another small boat appeared. These men appeared to fish in the cut right off the dock and then came to the house. Russ met them outside. These gave their names as White and Jones. They asked if we had stayed there through the hurricane and congratulated us on surviving. Then they, too, asked if we had received a hurricane warning. Russ held it as before. They followed the same pattern, but they offered *one hundred dollars* for the souvenir of the hurricane.

"You fellows are the second ones who tried to buy this hurricane warning–something damn fishy is going on." He took a step back and, folding the warning, put it in his back pocket.

Their anger was visible as they left. They also got into their boat and turned towards shore.

When we reached Fort Lauderdale, we read of the controversy regarding the storm warning. The Weather Bureau denied advance knowledge. I took our copy to the editor of the Fort Lauderdale *Daily News*. He was very surprised to see it. I said that if the Coast Guard had known about it, the Weather Bureau had also known. He agreed and asked for the message, so he could send it to the main office of the Weather Bureau in Washington. I hesitated until he called in his secretary and asked her to write out a receipt for it. It contained a description of the warning. Handing it to him then I explained my hesitation by telling him of the men who had wanted to buy it. He found it as strange as we had.

Later, when I returned and retrieved the message, it had been sent to Washington and, by the time it was returned, a second hurricane had occurred in Fort Lauderdale in November this same year. Up to that time the general public was not informed of barometric pressure and other signs of a severe storm. Storm warnings as we now have them did not exist. The fact is, the very short warning time before the Labor Day hurricane received by the very few people was hardly long enough to avoid loss of life or property.

Our warning disproved the supposed lack of knowledge on the part of the Weather Bureau. The terrible toll of almost six hundred lives lost so shocked the public that the Weather Bureau was trying to whitewash itself.

CHAPTER TWENTY-SIX

I Fluff Catching Ducks.
Captain W.R. Russell and Reno Only Survivors of Sponge Fleet.
Return to Fort Lauderdale. Load My Dad's Car. Chicken Story.
Russ' Evening with Hemingway. Visit by Investigator.
My Girl Friend's Story about Wilbur, the Dope Runner.
Wilbur Escapes. Flip Tells How Zigzag Path Was Used.

Sorting our possessions now, we had to go back mentally to what would be useful in town. The most useful thing we had on the Keys was the radio cabinet. I had become almost fond of that thing. It furnished small parts for many of our projects.

Clothing perfectly suitable for that area only went to the junk pile. All of my box furniture, pieces of Spanish cedar, precious jar containers were thrown aside. But the pile Russ was to take to the mainland, and the one we planned on taking by boat and skiff, loomed large.

Now we packed boxes that would fit in the car door. Russ was ready to leave on the chosen morning, and I packed the other things in boxes salvaged from our beach store. My last island beachcombing.

Russ returned much later than I expected and explained, "Mother and Dad arrived at the dock soon after I did and Mother supervised the loading of the car. We got everything stowed and they got in to leave. Then Dad got out again and said that he couldn't face the thought of driving eighty miles without being able to use his rear-vision mirror, at least a part of it.

"Everything came out again and Mother started re-packing boxes. She can certainly pack better than we did. While re-packing, she discarded enough boxes so that when we stowed the rest in the car, Dad had a tunnel through which he could see out the back. When it was finally done to his satisfaction, they left."

The skiff, loaded to the gunwales with the lifeboat cover lashed over it, was ready the night before we were to leave. The second skiff we left for Mr. Fossey. We planned on what we were to eat the next morning and then got out the remaining grits to cook with more fish obtained with a *brown fishhook* and fed the ducks. No breakfast for them. It might be too messy. Very tired that night, we couldn't decide what to do with our many canned things and went to bed.

We were awakened that morning by Captain William Reno Russell and Reno. They had just returned from Key West.

"It was very sad. When we sculled ashore, after anchoring in the harbor, we were met by so many women who asked if we had seen their men. We were the only sponge boat to return after the hurricane alive, just the two of us. Thanks to you!"

He only said a few words about his reunion with his wife, who had been in the crowd on shore. His expression said the rest.

The wives and families of sea-faring men have learned to depend a lot on faith and prayer. They also have great faith in the ability of their men to bring their vessels home safely. Most of the Key West homes facing the ocean at that time were constructed with widows' walks on the roof. When vessels were overdue, the families could be seen on them in constant vigil hoping to spot a late arrival.

In this case, the vigil proved fruitless, and symbolic black crepe hung on many front doors. Most fortunately Mrs. Russell did not have to go through this ordeal in their home on Olivia Street.

"Mr. Russell, I have been most thoughtless. I carry a calendar in the boat at all times but I completely forgot what my Pappy told me. We were almost to Key West when I remembered. He told me that anytime in the fall of the year, when there are five moon phases in one month, it's a hurricane month."

Coffee and pancakes were ready to serve now and I served them.

"Captain Russell, we have a problem you could help us with. We have about fifty pounds more than we can carry in the boat safely. Will you take care of it for us!"

"Be more than happy to do whatever I can. Where is it and what do you want me to do with it?"

"It's our extra groceries!"

When he heard that, he said he couldn't accept. Russ finally asked him if he had seen how low in the water the powerboat was. "Realize now, when I add the ducks, and our bedding, it will get lower."

"Thank you very kindly, I'd be happy to."

We all got boxes from the beach and, filling them with the food and jam, put them on the path to the dock. I gave the houses a final sweeping then and we were ready to gather the ducks, after Russ tied a hatch cover over the stove to protect it from the elements.

Then Russ put out a bit of food for the ducks to gather them and we all were supplied with burlap bags.

Now we all started grabbing ducks and shoving them into the bags. For a few startled minutes, they cooperated by standing still, then there was a mad scramble and it was rather hilarious as we chased them in the bent-over position necessary to capture them.

Of course, I stumbled. In falling, I managed to flatten two of the ducks. No longer laughing now, I lay there a minute. Captain Russell smiled but was too polite to join Russ and Reno in their laughter at the sight. I felt very bad about it, for a minute. It was only after I got up that I noticed the ducks didn't.

"Captain, those ducks are just fresh-killed," Russ said. "Maybe you and Reno would enjoy them for supper."

"We thank you kindly, Miss Charlotte." We put these aside and we waited for a time until the ducks became quiet again. A bit more food bunched them, and we got the rest. Now I had time to breathe and looked down at myself. I had smelled something, but didn't consider it was on me. It was. The only clothes I had now, except for my packed dress. Somewhere towards the bottom of the pile on the skiff, as I remembered.

Seeing my face then, Reno and Russell laughed again. They just hooted. Then Russ said, "Don't worry. It is warm enough today so you can take them off and drag them in the water a while. They'll get clean again and you can put them on before we get in to town.

Taking the ducks and the boxes of food to the dock didn't take long. There we handed Reno the food to stow and he returned to the dock to help Russ with our load. The crawfish car was tied to the load on the boat and the ducks put aboard in it. The lightweight Beastie had survived and was tied to the top of the skiff on the canvas.

Now, for the first time someone was seeing us off from the dock. It seemed strange! We promised to visit Captain Russell and his family in Key West and waved good-bye. Now, on our way back to civilization, I felt a bit sad. I think I would have changed my mind, if I had been asked right then. Things had been so interesting there. Not too many dull moments. Just some placid ones.

We went slowly because of our load and it was mid-afternoon when we arrived in Miami. Russ was familiar with the Miami waterfront and went into the slip where the large Mallory vessels docked. The end was just a few feet from Biscayne Boulevard. I threw the anchor onto the land there, nothing to tie to where we were. The irregularities in the wall helped me climb up. Russ boosted Fiddler up (he had to eat, too) and I grabbed his front legs, managing to get him ashore. Russ followed and put a rope leash on Fid's neck. It was his first time off the island, and he was a grown dog. Russ had put the empty water jug on his belt, before climbing.

My clothes were still damp as I had put them on just before we got into the river traffic. This time they had clean dirt on them from my climbing to land.

We were only a short distance from an eight-stool, short-order lunch stand. Russ went first and had started to order. Fiddler stood at his heels. Then a car drove up and stopped quite near us. Fiddler had never seen one before, and to him, it was a strange beast. He attacked and tried to bite the tires. He had always hated being laughed at and suffered greatly from it for the short time we remained there. Some people who hadn't seen it asked why others were laughing, and we soon had a small crowd around us. On our way to the slip, someone said, "Look, why are they going that way." Some followed us.

Russ handed me the cold drinks he was carrying and I put

302

them on the ground. I had six hamburgers in my hat. I got ready to hand Fiddler to him when Russ called. More people gathered when they saw him go over the edge. Now I had trouble with Fiddler but finally succeeded in getting him to go down. Next I tossed the drinks. Lastly, I lay on the ground and passed down the hat full of hamburgers.

"I'm holding the boat," Russ said. "Pass down the anchor."

I was aboard soon afterwards, and the end of the slip was now lined with people exclaiming about this and that, most especially, "Look at that strange thing perched on the skiff!" They all waved and called good-bye as we were on our way once more.

In the inland waterway, we reached Baker's Haulover just before sunset. The tide was going out. To anyone familiar with it, I wouldn't have to explain, but to you who aren't, I'll explain the tide is swift. With our heavy load, it was impossible to stay off the sandbar there. After going aground the second time, we gave up. Russ threw out the anchor, and we waited for the tide to change.

No room to stretch out, we sort of slumped against each other. When the tide changed some hours later, we were more than half-asleep. Starting the motor again, I pulled the anchor and using the flashlight to see the markers, we were on our way once more. Daylight found us near the pretty covered dock which was in the Sunny Isle Casino area. The rest of the trip was uneventful, except for quite a few times when speeding boats almost swamped our heavily laden one.

When we arrived, I refused to be seen in such dirty clothes, and Russ went to call my dad for his part in helping us move back. It wasn't long before he arrived.

He didn't mind when we loaded the back of his car with our assorted boxes and things, nor did he object (out loud) when we put the canvas on top of the car and hoisted the load of ducks onto it, but he did object to putting the lightweight, but clumsy, Beastie on the hood of his car.

"People will think I'm insane. The car looks like a gypsy caravan now!"

Although I knew there wasn't another Packard in town as big as his, I said, "But look, Dad. If we put the Beastie on the hood, it will get all the attention and no one will notice who is driving."

That did it! He cleared his throat, shifted his cigar to the other side of his mouth, and said, "You might have a point at that."

When it had been loaded and tied so it wouldn't interfere with his vision, Dad started off. No room for Fiddler except on Russell's lap with his head out the window.

I remember feeling a bit hurt at the expressions on his parents' faces. They didn't look at all pleased to see us, or our possessions.

We were surprised to find that their chicken coop was available for our ducks and quickly put them in it. Crowded as the ducks were, I don't think they would have lasted much longer without water. We put our assorted boxes in the garage and we started to untie the Beastie. Dad smiled now. Then, from Mother, "Leave that thing there. I absolutely will not have it around here. It's hideous–I'll have nightmares!"

Dad sat out the storm and then said, "I don't like it either, but I'll take it to the house and give it yard-room until tomorrow evening. You'll have to find another home for your treasure tomorrow."

Russ and I thanked Dad and told him we would be over for a while that evening. Thinking of that dignified man, and the expression on his face as he drove off with that monstrosity on the car hood, I can laugh again.

He was such a good sport about it. Mama told me later that he had taken all the back streets on the way home. Well, he hadn't gone on any busy ones on the long way to Russell's parents' home either!

When Dad had gone, Russ turned to his parents, "What happened to your fat and sassy chickens?"

We knew that they kept them primarily for an egg supply, no roosters. His mother and father took turns in telling the story. When one got to laughing too much to talk, the other took over. To fully appreciate it, you must remember his parents were Pennsylvania Dutch, the kind who scrub their sidewalks. "Cleanliness is *all*," that is, most important!

Here's the story:

While feeding the chickens one morning, Russ' mother noticed some of them scratching. Others were taking dust baths. Horrors! Not her chickens. Papa was disturbed, too, and went off to the feed store for something to kill the bugs.

He returned with Black Leaf Forty (concentrated nicotine), highly recommended by the clerk for killing mites. Mixed with lard, it was to be applied to the chicken's head and comb. "It will spread and take care of all the things on the chickens."

In their older clothing, the jar in her apron pocket, they were ready to apply the mix to their little egg-machines. In the coop, she grabbed the first chicken and held it while he applied the mix. Between them, they had captured and doused six chickens when she noticed the first one they doused. It was wobbling around in a small circle. Then the second. They looked on, dismayed. Soon, all six of the doctored chickens were down.

"Well", he said. "We know they were all healthy. It apparently entered their brains and killed them. Let's pluck and eat them."

They gathered the chickens and put them on the open back porch. She went to light the fire for boiling water to scald them, then got out a pillow cover for the feathers. "Waste not, want not!"

He briskly pulled the larger feathers off, and then found the smaller came out easily, and told her to turn the fire off. Now they were both occupied and talking about storing the chickens. The freezer compartment wasn't large. The pillow cover seemed to be getting quite full now and there were just the small feathers from the last chicken to add.

They were resting for a minute, looking at the row of naked chickens when, "Squawk!" One of the chickens, naked as a jaybird, was trying to stand on its feet. Another one was twitching.

In a mad dash to take them back to the pen before they ran away–the neighbors have dogs–Russ's dad took the two liveliest ones, while his mother grabbed the next two that moved. They passed each other laughing hilariously. When the last one was put into the pen, they were all standing and wobbling around.

Now, remembering the sight of all those naked chickens was too much for them and neither could talk. We laughed with them and waited to hear the rest of the story.

It got cooler, and the chickens were turning blue with cold. Russ' mother ran back into the house for her rag bag. Ah, an old flannel nightgown! She cut a pattern, then, on her trusty old

1912 model, treadle sewing machine, she sewed up a sort of chicken-shaped Mother Hubbard. With large safety pins in her pocket, she raced back to the pen. This was easy! The chickens just stood, staring unbelieving, at each other. Again, laughter slowed the telling of the story.

Putting the dresses on the chickens, they pinned a front and two side drapes together. This should keep them warm! Finished and back inside the house, they turned the radio on. A cold snap was expected that night. They went back to see how the chickens were doing. The chickens were no longer staring at each other–as though they could no longer stand that sight, they were standing sort of back to back, so they couldn't see each other. The two feathered chickens were slowly, silently walking in a ring around them. They were just fascinated. It was now long past time for them to be on their roosts, and their necks were just blue with cold.

(The chickens ended in the frying pan. All of them.)

We accepted the invitation to stay with Russ' parents until we found a place of our own and moved our things into the back bedroom. We visited with my parents for a short time that night and returned to get the first sleep in two days.

After breakfast, we fed the ducks and then Russ called me into the garage to give him a hand getting his old bicycle down from the wall where it was hanging. It was a 1916 model he had brought down from Pennsylvania.

He pumped up the tires while telling me that he was going to look for work. He mentioned that he might attend the political rally we had read was to be held that afternoon and evening at Stranahan Park.

When I said, "Oh, I wanted to see Mama and Jan today," his mother frowned. Dutch wives never interfere with their husbands' plans. I wasn't Dutch but I could see the sense of that.

I managed to occupy my time unpacking and sorting things for storage in the attic. (We stored more things in that attic until 1967. Then we got a few things out.)

Suppertime, Russ wasn't back. Bedtime, his supper in the warming oven, we all went to bed. I heard him shortly after ten-thirty. I got up and went to meet him, so did his mother. He came in, with an exaggerated sort of tiptoeing, a big grin on his face! His mother asked if he had eaten.

"No, Mama, I'm not hungry, thank you." The wind blew from him to us. Whew! She looked at him a minute and said, "Good night," not fussing at him for being under the weather. Heavens, she wouldn't admit her son would do such a thing!

In our bedroom with the door closed, he said, "I'm only slightly potted. I went to the rally and met some old friends. While we were talking, the public address system went phooey. Some guy called out for a radioman and my friends told him I was a radio engineer when I was fourteen. Well, I went over and told them they had to leave me alone in the truck, I needed quiet to work. I knew I could fix it in a couple of minutes. They had an old carbon speaker. Nobody gets paid for a minute's work though, so I smoked a cigarette, fixed the radio, then smoked another cigarette and went out. Told them to try it again. When it worked, the guy handed me five dollars. Not bad for a few minutes' work!

"When the rally was over, we went over to a bar on New River for a beer. I met an interesting little pudgy guy there. He had chin whiskers like an old sailing man. The other boys left but the pudgy man insisted I stay and drink beer with him. Imported beer yet! He said his name was Ernest Hemingway. He and I shot the breeze for over three hours. He bought all the beer–umpteen rounds. Funny I can only remember him telling one story, guess I did most of the talking.

"I managed to ride my bike all the way home, including that two-block, sand-trail approach to the house. I'm not really potted if I can do that!" With a last chuckle, he fell asleep.

(Later we read some of Hemingway's versions of our experiences.)

Some days later at my parents' home, Jan and I were in the back yard playing with the banty. It would fly to whoever called it, and it liked to land on her head. A delightful pet for a gentle child.

Mother seemed disturbed when she called me, "Charlotte, there is a border patrolman here! He says he wants to see you privately!" She seemed surprised when I smiled and ran past her to greet Happy or Al. It wasn't either.

"Department of Investigation," said the man. I requested his identification card. He showed it, and introduced himself. Then he asked if I would tell him of any unusual person we had met while on the Keys. To me, all of the native Conchs were unusual, and I wasn't about to tell him anything about our rum-running friends. I asked him to be more specific. He wanted to talk to Russ, he said, but since Russ wasn't available, he decided to talk to me.

No door to that room, Mama came in then. "Charlotte, Harry Kestner, the man who runs the sightseeing boat wants to see you."

I went out and he greeted me with, "Russ sent me to see if I like that bamboo Beastie of yours well enough to put it on my boat. Where is it?"

Mama said, "Oh, thank Heaven! Do come out back and look. I do hope you like it! We have it sort of hidden under a low tree."

I led the way and dragged the Beastie with its attached chain out from under the tree. The investigator had followed us. He and Harry just looked at it and grinned at each other.

Harry asked eagerly, "Can I have it?"

"Uh, uh," I said. "Possession only. We might get our own place soon to display it."

Mama watched happily as the investigator helped Harry tie it on the hood of his car. He said thanks and drove away.

Mama said, "I don't see why anyone would be happy to have possession of that thing."

(Harry displayed it proudly on his boat, and when we had a place for it, he offered free boat rides for rent of it. Thirteen years later in the storm of '48, it got washed overboard. Wonder what the people who found it thought when they saw those heads bobbing in the water?)

"Where in the world did you get that thing?" asked the investigator, who had followed me back in. He had an amused look.

I told him how we had made it on Elliott Key. He said, "Interesting." Then he took a little black notebook from his pocket.

"Our branch of the government has been requested to cooperate with other agencies, and we are seeking the whereabouts of Wilbur Roberti, approximately six feet, blue eyes, brown hair, youngish with a Bostonian accent."

"Yes, the description fits, but he is blond." I asked him then if he had a list of idiosyncrasies in his book. He nodded and I said, "Check off any of these: His favorite cuss word is 'shat.' He says people know what he means so he doesn't have to say it. His favorite story is about four Harvard graduates. His falsetto is perfect when he says, 'I'm the real McCoy.' As for clothing, he dislikes tucking in his shirttails and hates to wear socks." I was watching his face as I talked and could easily see he was a bit startled.

"All those things check and I can add the part about the socks."

I told him about meeting Wilbur in Sears & Roebuck and about the "polio" marks on his leg. The investigator looked startled, turned a few pages in the book, and asked me to describe the marks. He wrote while I talked. I also made the point of Wilbur having been a blond at that time.

The investigator wasn't convinced that Wilbur was the man he was looking for. It was then that I remembered an interesting visit with a girl friend a few days before. "Do you have time to listen to a secondhand story?" I asked. He nodded.

"I met an old friend a few days ago," I began. I told him she looked oddly ill and pale for someone usually well tanned. She told me she was just out of the hospital, recovering from an awful beating.

She had met a charming, cultured man on the beach. His name, was "Wilbur Roberti." His manners were impeccable. (The investigator made another checkmark in the book.) She was quite smitten. They met daily after she was through work, and they also had evening dates.

About a week after they met, he told her he had put his car in for repairs and asked to borrow hers. He offered to chauffeur her while he had the use of it. She thought she loved him and was happy to help him out. A few days later, he got his car back. However, he frequently arrived by bus, met her and drove her home, continuing to borrow her car.

"Now, listen closely," I said to the investigator. I said she told me that one day Wilbur fell asleep on the beach and for the first time she closely studied his handsome face. She is a beautician and it had seemed to her that something was odd about him. In the bright sunlight, she saw tiny scars, the kind left by an excellent facelift. His hair, blown a bit by the wind, showed whitish around the roots–a darn good dye job just beginning to grow out. When he awakened, she was lying alongside as usual.

Thinking of Wilbur on the Keys, I asked whether he had an accent.

"Yes," she said, "but not Italian, Bostonian.

I asked if he limped.

"Yes, it spoiled his complete recovery from polio and left such funny little puckered marks on his leg."

Then I knew she was talking about the greenhorn sportsman we knew on Elliott Key, the same man the investigator was looking for.

She loaned him her car that evening and he picked her up at work. Everything went as usual until she got into the passenger's side on the way home. After they got into traffic, she reached into the glove box for a Kleenex and out fell a large bundle of small packages, like Bromo-Seltzer packs without the name wrappers, held together with a rubber band.

"Put those things back and stop being so damn nosy," he snarled at her, and she was so shocked that she acted subdued rather than startled. She reached in again, got a Kleenex, and said, "I can't even get a Kleenex in my own car now, huh? What the hell is the matter with you?" Then she put the package back and closed the glove box.

He offered her all sorts of excuses for snarling at her. Then he stopped at Brady's drive-in and she let him buy her a beer. She allowed him to think she had forgiven him.

He dropped her off and she decided to learn the answers that night. All she thought was that he had another girl. She cancelled a bridge game and borrowed her brother's car. Right after dark, she drove near the apartment house in Rio Vista where he lived, and she parked and waited. She could see his car alongside hers.

Almost an hour later, he appeared, got into her car and drove off. She followed, without lights, at some distance. When he turned south on Andrews Avenue, she let three cars get between, turned on her lights and followed. He made a left turn into Croissant Park. She pulled to the curb and parked. When traffic permitted, she, too, turned down Croissant Park, slowly and without lights. The area was dark and deserted–sidewalks, but no houses, unlighted street lights–all abandoned by builders when the boom busted.

She was sure she saw her car about a block ahead of her on a side street. Only the dim lights were lit. Knowing that this area was a sort of lover's lane, she didn't expect to call any attention to herself if she parked. She turned left, in the opposite direction and parked in the middle of the block.

Now, very quietly, she opened the car door and eased out. She managed to get into the weeds near her car and then saw a car approaching hers head on. It stopped and a man got out, and went forward. Wilbur did the same. They met in between the cars. Wilbur, his hand in the light, was holding that packet from her glove box. The other man had a thick sheaf of money. Each reached forward for what the other held, and exchanged.

Then, under her foot, a small branch cracked, terrifyingly loud in the quiet.

He turned, saw her, and ran towards her, fairly screaming curses. As he beat her, he promised to kill her if she lived and talked. "I know he meant it!" she said.

She regained consciousness long enough to crawl to her brother's car. She managed to drive the few blocks to Andrews Avenue and shut the key off before passing out again. A passing motorist saw her blink her car lights when she recovered again. He offered to help, and she asked him to call her father, and gave him the phone number, but not the name. (Phone booths didn't exist then, and it was a half-mile to the nearest phone.)

She regained consciousness as her father and brother drove her to the hospital. She begged them for secrecy. With the help of the family doctor, they kept the matter from the police. And, a NO VISITORS sign was put on the door.

Her car was parked by the house in the morning. Sometime later, as she was recovering, a friend visited her and said Wilbur had been seen on the beach with a gorgeous blonde. Fort Lauderdale was a small town, then, so the occasional stranger was noticed. Her friend also said this particular stranger was working as a carpenter and acting very funny.

My friend hoped Wilbur would leave town, but he was watching her and hiding out. Sick and tired of saying she had been in an accident, she wanted to tell someone who wouldn't blab the facts to everyone.

"Now, sir," I said to the investigator, "You are the only one who will hear this from me. I'm telling you because my husband and I long ago decided to tell the authorities everything we knew if it would help catch a dope or alien runner!"

My friend knew a lot of people and she soon found out that the blonde was the daughter of a contractor Wilbur hired to build a duplex on a lot he bought. Wilbur offered an additional ten per cent of the cost to be put on as carpenter. His clumsy mistakes called attention to him.

During this entire story, the investigator hadn't interrupted me once. Now he demanded to know my girl friend's name and address, so he could question her instead of getting the information second hand. I refused, and he was quite bitter about it. He gave no credence to the thought that Wilbur might kill her. (Somehow, at the time, it never dawned on me that I had put myself in her position!)

"We can protect her from him!" he insisted.

"How will you do that? He might be a blond again by now; you were looking for a brunet. You don't know how big his organization is or if you can capture him. Incidentally, you don't even know his right name." I told him the name, and he quickly made note of it.

"Now, the address you want is right near here," I said, giving him the address of the building site. "One block north and two blocks west on the left side of the street. Go get him."

I had been so intent on getting those statements in the proper order, and watching his face as he took notes that I hadn't noticed Mama, who was just around the doorway listening. Her expression was something to behold. The investigator had risen and he too saw Mama and told her to say nothing of what she had heard.

(It could be that Wilbur was having Russ and me watched and left when he heard about the investigation—after all, a man in uniform isn't much of a secret. At any rate, when the investi-

gator arrived at the site, he was told that Wilbur had quit shortly before.)

"Charlotte, I thought that was a deserted island you and Russ
were on! How did you meet someone the police are looking for?"
Dear Mama had been so busy raising her nine children and
then caring for my Jan, that she had only read about such things.
Why, come to think of it, she knew as little about how other people lived as I did just two short years before.

That night we told the folks some of the funny things that
had happened, like cooling off Mugs' boat. We didn't mention
Bill until after three years had passed and we heard he had finally returned to Miami, and then, on to Dade.

We told them about seeing the S.S. Dixie. We had seen it
while making a last check at the dock, just before the storm hit,
Monday, twenty-four hours after we received our warning. The
ship had been heading south and as we watched, it started to turn
north. Strangely, it made a complete circle and continued on its
way.

An article in the newspaper when we returned from the Keys
explained the circle. The vessel had heard about the storm. The
captain ordered a return to Miami. While making the turn, the
owners demanded he continue on course.

The tremendous waves at that time picked up the boat and
set it down on French Reef. It came to rest, bow towards the
southwest, between two huge coral formations. They acted as
supports for the ship so she only received the damage caused by
the waves breaking over the vessel. Although some of the five
hundred or more passengers and crew on were badly bruised,
there was no loss of life, no serious injuries.

After the hurricane had passed, the Coast Guard removed all
the people aboard, except for a stand-by crew to take care of the
ship until salvage operations could take place. The coral formations were blasted to allow the ship to reach deep water. If the
Captain had been allowed to follow his original intention to
return to Miami, he would have saved all this confusion and
trouble.

The conversation got around to Wilbur. Russ told about
some of the dumb things Wilbur had done and said that we had

313

never guessed that the almost-always pleasant guy we had known on the Keys was, according to the investigator, the head dope runner of Florida and Georgia.

In November another storm was coming and we helped my parents prepare for it; then went to help Russ' parents. Finished and some tired, we were having coffee and watching the barometer go down when Russ noticed the chicken house swaying in the wind.

"Let's go, Charlotte."

We went out to fix it in spite of his parents' protest. They were afraid we might be injured in the terrible wind. Heck, we could walk against it. It wasn't bad. We got rope from our things in their garage. Our biggest struggle was getting the door closed against the wind. We managed by running at it together. We had to lean on the wind a little, but it was nothing compared to the last one we had been out in.

Working together, we laced the rope over the chicken house to the four corner posts. We were wet and a bit cold when we returned to the house and his worried parents.

In answer to their fussing about going into danger, "Why that wind isn't over 90 miles an hour. We had worse than that on Labor Day." As Russ talked, he looked at the barometer. It was going up. The storm was over.

Apparently Wilbur never returned to Fort Lauderdale. We found out later, through George Deen, that the blonde had taken Wilbur's Hacker-craft from the Coconut Grove Shipyard where he had kept it and most of his ready cash.

We never heard what happened regarding his lot and partially completed building on Broward Boulevard, but we did hear that his property on Elliott Key went for taxes. I don't imagine that particular loss bothered him though. He had only purchased it so he could cut the path across to the ocean.

Sometime later, when we visited Flip and Bertha, Flip told us the grapevine had it that Wilbur's boat had been chased many times prior to the Lauderdale happening, but he was never caught with contraband. He would run the bow of his boat aground on the ocean side, opposite his old camp. A runner would then make a quick pickup, out of the jungle and back again before the law could reach Wilbur's boat. When he was searched, he was always clean.

While they were searching Wilbur or the man running the boat at the time, the runner had reached the bay and another speed boat took off from the bayside exit. At Princeton, almost opposite, a car was waiting to take the contraband to a waiting plane at one of the many small deserted landing fields. The plane usually landed at an abandoned airfield south of Pompano.

Wilbur's limp had been caused by a bullet wound when he had almost been captured there. The police had staked out the area. One night, shortly after the plane landed, they closed in under the cover of the noise of an approaching car. The driver of the car went to the plane with a package. They sprang and called, "Hands up." No one stopped, so they shot. At first they heard sounds of distress and mumbled oaths. They approached the plane cautiously and found Don Bowen dead. Meanwhile, the driver of the car got away. A search the next morning by daylight disclosed evidence that a third person had lain bleeding for a long time in one spot.

They didn't know whom they had wounded until I told that investigator about Wilbur's leg. Months later, Happy and Al told us that Wilbur was still at large.

The strangely fogged pictures Wilbur took were explained when my girl friend said the same thing happened to her. She was never able to get a good picture of him. He took care of delivery and pickup of all photos. All of his *fogged*.

Bridge at Boca Chica Over-the-Sea Auto Highway to Key West
- *Photo Courtesy of Monroe County Public Library*

EPILOGUE

A Trip Down the Keys to Key West–Sad Changes.
Visit Captain W.R. Russell Family in Key West.

Questions Answered about the Ball and Chain. Why Mayor
Fossey Couldn't Get Re-elected. To a Certain Group in Miami,
We Are THOSE PEOPLE.

In the winter of 1938, we went to Key West to visit Captain William Reno Russell. We now owned a secondhand 1929 Cadillac Sport Phaeton. The car was a four-seater and a prestige car of its day. It had wire wheels and two spare wheels were mounted in wells in the front fenders. The top was a manually operated cloth fold-down and the seats were covered with genuine hand-crafted leather. On the trunk rack in the rear was mounted a very well-made trunk, complete with canvas dust cover.

The V-8 engine had tremendous power. The wheels were, by today's standards, quite monstrous. And the tires commanded a premium price. We bought excellent secondhand ones from a truck company–32 by 6 high-pressure truck tires that fit perfectly and gave wonderful service.

The car burned low-grade gasoline and had a twenty-five gallon tank. In fact, it was a premium car. Shortly after we bought it, we found it had a built-in holster, easily reached by the driver if he put his right hand forward and slightly under the dashboard. The car was immensely heavy–the metal was as thick as a truck body.

The state of Florida had acquired the old Florida East Coast

Railroad right-of-way from Florida City to Key West. "The Railroad That Went to Sea" was a thing of the past.

Using material salvaged from the old railroad, and building directly on the old railroad bed, with temporary one-way wooden bridges over some of the railroad trestles, the state road department had made it possible to drive to Key West by using several ferries to cross the water at the larger uncompleted portions of the road.

In most places the road followed the right-of-way. However, there had been some wooden bridges extending a road up the Keys from Key West, and a wooden bridge connected Big Pine Key with No Name Key. The State continued to use these bridges to avoid building new, hard surface roads to connect them to the existing roads. The bridges became progressively narrower, longer, and more rickety as one drove south from Florida City towards Key West.

On the longer keys, such as Key Largo, Plantation and Key Vaca, small roads for local travel had been built years before. These were narrow, but surfaced with macadam. The newer roads were crushed coral rock, quite smooth.

There were a few towns on the larger keys, and at any important bridge or channel, one could find a frame building, generally painted white. Here it was possible to rent a rowboat, a cane fishing pole, and to buy bait. They quite often sold meals, but the menu was seafood and grits. Beer and soft drinks were also available. Drinks were expensive and the food was cheap. Some places close to a town had electricity, others made do with the crude generators of that period and had kerosene-burning refrigerators. These people found it difficult to show ten dollars total income for a week of hard work.

Our life with the Conchs on Elliott Key had provided us with enough of the speech and mannerisms of the Keys' people so that we had a pleasant trip and no difficulties. We explained the unusual car, "It was in storage in a garage, awaiting settlement of a wealthy person's estate. We heard there was $125 storage against it and managed to buy it. The garage owner had been hoping to acquire it for storage bills and was reluctant to let it go. He had intended to make a wrecker from it because of its tremendous weight and excellent motor."

The ferryboat operator grumbled when we drove aboard his craft. He seemed to think we should pay truck prices for our passage. However, we were finally accepted. Monroe County was not trying to operate these ferries at a loss. For that period of short running, the fares were high. The short hop ferry cost $1.75 minimum and the longer was $2.50 minimum.

These water trips were very pleasant and the relief from driving on the narrow bridges, the crossing of which gave me the nervous jitters, helped Russ enjoy the trip more.

After getting off the last ferry at No Name Key, we crossed over the wooden bridge to Big Pine Key and were then on the Old Road, which had been built many years before. We had to cross several small wooden bridges to reach Stock Island before entering Key West.

At that time, the old City Ice and Fuel plant was operating. Along with their other activities, they made goat's milk ice cream—there was a large herd of goats on Stock Island—and it retained its shape when warm because of added gelatin. The ice cream was flavored with many of the tropical fruits, among them soursop, mango, sapodilla and fresh coconut. These were just strange names to a northerner, but sheer heaven to a native.

I hadn't been to Key West before, but Russ said he was dismayed to see the changes that had taken place in the last few years. The cigar factory, which had been world-famous and a mainstay in the Key West economy, was closed. It had moved to Ybor City, near Tampa, the locals said, "Lots of folks followed it."

Only a relatively few people were left on the U.S. Navy base. Older hotels, such as the La Concha on Duval Street, had closed their doors. To replace their facilities were a few small *motels*, a completely new concept for Key West. The big-spenders, who had come by railroad, would not make the long trip by car.

At the old Mallory docks, there were still very large freshwater storage tanks. These had been necessary when there was an influx of visitors, as the natives had only their rainwater cisterns and couldn't provide any fresh water for others. (Now, all the water on the Florida Keys comes by Navy pipeline from the same well in Florida City. This 30-inch pipeline was designed to carry about one and a half million gallons of water a day. Because of its length, it took several days before the first water reached

Key West.)

Most of the older buildings in Key West were built of wood. Some few of these houses were built in the Bahamas, dismantled, and shipped to Key West in sections on sailing vessels. Invariably, they were embellished with very ornate gingerbread woodwork, iron grillwork, or both. The windows were very tall and narrow, quite often reaching from the floor to the ceiling, and they always had outside louvered Bahamian shutters that could be opened for ventilation, and excluded the sun. Most of them were painted white.

The masonry buildings, either brick or cement, were mostly business offices. Most of them had very ornate hand-forged iron-work grills and balconies, reflecting the Spanish influence.

We stayed at a small motel a few blocks from the old monastery, which later had an attached convent.

The turtle kraals had always been a part of Key West, as well as the sponge dock and warehouses. They will always be a part of the Conch way of life.

As we had arrived in late evening, we planned to visit with the Russell family the next morning and went to one of the older restaurants for supper. The seafood was fresh and very well flavored; the Cuban inspired touches changed perfectly ordinary food into a gourmet dish. The dessert was Key Lime pie. The entire meal, not cheap for those days, cost eighty-five cents per person.

The restaurant was open to the sidewalk with a series of hinged doors on both ends of the building. Our table was near the sidewalk. Of course, we were soon spotted by the many small street urchins–sometimes raggedy, but always clean–who always seemed very happy to perform their little specialties for anyone who tossed them a few coins. One little colored boy did a sort of soft-shoe dance–in bare feet, but with bottle caps firmly clamped to the soles of his feet. This gave a weird tap dance effect to his barefoot dancing. He seemed to thoroughly enjoy his performance and was happy to show what he could do even without the incentive of the few coins we threw him.

Captain W.R. Russell's house was typical to Key West. It was a white frame house with gingerbread porches on the front and one side. On top were a cupola and a widow's walk, the low

LaConcha Hotel, Duval Street, Key West
- Photo Courtesy of Monroe County Public Library

Turtle Kraals, Key West
- *Photo Courtesy of Monroe County Public Library*

ornate railings matching that on the porches. The windows were full height with Bahama shutters.

Inside, everything was shipshape. Shining white paint with contrasting dark mahogany floors, stair treads and rails. It was not a large house but seemed spacious because of the paint and the arrangement of the furniture.

During coffee and cake, Mrs. Russell thanked us profusely for having saved the life of her husband and son at the time of the hurricane. Then she said that she had noticed my admiring glances at her ruby glass and would like to give it to me for a thank you. I was amazed.

On the buffet to my left was a magnificent set of Bohemian ruby glass. A set of six glasses, two decanters and a water pitcher. I could see from the way they were displayed that they were her most prized possessions. I told her that I appreciated it very much, and would like to have them but didn't want to deprive her of them—then I asked if she would leave them to me in her will.

Her expression was delightful. She thanked me for my thoughtfulness and said, "I would be happy to!"

Just before we left, at the car now, Captain Russell told us that Reno had died in a barroom brawl.

Some events occurred which caused us to lose contact with them, and we never heard from her or the captain again.

A few years after leaving Elliott Key, Russ left for Saint Mary's, Georgia, to work as a machinist on a construction job. He telephoned me about a week later to say that he had located a house where we three could get room and board for the grand total of eight dollars a week. He would expect us to arrive at Kingsland, Georgia, the nearest bus stop, on Sunday. Saint Mary's was off the main road and had no bus connections.

More of our possessions were stored in his parents' attic and our clothing packed—I was ready to go. It was a tearful good-bye between Jan and my parents. This was the first time they faced being separated for more than a week.

Dad suggested that I buy reserved seats. I took his advice and it was most fortunate I did so. This bus trip to Kingsland was a long one, and it seemed all South Florida was traveling that day.

The bus driver allowed only twenty-two standees, and they were packed in the aisle. Most of our luggage was in the baggage compartment beneath the bus, but I had several small, precious packages and suitcases riding in the seat with Jan and me. Jan was busy with her funny books and I with my magazine when I was suddenly crowded sideways by a lardy man sitting on the armrest—not quite on my lap—scrunching Jan and me against the window.

"You don't mind, do you?"

"Hell, yes, I mind!" I rammed him with my elbow.

He grunted and stood up cussing. Then the other passengers remarked in various ways about his rudeness. He shut up, and things went on in a normal fashion.

A two-hour stop in Jacksonville, Florida, gave us a chance to eat a hot meal and stretch our legs, but when it came time to get back on the bus, we were in trouble. More than fifty people blocked our way. They hoped to get some of the standing room. The bus driver was calling for all passengers with reserved seats, and I couldn't move.

My arms were full and I was unable to carry little Jan or hold her hand, so I instructed her to get in back of me and hold onto my dress on both sides.

Then the bus driver announced that servicemen would have preference on the standing room. I called to some husky-looking sailors in front of me and told them that I had two reserved seats. "Please help my daughter and me aboard the bus!"

"Your daughter?"

I raised my arm and Jan peered out.

They grinned then and looked at the crowd between us and the bus door. "Okay, lady, we'll try it."

One of the boys picked up Jan and sat her on his shoulder. The other got in back of me and I was slowly scrunched forward. The people in front of me were made too uncomfortable to retain their positions and moved sideways. Slow, but steady, progress got me to the door. Pinned firmly against the open edge, I couldn't move. I hurt a bit. I managed to get enough breath to say, "Push me to port."

They laughed and pushed me sideways as they said, "A sea-going gal!"

The sideways push turned me around partway and I was then pushed backwards to the bus step. I would have fallen except for a quick assist from the bus driver. Jan laughed. I guess I did look funny.

We were the last passengers with reserved seats and the bus driver allowed the sailors to enter with us. Somehow I had managed not to lose anything I was carrying, but I was exhausted. Jan had a grandstand seat through it all, and had loved it. I thanked the sailors and told them to stand right by our seats so they could claim them when we got off at Kingsland, just thirty miles up the road. The big sailor grinned and said, "Believe it or not lady, we enjoyed it. Besides, you got us aboard!"

Russ was waiting for us when we arrived at Kingsland and it seemed to take us ten minutes or more to get through the standees, Jan again hanging onto my skirt in back of me. Our luggage was in the car by the time we got there. It seemed so good to get out in the open where there was elbowroom and fresh-smelling air.

The road to Saint Mary's, east from the highway, was unique. I had never before seen a red brick road like that one. It was narrow but not too bumpy. It hadn't been necessary to make a wide road back when it was built for carriages.

When we reached the little town, Jan and I were fascinated. It was necessary to drive very slowly to avoid the cows roaming the streets. I couldn't decide what was so different about it. Then it registered. Each house was separated from the others by a lawn and was surrounded by a white picket fence to protect it from the roaming cattle.

Saint Mary's had been a booming little town in the days of the sailing vessels, and had almost fallen asleep now. They had refused Flagler access to their town for his railroad, and now one road led to and from Saint Mary's. It was at the end of the road.

Jan and I looked for things to occupy our time during the day. Swimming was one of those. Rose, who had arranged our room and board, directed us to the river. We went there and found that we were allowed entrance to the pool free because we were residents of Saint Mary's. A floating gangplank with side rails led to a strange contraption out in the water. Four telephone poles had been driven into the bottom mud and a fifteen-foot square railed platform floated out and fastened to the poles. You might think that swimming in coffee colored water is fun, but not after one of the natives tells you that the platform is railed and raised because of the monstrous sharks.

When visiting in the evening, Russ would tell us of any unusual events that had taken place at work. I heard more and more about the disputes between the machinists and the boilermakers. The boilermakers claimed the right to install machinery in machinists' territory.

One evening I asked Russ if he personally had gotten into a dispute with the boilermakers. He said, "No. And I'm not of a size to talk to those big bruisers about anything. They all weigh at least a hundred pounds more than I do. When it becomes necessary, I'll do my talking with action. My way."

"What do you mean?"

"Never mind. Wait and see!"

My brother Dode was also working in Saint Mary's and that evening he came over to tell us that he had at last found a large room in a private house for his wife and small son. He planned to leave for Fort Lauderdale on Friday night to get them right after work and return in time for work on Monday.

"Do you want to go along?"

We did!

We planned to go in his Chrysler rather than our car, which lacked the front side curtains. It was colder now. We started off, and the blacktop road retained some of the day's heat. Except for narrowly missing some of those cows lying on the warm road, the trip was uneventful. Jan slept all the way.

During the ride, Dode told the story of one of his working buddies who had hit a cow one night with a new car. His car was totally demolished, but the owner of the cow took the man to court. There wasn't any hope of a "foreigner" getting justice in the courts then, and he was forced to pay twice what the cow was worth on the market. He realized only a few dollars by selling the tires off the remains of his car and was furious about the injustice of it all.

He announced to anyone who would listen that he was going to get even! That night he borrowed a gun and in a friend's car, he went back to the wreck location so as to get a cow from the same herd. He killed two cows, and returning to Saint Mary's, he bragged about it.

He was arrested and a court trial was held. All six of his buddies stayed away from work that day and went to court with him. The owner of the cows presented his case–and it was the same man who had collected double the value of the first cow.

"He said he would get even," he told the judge. "No, Your Honor, I didn't see him do it, but he bragged about doing it–all over town. I feel it's an open and shut case."

When the judge put the accused construction worker on the stand and asked him to give his side of it, he said, "Your Honor, I've got a great big mouth! Sure, I was mad when I had to pay double for that cow–and no one gave me a penny for my car. It was worth more than six of his cows. Howsoever, you can't believe a word I say. I'm a hell of a liar and I've got witnesses in court. Ask them."

Then the judge put one of the other workers on the stand. He said, "Your Honor, we just listen to him 'cause he tells the most fantastic and interesting stories."

The case was dismissed. For lack of proof.

Dode dropped Russ off at his parents' home and we went to ours. Dad was psychic and had awakened Mother shortly before we got there saying, "I expect two of our wandering children soon. Make some pancakes."

Mom had things ready to eat when we got there. We ate and slept for a little while.

Dorothy, Dode's wife, had everything packed except for last-minute clothing items, and we helped find a spot for them in the two-wheeled trailer.

Tearful good-byes again and we were on our way to pick up Russ. For that few miles, we had a little spare room in the car. But when Russ got in, we had to juggle around a bit. Dorothy and I were in the back seat with the two children. It was my turn to hold Joey, and it was a pleasure. Jan sat between us. Fruit, cookies, and candy snacks were put on the ledge by the back window and we were ready.

Everything went smoothly until we were about fifty miles

south of Jacksonville that night. Jan was sleeping with her head on Dorothy's lap and I held Joey. We had been averaging around fifty-five to sixty miles an hour, and the trailer was behaving beautifully.

We closed the gap between ourselves and an army convoy that was traveling more slowly than we, forty-five miles an hour. The huge trucks were spaced so that if oncoming traffic permitted, we could pass one or two of them at a time. Finally, there were only two more left to pass.

Dode was a careful driver—he had his loved ones aboard! He waited until there were no lights of oncoming cars for at least two miles, then he gave it the gas and pulled out to pass the large trucks. We were returning to the right side of the road when we hit a cow—broadside. Thank God Dode had the strength necessary to hold the wheel straight and the car was a Chrysler of that pratfall year when they sealed the underbody as well as a toaster crumb-catcher.

We were thrown around like popcorn. I gripped Joey so firmly that he cried. When the car landed on its front wheels after sliding over most of the cow, we could hear the crunch of its ribs like dry sticks as the back wheels took hold and pulled us over. Then, the trailer bounced into the air and followed us. We could hear the sound of breaking glass, or dishes.

Once we were safely over and still on the highway, I looked around for the cigarette I had been smoking. The neatly stacked things on the floor had firmly packed themselves around my legs. I located the cigarette by the heat on the back of my right leg. Holding the baby as I was, my hands weren't free, and I saw the upholstery smoldering. Without a second thought, I put it out by pressing my leg against it. I still have the scar.

Jan was crying from the bump she got on her head. But she had landed on Dorothy's lap, and Dorothy was soothing her.

Dode said, "Look at that." This was wartime and even with the dim lights required then, I could see it in the rearview mirror. "Every one of those trucks is making a slight turnout and flattening out that cow still more."

While we were talking about the cow rug that would be on the highway the next morning, I realized that I felt very uncomfortable in addition to the pain of the burned leg. I had been too excited to realize it before. I asked Dorothy to take Joey. She did, and that put Jan between us again. I raised myself and found the reason. The peaches had been squashed, some of the seeds were in an upright position, held there by the remains of the cookies, crackers, bananas, a small camera, and everything else that had been on the ledge under the back window.

Separating the camera and the Kleenex from the rest of the stuff, I scooped up handfuls of the mess and threw it out the window. I had to ignore the remaining paste on the upholstery, and it was too late to worry about the paste on my dress. Enough of the Kleenex was untouched so I could partially clean the camera.

Dode now drove a bit more slowly because of the possible damage from the bumps. At Saint Augustine, he found an all-night filling station. He asked the attendant to put the car on the grease rack. He and Russ got out. The rest of us stayed where we were. By now the children were again asleep.

Now Dode said that he just wanted the man to give the grease fittings up front a shot. They stood in back of him when he did this.

In another couple of minutes, the car was lowered to the ground. When he had paid the man and we were again on our way, I asked if there was any visible injury to the car.

"Clean. No road dust at all."

"Hells bells! Why did you pay that man all that money just for a shot of grease?"

"I didn't want him to see cow hair. He would have reported it to the highway patrol."

Just before we reached Butler's, a juke joint near Kingsland, the left tire on the trailer blew. Dode pulled over to the left side of the road and both men got out to fix it. In a few minutes they returned to say that it was impossible. They couldn't find the tube—just a few little hot shreds.

"We'll have to leave the trailer and come back for it. I'll try to make a deal with Butler."

We dragged the trailer there and Butler agreed to watch it—for two dollars in advance. We pulled it to the back of his place, right up against the building. More sounds of breaking dishes now. Later, we found only five small plates had survived.

We stopped at every open filling station on the way to Saint

Mary's, looking for a tube. It was hopeless. In wartime, you had to know somebody important to buy anything like that. We were out of familiar territory.

While we were discussing this, Russ said, "Dode, I think we can get the trailer wheels on the Cadillac trunk rack and bring it here. Then we can take our time getting a tube."

Dorothy and Joey were taken to their new home and bedded down. I put Jan to bed at the Captain Keating home where we boarded, and changed my clothes, while the boys were removing the trunk from the Cadillac. It was left on the porch.

Back at Butler's, the boys beefed the trailer around and folded down the cloth top of the car. The trailer had been tilted over until the tongue was in the air. Dode and I used our combined weight to hold it that way while Russ backed the car under the tongue and set the brakes. For a time it seemed impossible, but we finally managed to hoist the wheels onto the trunk rack, pull the tongue down, and fasten it to the rail used to hold the lap robe. We secured it further with ropes to the door handles, and rocks under the wheels, and we were ready to roll. Three on the front seat, we returned to Saint Mary's in time for supper and a well-earned rest.

During supper Russ said with a grin, "Well, Charlotte, I won. Three boilermakers came to run me off an assembly job I was working on alone. After we install the machinery, other men finish the floors and put up the walls, so I was working on a kind of scaffolding. I was above them and started throwing one-inch bolts. The bolts weigh a pound apiece, and I really clanged them off their hardhats. They finally got enough of it when some of them got body hits and they went off and let me alone. I would recognize one of them again. He was a particularly large Irishman with some white in his red hair."

There was nothing in the way of entertainment in Saint Mary's. Most of the workers went to Butler's for recreation, beer, juke organs, and slot machines. On the highway a few miles north of Kingsland was a much better class place named Chief Tomachichi's. This was the type place where men could take their families.

Brunswick, Georgia, was the closest large town with a news-paper and we subscribed to it. Not too long before, we had read about some vandals who had destroyed several slot machines and mistreated the owner of Butler's juke joint. The slot machines had been removed from the building and were found broken on the public highway in front of the place. Coins, machine parts and broken slot machine cases were strewn all over the road. They had been found by a passing motorist who reported it to the sheriff's department. No statement was made regarding the manner in which Butler had been mistreated.

We were in the habit of going to Jacksonville at least once a week on their day off now that Russ had converted the car to run on diesel fuel. Because diesel fuel gave better mileage and cost less than gasoline, we could travel almost three times farther for the same amount of money.

Jan and I were ready to visit Fort Lauderdale again one Sunday, Russ' day off. It was a twelve and a half mile trip to the highway. This trip was to be different. Instead of our returning by bus, Russ would drive down to pick us up and have a short time to visit with his parents.

He left right after work a week later arriving in Fort Lauderdale, he had an hour's visit with his parents, then he drove over to pick us up. A hurricane was expected that day and we didn't want to get caught in it.

On our way for a few hours, we stopped to eat and heard on the radio in the restaurant that the hurricane had bypassed Fort Lauderdale and might go in by Fort Pierce. Russ put down our fragile car top, got out the lifeboat cover that he carried for emergencies, and tied it to the top of the windshield. We climbed in, tucked the canvas in back of us, and were on our way, prepared to get wet.

We followed the Greyhound bus quite closely for the next hour as the storm got worse. When it pulled off the side of the road because of low visibility and wind gusts, we pulled in behind it and sat out the hurricane. During the lull, we passed the bus and were on our way. Supper at Chief Tomachichi's and then home.

When we arrived there, contrary to all other arrivings we

were met by Rose. She was sullen and said, "Follow me."

In the parlor she introduced us to "Mrs. Keating, the owner," a dignified lady, who for the first few minutes was very brittle.

"How long have you been in my home? What rent do you pay? What arrangements have been made regarding payment for food?"

Russ explained that Rose had rented us our room and told her that we had been there several months. Then he told her what he had been paying. Further questioning regarding our future plans caused Russ to ask her reasons for questioning him.

"Rose is my housekeeper and did not ask me if she could rent a room, or make any other arrangements. I don't mind occupying my own guest room. It is fully as nice as my own room, but it is disconcerting to find that during my absence in Europe, strangers have moved into my home. I'll make no decision for a week. We'll see how this arrangement works out. I know how difficult it would be for you to find another place to live. This town hasn't had this many people in it for fifty years!"

Our probation period was soon over and Mrs. Keating announced that she enjoyed having us in her home. The only change made was that in the future the rent was paid *to her*. (Rose finally stopped sulking.)

Some two months passed and we were planning another trip to Lauderdale. The day arrived and when we got to Kingsland, we found that we were fortunate in getting seats across the aisle from each other. All window seats were occupied. Placing Jan in the seat next to an elderly woman, I took my seat on the right side, next to a large, red-haired man.

Jan was looking at a comic book now and I was reading the *Saturday Evening Post*. We soon arrived at the next bus stop. It was about five miles down the road at a filling station. The red-headed man was staring out the window, and as the bus slowed down to make the stop, he snatched the magazine from my hands. I looked around, startled, to see him holding it in front of his face, partially towards the window. I don't know why I didn't do or say anything. In only a few minutes we loaded the passengers, and I was surprised to see the last man aboard stand there and look around the bus, then he turned and went back out.

A minute or so after we were on our way again, while I was staring at the redheaded man in perplexity, he handed my magazine back to me. "Thanks, little lady. That was a big help! I suppose you'd like to know what that was all about?"

I had been indignant when he grabbed my book and guess I sounded like it, "I certainly would!"

He was grinning, "Well, I suppose you read in the paper about that Butler thing. Let me tell you the truth about it.

"Six of us boys travel together and we been going to Butler's every night, playing his slot machines and having a few beers there. After about a week of that—one night we sort of got together and talked about our take. You know, it came out then, not one of us had ever hit one of those machines for more than five coins! Mostly we played the quarter and half-dollar machines. Butler had the house percentage set so damn high that you couldn't ever break even, much less win!

"Well, we studied it over and made a plan. Come payday night, we each put fifty dollars slot machine money in one pocket and a couple dollars beer money in a different pocket. We checked each other out. Got to be fair, you know!

"That night, we started off at Chief Tomachichi's place, having supper there and a beer. We lazed around and took our time so it was kind of late when we got to Butler's. We figured to sit around and kind of outlast the crowd. Around eleven-thirty when most of them were leaving, we bought another beer apiece and then began playing them slot machines. We each played until we used up our fifty dollars. Then we went over to the counter and nursed a beer. Pretty soon, all six of us was sitting there, and word passed around. Not one of us had a cent left—except beer money! About that time, the last of the other customers went out the door.

"Then, we told Butler that we knew he had his machines rigged and we wanted our money back. Told him nicely. Told him there wouldn't be no trouble if he kicked over with the money.

"Say, do you know, he got real belligerent! Cussed at us and started for the telephone on the back wall. Guess he would have called the Mon, but two of the boys jumped over the counter, grabbed him and tied him with strips they tore off his bar cloths.

Then one of the boys guarded him and the rest of us grabbed those clumsy machines and wrestled them out to the middle of the highway. That's public domain, you know.

"We sort of figgered that old Butler would act that way so we had a 'can opener' in the trunk. That sledgehammer made it real easy to break up those machines so we could get our money. Then we started counting half dollars so as to pay ourselves back. We were really working fast, now, in case some car might come along. One of the guys got a leather jacket and put it on the road—we threw them coins in it for a quick getaway if we had to. Had to count in some quarters, too, but pretty quick we each had counted out our fifty dollars and then we each got some to make up our guard's money and ten dollars extra for him for standing guard. Believe me, it made quite a heavy bundle. It took two of us to carry the money and the sledgehammer over to the trunk of the car.

"Boy! All that work just to get our money back. We was mad! Went in to Butler's then to tell our guy we got our money back—and I had an idea.

"You shoulda heard Butler—he yelled like a stuck pig all the time we was undressing him. When he was naked as a plucked chicken, we took him out back of his place, walked him through all those sandspurs barefoot for about seventy-five feet. He was yelling something fierce then—guess he thought we was going to kill him.

"Then, we just tied him to a pine tree back there and left him. That was during mosquito season, you know. All the way back to the car we could hear him yak-yakking about what he was going to do when he caught up with us.

"We all piled in the car and took off. All of us was laughing like mad and thinking how much skinnier Butler would be when those mosquitoes been working a while.

"We left all that silver money in the car trunk and went to Chief Tomachichi's and had a hamburger and another beer. That used up about a half-hour and I figured old Butler been punished enough. I went over to the phone when no one was around it and called the sheriff's office. Changed my voice much as I could and told them where they could find Butler.

"They started askin' questions and I hung up on them. We

guys figgered that by the time they found him and got him inside again with all them sandspurs making it tough for him to walk, old High-Percentage Butler would have enough punishment. Hear tell, though, he was yelling mighty loud and it didn't take them long to find him!"

I tried to laugh more silently as he went on.

"Well, do you know, ever since then that silly bastard had been renewing a John Doe warrant for me? The other guys are kinda average looking but he knows what I look like, all right! I been real careful about not letting him spot me. Some of the guys told me that he watches every bus heading south. Different bus stops all the time. He was back there at that bus stop where we was when I snatched your book!"

"Oh, one man got on the bus, looked around and then got off." I described him.

He laughed. "That was him! Son of a gun! He sure would have spotted me if you had made a fuss about your book. Thanks again, little lady!"

I joined him in his laughter. I had enjoyed hearing the story as much as he had enjoyed reliving it as he told it.

I asked the usual traveler's questions about destination and he answered, "Miami is my home."

I told him that my daughter and I were going to Fort Lauderdale. No names were exchanged, then, or later.

"If you live in Miami," I said, " maybe you know Mayor Fossey."

He chuckled. "I surely *did!* That was some smart, little guy. But say, we just couldn't let him get elected mayor again. He was too honest. You know, that little son-of-a-gun wouldn't take a bribe?" He said that as though it was impossible to believe and very irregular.

"Let me tell you about him. About then, I was Acey-Ducey's bodyguard."

"Who is Acey-Ducey?"

He looked incredulous. "Why he was *top* gambler in Miami, then, still going strong. I was Acey-Ducey's bodyguard. I'm hidin' out now, workin' as a boilermaker. Nobody would think of *me* doin' *that!* I'm *hot!* Well, to get back to Fossey–he planned a great big raid on our joint, but we had the police and the sheriff's department all bought off so they told us about it. Here's the way we worked it:

"Just before raid time that night, all sorts of calls got phoned in to the law, asking for men from both those departments. All them calls got put on the book the regular way and they show them to Fossey when he comes in to collect the men for the raid. He's wearing–of all things–a white Palm Beach suit. Everyone was out on emergency duty.

"That little banty rooster is only five feet, one and a half inches tall, you know! He really stormed around there for a few minutes! Then he shoved out that chin of his and demanded two guns–loaded ones. Naturally, the guy on duty got them for him, and told Fossey again how very sorry he was that there were no men there to go along with him. Did you know he used to captain a big English sailing vessel on the Australian run? Well, guess he figured he could captain that raid.

"The next thing we know about it, our door tender sent back word that Mayor Fossey had just driven into the parking lot of our joint in his old car. We tried quite a few times to give him a new one, but he just wouldn't take it. Too honest. Say, I even heard tell he was buying a new refrigerator on time payments!

"Anyway, Acey-Ducey sent word out front to let Fossey come in. We waited and he just came a-stalkin' in, ten feet tall like. The coat pockets of his white suit was just a-saggin' from the weight of those guns. He just stood there for a minute, then, and glared at us. All of us was bigger'n him and we just sort of stood there, still like.

"Well, sir, damned if he didn't walk over to a table, then, and pull a chair away from it. Then, he used the chair for a step and got up on the middle of the table. Taller'n us then. He pulled out those big guns and barked, 'The joint's raided!'

"Say, do you know, we admired his guts so much that we let ourselves be raided! He is a real gutsy guy. Too damn honest, though. We just couldn't let him get elected again."

As I listened, it was a bit difficult for me to picture the man whom I had known as a very mild-mannered person being so aggressive. But, I realized that a sailor does not become a captain unless he has the superior intelligence, ability, and leadership qualities.

After a few silent moments, he asked what work my husband did at Saint Mary's. I told him that my husband was a brunet, my height, and a machinist. Then I told him about the boiler-makers trying to run him off a machinist's job and how he threw the bolts at them to keep them too busy to climb up to the level where he was working.

He startled everyone in the bus then. He threw back his head and just roared with laughter. When he had finally stopped laughing, he explained. "That's a right gutsy guy you got, too! That's why we let him win. Hell, us guys all outweigh him two to one!"

Then, remembering what he had said about his associates, I thought he might be able to explain the very odd experience we had in Miami during Prohibition. It had always puzzled us and I hate unfinished stories.

I recounted the Ball and Chain episode, forgetting at the time to mention the name of the place. When he asked for it, I told him—and added we lived on the north end of Elliott Key at that time.

This time when he turned to look at me it was different—a very friendly, approving look.

"Let's see now. That Ball and Chain joint was about Sixteenth or Seventeenth Avenue—in a house, wasn't it?"

"I'm not sure of the address, but it was a house, and on the Tamiami Trail."

He grinned. "Sure, I can explain. I know why that guy gave you the red carpet treatment. Any of us would have done it. You're *those* people. All the time you lived on the north end of Elliott Key during the rum-running days, you were really on the spot. And, you never saw anything and you never talked! Except about those dirty alien runners. You never, never hurt no one. Heard tell you fed the rum runners, too, and they told it that you never even asked for a bottle.

"Why, everybody knew how you were friends with the Border Patrol, too, and that day when they had coffee with you when Big Erskine was down the beach, you managed to not let them go and take a look!

"You even cooled off Mugs' boat for him."

Then, he said, his voice full of disbelief, "Say, didn't you people know that you could just about *have* Miami? Just let the big boys know. They'll finance you. You can just about have the town, 'cause you mind your own business. Look me up! If you do, I'll be around to help you, too."

To him it was unbelievable that we had never asked for any favors or material things.

Then he put out his hand and shook mine. "I'm real proud to know you, little lady. Didn't know there was a woman alive who could keep her mouth shut like you did.

"I draw a little weight with the boilermakers, too, and I'll see that they don't give your husband a hard time from now on. I'd like to meet him, too. He is quite a guy!"

What an amazing way to get the final answers to our questions.

When the bus reached Fort Lauderdale, he insisted on shaking hands again and thanking me again.

After visiting for a bit with my parents, I wrote Russ a letter and told him all about my interesting bus trip.

His reply was "I just sat and grinned for a while after reading your letter. It's nice to know that we were appreciated after all."

GOD BLESS

INDEX

ABOUT CHARLOTTE
1910 - 1983

"She was extraordinary. Magnificent!" her friend recalls. "Charlotte had long, slim legs, and a voluptuous figure. When she traveled off the island alone, she bound her breasts and dressed as a boy!"

She was "both a small town and a city girl," another friend said. As a child in Wisconsin Rapids, according to her hometown paper, she could often be seen scooping polliwogs and minnows from Arpin Creek." Among her circle of friends in Fort Lauderdale, she was "a stylish flapper" and "a high fashion pacesetter." Charlotte married for the first time at sixteen. She was still very young, with a toddler in tow, when she met and married Russell.

So what was a girl like that doing on a remote island, living like a frontier woman?

With courage of her own and trust in her exceptional husband, she was turning Depression living into a romantic adventure.

Charlotte was game. Growing up one of nine children, "she could do anything her brothers could do—swim, dive, ride horseback, climb trees. A poker face often hid her fear then, and later on the keys." Russell thought her greatest challenge on Elliott Key was "to conceal and ignore her culture and accept the speech, mannerisms and habits of people with an entirely different mode of living. She may have been terrified at times," he said, "but she was brave enough never to give other people the advantage by letting them know it."

In their forty-four years together, she and Russell never settled for ordinary life. They lived on their second island paradise, Lignum Vitae Key, from 1953 to 1975, and a boat after that. Russell's study of the natural history of Lignum Vitae, an island forest of virgin hardwood, was so detailed and valuable—and the State of Florida's eviction of the Niedhauks so untoward—as to inspire a Cornell doctoral dissertation and the widespread attention of the press.

About her story, she says, "As I write this, my husband and I have been on Lignum Vitae Key twenty-one years." She had kept notes and memorabilia, "but without Russ's photographic memory, it wouldn't have been possible. Russ remembers everything, every detail of an episode, even the props and where each episode comes in sequence." Charlotte retyped her manuscript eighteen times on an old Royal. "He made me rewrite a page because I had added six inches to the length of a moray eel."

The pristine islands Charlotte loved are preserved for all of us: Elliott Key in Biscayne National Park and Lignum Vitae Key, a Florida State Park.